W9-CJK-058

11/20/12

From Jodi

Chief Left Hand

THE CIVILIZATION OF THE AMERICAN INDIAN SERIES

" . . .the places that knew them in their pride shall know them no more forever."

E. N. H. Patterson
journalist, traveler
1859

CHIEF
LEFT
HAND
Southern Arapaho

Margaret Coel

University of Oklahoma Press
Norman

For George, Kristin, Lisa, and Bill,
who came with me on the trail of the
Southern Arapahos across the central
plains; especially for Bill.

BY MARGARET COEL

Chief Left Hand (Norman, 1981)
Goin' Railroading (Boulder, 1985)

Coel, Margaret, 1937–
    Chief Left Hand, Southern Arapaho.
    (The Civilization of the American Indian series; no. 159)
    Bibliography: p. 319
    Includes index.
    1. Left Hand, Southern Arapaho chief, ca. 1880–1864? 2. Arapaho
    Indians—History. 3. Arapaho Indians—Biography.
    I. Title II. Series: Civilization of the American Indian series; no. 159.
    E99.A7C63 1981   970.004'97   [B]   80–5940
    ISBN: 978-0-8061-2030-0 (paper)

9 10 11 12 13 14

Contents

Illustrations

Maps

Author's Note

Chief Left Hand, Southern Arapaho is the first biography of a remarkable Indian leader during the turbulent years of the Colorado Gold Rush and settlement. In telling the story of this man, also known by his Arapaho name, Niwot, I relied upon primary sources, many of which had not been published previously. The accounts of men and women whose paths had intersected with Chief Left Hand's tell of his tireless efforts as a diplomat, negotiator, and peacemaker, efforts that would place him and his band at Sand Creek on the fateful day of November 29, 1864, when the U.S. Army troops led by Colonel John M. Chivington attacked the Arapaho and Cheyenne camp and massacred about 150 men, women, and children.

When this biography was published in 1981, scholars had been arguing for more than a century over whether Chief Left Hand had survived the Sand Creek massacre. Those who believed he had survived pointed to the fact that his body was not identified at the site. Furthermore, an Arapaho chief with the same name had become prominent in Oklahoma in the 1880s. Could this not be the same man?

Other scholars believed that Chief Left Hand had been killed. They pointed to the fact that, in the years immediately following the massacre, no mention of him appears in the records. Had he survived, they claimed, he would have continued to speak out for his people.

I spent four years searching for the evidence that would prove conclusively that Chief Left Hand was killed at Sand Creek. Eventually I located the first documentary proof to be published about his fate. The proof consisted of three obscure letters written by George Bent to his biographer, George E. Hyde. Bent had been at Sand Creek and had witnessed Chief Left Hand's actions as the troops swept into the camp. In careful detail, Bent tells what happened to the chief on that fateful November day. He also distinguishes Chief Left Hand from the Arapaho man who would later become a chief in Oklahoma.

In the years since this book was published, I have been gratified by further substantiation of the conclusions I had reached. Numerous George Bent letters in the archives at Yale University have been found that corroborate the statements in the letters referred to in this book. Still other important evidence came to light in September 2000, when two letters were donated to the Colorado Historical Society. Written within a month of the massacre by Lieutenant Silas Soule and Lieutenant Joseph Cramer, both eyewitnesses to the massacre, the letters provide detailed accounts of Chief Left Hand's fate. The accounts confirm the information in the Bent letters.

On November 7, 2000, President Clinton signed into law a bill designating 12,480 acres in southeastern Colorado, where the massacre occurred, as a National Historic Site. With this designation, land that has been considered sacred by the Arapahos and Cheyennes for more than a century will be preserved so that future generations may be able to understand the past. The Sand Creek historic site is a fitting memorial to the innocent people who died there, as well as to Chief Left Hand and the other Indian leaders who had pledged themselves to peace.

Boulder, Colorado
December 2000

Acknowledgments

I am indebted to many individuals for the help I have received in preparing the present volume, among whom, especially, are the Southern Arapahos of Geary and Concho, Oklahoma, for their kindness and hospitality; Virginia Cole Trenholm, Kent Ruth and Helen Ruth, and Stan Hoig, for their encouragement and advice; Gladys Doty and Jane Fitz-Randolph, for reading all or parts of my manuscript and for suggesting ways of dealing with what appeared to be an unwieldy amount of material; the National Park Service officials at Fort Larned, Fort Kearny, and Fort Laramie; and countless librarians who aided my research at the University of Colorado Library, in Boulder; the Colorado State Archives; the Colorado State Historical Society; the Denver Public Library; the Federal Regional Archives, in Denver; the University of Oklahoma Library, in Norman; the Indian Archives of the Oklahoma State Historical Society, in Oklahoma City; the Kansas State Historical Society, in Topeka; the Nebraska State Historical Society, in Lincoln; the Public Library, in Council Bluffs, Iowa; the Pioneers Museum, in Colorado Springs; the National Archives, in Washington, D.C.; and the British Museum, London.

Margaret Coel
Boulder, Colorado

Introduction

This is the story of one of the most famous Indians of the plains, a man about whom legends were made. In 1858, Chief Left Hand astonished the early goldseekers in Colorado by greeting them in their own language. They were not the first white men he had known. He had dealt with whites all his life and had learned to speak their language as a child.

The white men never forgot him. In time they gave his name to some of the places he had called home: Left Hand Canyon, in the foothills near Boulder where he had spent each winter; the town of Niwot, his Arapaho name, close to where his village had stood; and Niwot Mountain, which rises to the clouds among the Indian Peaks of the Rockies.

This is also the story of his people, the Southern Arapahos, during the most fateful years of their history. They were a gentle people, for the most part, deeply religious, friendly, and generous. They were also canny businessmen, carrying on an extensive trade with whites and Indians across the central plains. They called themselves Inuñaina, which means ''Our People,'' but their English name comes from the Pawnee word *tirapihu* (''trader'').

As traders they preferred peace—and the uninterrupted flow of business—to war. Although young Arapaho warriors fought against their traditional enemies, the Utes and the Pawnees, and eventually took arms against the whites, the Southern Arapahos as a tribe spent far more time and energy in maintaining peace than in making war.

Both the Southern and the Northern Arapahos had preceded the white man to the plains by only about fifty years. Sometime in the dawn of their history they had migrated westward from the mother tribe to which they belonged, the great Algonquins, and in the intervening centuries had evolved their own language and customs. Before the last half of the 1700s they had lived in the

Red River country of Minnesota for as long as a thousand years.

When other tribes and white men began moving into the Red River country, the Arapahos and the Cheyennes, also part of the Algonquins, began moving out. The direction of their steady migration was south and west until around 1790, when they arrived on the central plains of Colorado, Kansas, Nebraska, and Wyoming. The ponies they acquired from the Comanches gave them the freedom to follow the buffalo vast distances across the open prairie, and by 1800 both tribes, now close allies, had settled in a new homeland.

Shortly thereafter, the Arapahos and Cheyennes both separated into their northern tribe, that half of the people who preferred the cooler climate around the Bighorn and Powder rivers, and the southern tribe, those who liked the milder, warmer temperatures south of the Platte. The separation was merely geographical; the Southern and Northern Arapahos remained one people. They traveled back and forth to visit one another, intermarried, and maintained close relationships, as did the Southern and Northern Cheyennes.

When hordes of white men began migrating to the central plains in the mid-nineteenth century, there was no place left for the Indians to go. The Southern Arapahos hoped to make an arrangement with the newcomers that would allow two different cultures to share the same vast land. To do this, they relied upon Left Hand, the chief who could glimpse the white man's mind because he understood his language.

This is the story of that chief and his people during a time of change, a time that would alter their lives and the face of an entire region, a time of endings and beginnings.

The People,
The Land

Abbreviations Used
in the Footnotes

BIA Reports: U.S., Department of the Interior, Bureau of Indian Affairs, *Reports of the Commissioner of Indian Affairs.*

"Cheyenne Massacre": U.S., Congress, Senate, "Massacre of the Cheyenne Indians," *Report of the Joint Committee on the Conduct of the War,* Sen. Report 142, 38th Cong., 2d sess., 1865.

"Chivington Massacre": U.S., Congress, Senate, "The Chivington Massacre," *Reports of the Joint Special Committee on the Condition of the Indian Tribes,* Sen. Report 156, 39th Cong., 2d sess., 1867.

Evans Letters, CSA: John Evans Collection: Indian Affairs, Colorado State Archives, Denver, Colorado.

OIA: Office of Indian Affairs

"Sand Creek Massacre": U.S., Congress, Senate, "Sand Creek Massacre," *Report of the Secretary of War,* Sen. Exec. Doc. 26, 39th Cong., 2d sess., 1867.

WRR: U.S., War Department, *The War of the Rebellion: A Compilation of The Official Records of the Union and Confederate Armies.* Four series, 128 vols., Washington, D.C., 1880-1910.

Wynkoop manuscript: Edward W. Wynkoop manuscript, Colorado State Historical Society, Denver, Colorado.

My children,
My children,
Here it is, I hand it to you
The earth,
The earth.

1

Southern Arapaho song

In the early 1820s a Southern Arapaho woman gave birth to a male child who was destined to become a leader of his tribe during the most critical period of its history. The place of his birth was a village spread among giant cottonwood trees along one of the streams that crisscross the central plains of present-day eastern Colorado, western Kansas, and parts of Nebraska, Wyoming, and Oklahoma. Although the exact location and date of the child's birth are not recorded, Southern Arapaho customs, handed down from generation to generation, provide a glimpse into the probable circumstances.[1]

Every birth in the tribe prompted a joyous celebration. Southern Arapaho parents looked upon the arrival of children as a sign that their lives had been richly blessed. The father would have walked through the village inviting friends and relatives to his lodge, or tipi, to help celebrate his good fortune and marvel over his son. After the guests had feasted and toasted the child's health and long life, the father would make them gifts of the finest ponies in his herd. He would select an exceptionally beautiful pony as a gift to the child.

Southern Arapaho mothers kept their infants wrapped in fine deerskins which they had tanned with particular care. They packed ground buffalo chips around the lower part of the babies' bodies to keep them clean and to prevent rashes. When the children cried, they would be firmly but gently pinched on the

---

[1] Sister M. Inez Hilger, "Arapaho Child Life and Its Cultural Background," Smithsonian Institution, Bureau of American Ethnology Bulletin no. 148 (1952), pp. 6–78; Alfred L. Kroeber, "The Arapaho," American Museum of Natural History Bulletin 18, nos. 1–4 (1902–1907). Information on Left Hand's probable early childhood is drawn from these sources; I have assumed for Left Hand a normal Southern Arapaho childhood.

nose and mouth, so that their sounds would not give away the village's location to an enemy who might be nearby.

The infants of the Southern Arapaho tribe were not breast-fed until one of the older women of the tribe had sucked away the colostrum, which they believed was harmful to the child, and had drawn from the mother's breast the pure, blue-white milk. The children were nursed until they were around four years old.

Until Southern Arapaho children learned to walk, they were strapped to their mothers' backs on skin cradles. These were sewed and embroidered with black cattail roots and porcupine quills dyed in vivid colors. In cold weather children were slipped inside tanned wildcat skins so that their arms and legs filled out the skins' legs and their faces peered from the heads.

The father honored an esteemed family member, perhaps his own father, by inviting him to give the child his first name. This name probably referred to an unusual natural occurrence or to an outstanding deed performed by someone in the tribe.

When the child grew old enough to demonstrate distinct physical characteristics, he received a personal name. This particular baby, who stuffed chunks of dried buffalo meat into his mouth with his left hand or stretched that hand toward his mother, received the name Niwot ("Left Hand"). Although Southern Arapahos customarily changed their names throughout their lives, Left Hand would always keep that name.

Left Hand was not the only child of his parents. At the time of his birth his sister MaHom, or Snake Woman, was about six years old. Left Hand also had a brother, Neva, and from an early age the two boys were close companions, romping and playing together through the village and cementing a lifelong bond of friendship.

The world must have seemed an open, friendly place to Left Hand as a young child. He had been born into a tribe that loved and outrageously spoiled its children: he had a deep sense of belonging, not merely with his parents, but with the larger family of grandparents, aunts, uncles, and cousins, all of whom accepted him as one of their own children. From his earliest awareness of his surroundings, he understood that he was as welcome to play, eat, or sleep in the lodges of his relatives as in his parents' lodge. He even called his father's brothers by the name "father," and his mother's sisters, "mother."

They were a handsome people, the Southern Arapahos. The men were from five feet, eight inches to six feet tall, the women a few inches shorter.[2] Both had slender, delicate bone structures, with medium-dark complexions, prominent aquiline noses, sleek black hair, and long, graceful hands. They walked proudly erect to dramatize their height and always took a keen interest in their appearance, bathing daily in the streams and combing and dressing their hair. Most of the men wore braids, and the women let their hair hang loosely about their shoulders and sometimes painted it.[3] They were fully aware of their good looks compared with other plains tribes and, in fact, considered the Comanches bandy-legged and graceless. They suspected the short, swarthy Utes of coveting Southern Arapaho women to improve Ute stock.[4]

Women wore ankle-length dresses of soft skins that were decorated with porcupine quills and beads, and their moccasins were attached to long leggings. For warmth they wrapped themselves in wool blankets they had obtained in trade from other tribes. Men dressed in tanned-skin shirts, leggings that extended from the ankles to the hips, breechcloths, moccasins, and blankets of tanned buffalo skins.[5]

When a Southern Arapaho child was about four years old, his father would teach him to ride the pony he had received at birth. No doubt Left Hand fell off many times, only to be set back on again and again, until he learned to bring the animal under control. Boys in his tribe were expert riders by the age of five. A similar practice turned them into excellent swimmers. As soon as their fathers believed they were old enough to swim, they were thrown into a stream and, when they emerged sputtering and choking, thrown back again, until finally they began to paddle and kick.

Despite such rigorous and early practical training, Left Hand,

[2] Virginia Cole Trenholm, *The Arapahoes, Our People*, p. 4.
[3] Kroeber, "The Arapaho," pp. 23–28.
[4] Trenholm, *Arapahoes*, p. 234.
[5] Kroeber, "The Arapaho," pp. 23–28. When the explorer John Frémont encountered a band of Arapahos on the Platte in 1843, the men were naked except for a breech cloth and the women were naked "from the knees down and the hips up" (John C. Frémont, *Memoirs of My Life*, 1:115–19).

like other Southern Arapaho children, was reared by what the tribe called the "easiest way."[6] This meant, simply, that parents and other adults spent long hours patiently advising and counseling the young boy, talking to him about the right things to do and the right way to live. He was never spanked or whipped, since harsh physical punishment was not considered appropriate for children. To strike a child, the Southern Arapahos believed, was to break his spirit. Instead, every effort was made to teach a child by example and counsel to be kind and friendly, outgoing and generous, and always ready to extend hospitality. "Be sure to have fat horses," children were told, "no matter how poor your saddle." Another maxim was: "Never allow your heart to tire of giving and you will be loved and respected by other people."[7]

Left Hand's home was a comfortable lodge, warm in winter and cool in summer, about eighteen feet in diameter, constructed of buffalo skins sewed together and draped around sturdy cedar or pine poles, its flap facing the rising sun. Along the lodge's southern side, with its head to the west, was the father's bed, made of woven willow branches. Above the bed on the lodge wall were delicately painted pictures depicting events in his father's life. The beds of other family members lined the western and northern walls. Heavy buffalo robes, comfortable to sit upon during the day and warm to sleep under at night, lay over the beds and the lodge floor.

A fire burned continuously on the flatstones in the center of the lodge. Usually the fire was built of wood gathered near the streams, but when wood was unavailable, buffalo chips were used. An iron pot, received in trade with the white man, balanced on stones over the fire. Chunks of buffalo meat and wild vegetables simmered all day in the pot, ready to be eaten whenever the family was hungry.

Although there was no regular mealtime, Left Hand's family probably observed traditional customs before eating. As the family gathered around the steaming pot of food, the father would place a piece of meat on the flatstones as a burnt offering. Holding another piece on a stick above the offering, he would

[6] Hilger, "Arapaho Child Life," p. 78.
[7] Ibid., p. 100; Trenholm, *Arapahoes*, p. 4.

speak to the Great Being whom the tribe called Man-Above. Then, lowering the stick toward the ground, he would ask Mother Earth for strength.[8]

Left Hand's lodge stood in a small village occupied by his band, which comprised all those family members who lived, hunted, and traveled together across the plains. Carl Sweezy, a Southern Arapaho, later described the villages as sociable, friendly places.

> Dogs played around the doorways; ponies grazed in the open spaces; children romped with the dogs and climbed on the ponies, women sat on the ground sewing moccasins or beading pouches; men straightened arrowwood or strung bows or combed and dressed their long hair.[9]

The daily work in the village fell solely to the women, who set up and broke camp, packed and moved family belongings on their backs—including the heavy skin lodges and poles— tanned and sewed skins for clothing, prepared all the food, and gathered much of it. An early plains traveler, Thomas J. Farnham, struck by the relentless drudgery of a Southern Arapaho woman's life compared with that of her husband, was moved to comment:

> His wife takes care of his horses, manufactures his saddles and bridles, and leash ropes and whips, his moccasins, leggins, and hunting shirts from leather and other materials prepared by her own hands; beats with a wooden adze his buffalo robes till they are soft and pleasant for his couch; tans hides for his tent covering, and drags from the distant hills the clean white pine poles to support it; cooks his daily food and places it before him. . . . His sole duty, as her lord in life, and as a citizen of the Arapaho tribe, is to ride the horse which she saddles and brings to his feet, kill the game which she dresses and cures; sit and slumber on the couch which she spreads; and fight the enemies.[10]

Among these many tasks the preparation of food for winter was

[8] Hubert Edwin Collins, *Warpath and Cattle Trail*, p. 194.

[9] Carl Sweezy, *The Arapahoe Way*, p. 26

[10] Thomas J. Farnham, *Travels in the Great Western Prairies*, vol. 28 in *The American Scene Series*, pp. 266–67.

necessarily the most important. Throughout spring and fall women gathered and dried wild chokecherries, squawberries, currants, haws, and cattail roots. They made pemmican by pounding strips of buffalo meat with fat, marrow, and choke-cherry paste and then wrapping it in skin casings like a sausage or patting it into small cakes.[11] During the long, harsh winters pemmican and dried fruits kept the Southern Arapahos free of scurvy, a disease that continuously plagued the white man who did not know how to recognize or use the wild fruits and vegetables of the plains.[12]

Like other Southern Arapaho bands, Left Hand's people moved their village across the central plains, following the seasons and the buffalo herds. Some of the white men who, like Farnham, ventured into the region left vivid descriptions of the vast, empty land that sloped upward from the Missouri River to the base of the Rocky Mountains, a distance of about six hundred miles. Crossing present-day Kansas and Nebraska, these travelers wrote of the unbroken horizon that stretched in every direction as far as the eye could see. Moving into today's eastern Colorado, they were awed by mile after mile of the treeless bluffs that seemed to roll toward the mountains like some great ocean. The bluffs were broken only by deep and, as some travelers learned, treacherous arroyos that had been cut by mountain streams as they cascaded out of the canyons each spring.

The climate was as forbidding as the landscape. Through the summer months and into late autumn the relentless sun scorched the earth, and the winds frequently whipped up blinding sand-storms. In winter, penetrating cold settled over the land, and freezing winds drove the snow into ever-deepening drifts.[13] Between these extremes, however, fell long periods of warm, dry days under clear and brilliant skies.

Vegetation was sparse on the plains. Berry bushes and wild vegetable plants grew near the streams, and clumps of wild roses and thistles dotted the landscape. About the only growth that

[11] Trenholm, *Arapahoes,* p. 66

[12] One report of the hardships of scurvy suffered by white men on the plains is contained in LeRoy R. Hafen, ed., *Relations with the Indians of the Plains,* vol. 9 in *The Far West and the Rockies Historical Series,* p. 273.

[13] De B. Randolph Keim, *Sheridan's Troopers on the Border,* p. 17.

could be said to thrive was a thick grass, two inches high, that required little moisture.[14] Immense herds of buffalo, estimated at thirty million head in the early part of the nineteenth century, were sustained by this nutritious grass. Buffalo ranges heaved with black masses of animal flesh, and, it was said, an Indian could ride all day and not cover a herd from end to end.[15]

The two major rivers that flowed across the central plains formed natural territorial boundaries for the various tribes. The wide, muddy Platte—its north and south branches converging near the present-day Colorado-Nebraska line—cut across the northern edge. Along the southern edge rolled the mighty Arkansas. Smaller streams and rivers, including the Republican and the Solomon, also wound through parts of the region. The only timber was the cottonwood tree, known as "the tree of the desert" because of its stubborn hardiness in an inhospitable environment, and occasional stands of cedar. Both grew along the waterways.

The Southern Arapahos shared the land between the Platte and the Arkansas rivers with the Southern Cheyennes and located their villages in the shelter of giant cottonwoods on the banks of various streams. One of their favorite campgrounds was the large, triangular site formed by the confluence of the South Platte River and Beaver Creek, near today's Brush, Colorado. The site was a kind of plains oasis shaded by clumps of large trees. Water was easily accessible, grass for the ponies plentiful, and large buffalo and antelope herds could be found nearby.

In late fall the Southern Arapahos moved their villages to campgrounds on the present sites of Denver and Boulder, near the foothills. Here, in the lee of the mountains, they were protected from the severe blasts of winter that were so punishing on the open plains.

Campsites were also selected with an eye to the tribe's principal interest—trading with other people. Clever and practical in matters of commerce, the Southern Arapahos had long conducted an active, far-reaching trading business, establishing themselves as the medium through which goods were exchanged between

[14] Albert D. Richardson, *Beyond the Mississippi,* pp. 248–49.
[15] Ernest Thompson Seton, *Life Histories of Northern Animals,* 1:292; S. L. A. Marshall, *Crimsoned Prairie,* p. 6.

northern and southern plains tribes. The Beaver Creek site, for example, was not only a pleasant oasis, but also, with its central location, an ideal trading base.[16] There they could count on exchanging goods with a steady stream of Northern Arapahos, Cheyennes, Sioux, and friendly bands of Shoshonis, Blackfeet, and Pawnees, so that at times the village resembled a busy market town. When business slowed, the Southern Arapahos moved south toward the Arkansas, stopping to trade at Cheyenne camps along the way. Crossing the Arkansas, they conducted a brisk business with the Comanches, Kiowas, and Kiowa-Apaches.

The commerce carried on by his people gave Left Hand, from his earliest years, an opportunity to mingle with other tribes and become familiar with customs other than his own. He was probably an outgoing, friendly boy, exhibiting those traits that would mark his adult personality, and when trading parties visited Cheyenne and Sioux camps he busied himself by learning these languages. Eventually he would become fluent in both, making him one of the few Plains Indians who was ever interested in learning the spoken languages of other tribes. Most relied upon a highly complex sign language for intertribal communication. Even the Southern Arapahos and Cheyennes, close allies who often camped and hunted together, communicated by signs.[17]

Throughout Left Hand's boyhood his people also carried on an extensive trade with white men, a circumstance that early introduced him to rough-edged trappers and adventurers who had exchanged civilization in the states for a nomadic life on the plains. Traipsing across Indian lands, these white men were mainly in the business of gathering beaver pelts for men's fur hats, fashionable during the 1820s and 1830s. The more enter-

[16] James Mooney, "The Ghost Dance Religion and the Sioux Outbreak of 1890," Smithsonian Institution, Bureau of American Ethnology Fourteenth Annual Report, no. 2 (1896), pp. 1013–1014; James Mooney, "Arapaho," in *Handbook of American Indians North of Mexico,* ed. Frederick Webb Hodge, Smithsonian Institution, Bureau of American Ethnology Bulletin no. 30, 1 (1907):73; LeRoy R. Hafen, "Fort St. Vrain," *Colorado Magazine* 39 (1952):241–55.

[17] Sweezy, *Arapahoe Way,* p. 3. There is some evidence that many Arapahos could at least understand Cheyenne, if not speak it. See Hugh L. Scott, "The Early History and Names of the Arapaho," *American Anthropologist,* n.s., 9 (1907):548.

prising and stable whites established permanent posts where they bought pelts from itinerant trappers, transported them by wagon across the plains to St. Louis, and sold them for a price high enough to cover their costs and bring in tidy profits.

One of these early trapper-traders was a Missourian by the name of William Bent, who, with his brother Charles and their partner Ceran St. Vrain, constructed Bent's Fort about 1833 on the Arkansas River near present-day LaJunta.[18] The fort soon grew into a busy, gaudy outpost of civilization where, amid a babble of languages, the Southern Arapahos traded with white men from the states, French Canadian trappers, Mexicans, and other Indian tribes.

Sometime around 1838, William Bent and St. Vrain also established Fort St. Vrain, originally called Fort Lookout, on the edge of a bluff overlooking the South Platte about six miles from today's Platteville. The fort proved a convenient halfway stop for traders making their way between Bent's Fort and another major trading post on the Platte, Fort Laramie. About the same time, smaller posts sprang up within ten miles of Fort St. Vrain—Forts Lupton, Vasquez, and Jackson. This network of white commercialism crossing Southern Arapaho lands thrust the tribe into continuous contact with white men and gave Left Hand the chance, as he said later, to learn English.[19]

In 1833, Left Hand's sister, MaHom, then about fifteen or sixteen years old, married one of the white traders, John Poisal, a twenty-four-year-old Kentuckian who worked for Bent.[20] Poisal's occupation had naturally placed him in Southern Arapaho villages, and, in fact, he had probably begun living with the tribe by about 1830.[21] In any case, Poisal took an interest in MaHom's younger brothers, overseeing an education of sorts. Impressed by Left Hand's ability to pick up languages, Poisal began tutoring him in English. Between Poisal's instruction and the frequent opportunity to practice English in conversation with

[18] David Lavender, *Bent's Fort,* p. 386 n. 12; Donald J. Berthrong, *The Southern Cheyennes,* p. 25; George Hyde, *Life of George Bent,* p. 59.

[19] Richardson, *Beyond the Mississippi,* p. 190.

[20] "Thomas Autobees Interview of F. W. Cragin," November 8, 1907, Cragin Collection, Pioneers Museum, Colorado Springs, Colo.

[21] LeRoy R. Hafen, *Broken Hand,* p. 274.

the other traders, Left Hand soon began speaking the white man's language fluently. Neva also benefited, gaining the ability to understand English and to speak it to some extent.

It was an extraordinary accomplishment for two young Southern Arapaho boys. At this time, and in fact for many years to come, no other Southern Arapaho could speak English.[22] It was this accomplishment that would later help to mark Left Hand for leadership.

Aside from learning other languages, Left Hand's activities were the same as those of other Southern Arapaho boys. Growing up as nomadic people in a boundless land must have instilled in them a deep, abiding sense of freedom. There were always opportunities to test their independence by racing their ponies wildly across the plains, whooping and hollering, far away from the security of the village. There was always time to tease and chase one another, to run footraces, or to join in such favorite games as spinning bone or wooden tops from a piece of buckskin or sliding toward some target they had marked in the earth the painted sticks they had made and tipped with buffalo horn.[23]

By the age of nine or ten Left Hand, like other boys, began to assume responsibilities, including such chores as watering the ponies at the streams and herding them close to the village in the evenings. Sitting outside his lodge with his grandfather, father, and uncles, he learned to straighten arrowwood and chip sharp arrow points from flint. He also learned to stalk and kill rabbits and squirrels; hunting gave him his first sense of pride in providing food for his family. At the same time it taught him the skills he would later need to bring down the buffalo.

There were many sociable, exciting events for a young boy to look forward to each year. Among the great events were the major buffalo hunts, when the Southern Arapaho and Cheyenne warriors joined forces to kill enough animals to feed both tribes for at

---

[22] The Northern Arapaho Friday, a contemporary of Left Hand, was adopted by Upper Platte Agent Thomas Fitzpatrick and sent to school in St. Louis, where he learned to speak fluent English (Hafen, *Broken Hand,* p. 86; Trenholm, *Arapahoes,* p. 117); extensive research has revealed no other Arapaho who spoke English at this time. It has been reported that even in 1881 Friday was the only English-speaking Arapaho (Evadene Burris Swanson, "Friday: Roving Arapaho," *Annals of Wyoming* 47 [1975]:59–68).

[23] Mooney, "Ghost Dance Religion," pp. 1006–1008.

least six months. By the age of twelve or thirteen, Left Hand was allowed to join his father and the other men in the hunting parties and take part in the feasting, dancing, and singing around the blazing bonfires that followed successful hunts. These were times of deep satisfaction, accomplishment, and joy.

The Southern Arapahos, along with other plain tribes, depended upon the buffalo to provide for all of life's necessities and used every part of a slain animal. The hide was turned into lodge coverings, warm robes, clothing, war shields, and parfleches—the small, slightly stiff trunks that were used to store and transport family goods. The pouch served as a pail or bowl. Ornaments were fashioned from the tail and hooves, and spoons and tools from the horns. The sinews were useful as cords or thread. Flesh, fat, organs, blood, and bone marrow were consumed; brains and liver, great delicacies, were eaten raw. Even buffalo chips were either put to good use as fuel or were ground into a soothing baby powder.[24]

The times of the buffalo hunts were equaled in excitement only by those days when the warriors painted themselves and prepared to ride out to raid the pony herds of enemy tribes. From the time he learned to ride, Left Hand must have badgered his father to take him along, since, like all other boys, he longed to be counted among the men, doing men's work, rather than to stay behind in the village with women and children.

Although the Southern Arapahos were primarily interested in carrying on a successful trading business, they also maintained a warrior society similar to that of other plains tribes. In such societies courageous deeds in the face of danger counted above all else. A man's reputation was built on his fearlessness in counting coups (touching enemy warriors) and on his prowess in stealing ponies. A tribe gauged its wealth by the number of ponies it possessed.

Pony raids, of course, led to skirmishes, battles, and retaliatory raids that left warriors dead and wounded and sometimes brought attacks on whole villages. For this reason, guards were always posted outside the villages to warn of an approaching enemy.

To the Southern Arapahos, the Utes were dreaded and de-

[24] Sweezy, *Arapahoe Way*, pp. 28-29.

tested enemies. Left Hand said later that he could not remember a time when his people were not warring against the tribe that lived in the mountains.[25] From time to time they also counted the Pawnees, Comanches, and Kiowas as enemies, usually because those tribes encroached on Southern Arapaho buffalo ranges. At other times their alliance with the Southern Cheyennes embroiled them in Cheyenne battles. Such was the case in 1837, when some of the Southern Arapaho warriors joined the Cheyennes against the Kiowas and Comanches in the Battle of Wolf Creek, the last major Indian battle on the southern plains.[26]

Nevertheless, the Southern Arapahos endeavored to strike a balance between the demands of a warrior society and the necessities of their trading businsess. As a tribe they preferred peace to war, since peace was more conducive to successful commerce. Even during periods of intertribal tension they worked at keeping the avenues of trade open. Only shortly before the Wolf Creek battle, for example, a Southern Arapaho trading party had visited the Kiowa and Comanche camps.[27]

If raids offered young warriors the chance to prove their mettle, the Sun Dance, held each summer when both the northern and southern tribal bands gathered together, was the time of contemplation and spiritual rejuvenation. A deeply religious people, the tribe believed that the first created man had been an Arapaho. Only later did the Creator give life to other tribes and, still later, to the white men beyond the waters.[28] It was during the Sun Dance that the people put themselves in touch with the spirit of the world in which they lived and with the spirit of the Great Being, Man-Above.

To a young boy the eight-day ceremony meant a time to romp with children from other bands and to run important errands for adults who were busy constructing the ceremonial lodges for the sacred rituals. The fourth day of the ceremony was the best, with the warriors fighting a mock battle to determine who would carry

[25] Horace Greeley, An Overland Journey, p. 149–50.
[26] Berthrong, Southern Cheyennes, pp. 82–83.
[27] Ibid.
[28] See George A. Dorsey and Alfred L. Kroeber, "Traditions of the Arapaho," Field Columbian Museum Anthropological Series no. 81, 5 (1903):1–7, for a full explanation of the Arapahos' religious beliefs.

the central pole for the Offerings Lodge. Not until the lodge was built did the actual dancing begin. Before dawn on the fifth day, the warriors, their bodies painted and decorated with eagle feathers, would form a long line facing the east and dance throughout the sunrise.

Even more impressive to the young boy was the self-torture of the man who would hang himself from a pole by thongs pulled through his chest muscles and slowly twist in the air until the muscles ripped apart. Left Hand understood from his elders that this warrior willingly underwent such suffering as a symbolic expiation for the whole tribe.[29] It was a way in which one man took upon himself a special responsibility for others, and it was a teaching that deeply impressed Left Hand.

Around 1840, Left Hand reached the age of seventeen, the threshold of manhood for Southern Arapaho youth, and became eligible to join the Fox Men, the first of the tribe's age societies.[30] The eight progressive societies constituted a well-organized political system whereby order was maintained, laws enforced, and responsibilities delegated. Nearly all men in the tribe belonged to a society, taking part in its secret instructions and rituals, although membership was not compulsory. Since only members were entrusted with tribal duties or allowed to participate in tribal ceremonies, the rare individual who refused to join was, in effect, socially ostracized.

Members of the Fox Men, or Nuhinana, were between the ages of seventeen and twenty-five. They were charged with duties benefiting the entire tribe: hunting, fighting enemies, and guarding the villages. When a man entered his late twenties, about the time he accepted the additional responsibility of a wife and family, he graduated into the next order, the Star Men. Members of the third society, the Club Men, were in their mid-

---

[29] For a complete explanation of the Arapaho Sun Dance see George A. Dorsey, ''The Arapahoe Sun Dance,'' Field Columbian Museum Anthropological Series no. 75, 4(1903); see Trenholm, *Arapahoes*, pp. 71–76, for a concise explanation.

[30] Hilger maintains a boy of twelve could join the first society (Hilger, ''Arapaho Child Life,'' p. 118); Mooney's study, which predates Hilger's, places the age at seventeen, probably the required age during Left Hand's time (Mooney, ''Arapaho,'' pp. 72–73).

thirties—the prime of life—and were valued for their strength, their growing wisdom, and their experience. Following that order came the society of the Spear Men—mature, accomplished warriors, responsible for police duty in the tribe and for enforcing the chief's orders if necessary. Members of the Crazy Men, the next order, were more than fifty years old and were graduates of the lower orders. Then came the Dog Men, who were highly respected elders entrusted with the tribe's sacred rattles. The highest order to which a man might aspire was that of the Water-Pouring Men, made up of seven venerable priests who were instructors of the lower orders.[31] Only a few would reach this last order.

With his acceptance into the Fox Men, Left Hand began to shoulder adult responsibilities. From this point on, the welfare of others would depend upon his judgment and the way in which he carried out his duties. Whereas before he had brought home small game and shared the excitement of the buffalo hunt, proud to help provide food for his family, he now accepted the burden, along with other men, of supplying food for the entire tribe. Should he fail, others would suffer. Whereas raids on other tribes had been high adventure, they now became the means by which he must prove his courage and soundness while, at the same time, enriching his own people.

About the time Left Hand became a Fox Man, the Southern Arapahos and the Cheyennes made a lasting peace with the plains tribes south of the Arkansas. According to the Cheyenne historian Donald J. Berthrong, those tribes, under increasing pressure from Texans expanding into their territory, sought the peace in order to free their resources for a stand against the whites. In 1840, Little Raven, the thirty-year-old principal chief of the Southern Arapahos who was married to a Kiowa-Apache, acted as intermediary in bringing together the Southern Arapahos, Cheyennes, Kiowas, Comanches, and Kiowa-Apaches at a site near Bent's Fort. The treaty that the tribe agreed upon included the right to hunt on one another's ranges—a provision offering relief to the beleaguered southern tribes. The peace pledged at this time would never be broken.[32]

[31] Mooney, ''Arapaho,'' pp. 72–73.
[32] Berthrong, *Southern Cheyennes*, p. 83.

Six years after the truce Alexander Barclay, a trader who had established a post at the present site of Pueblo, Colorado, recorded in his diary the first written account of Left Hand: "June 10, 1846," Barclay wrote, "Arkansas up very high. Poisal's Indian Namus [Left Hand]...sent for help to cross the Arkansas."[33] As succinct and uninformative as Barclay's mention of Left Hand is, it nevertheless alludes to two important aspects of his character: his continuing friendship with his brother-in-law, the white trader Poisal, and his willingness to render assistance to the white man.

At this time Left Hand was about twenty-three years old, in the first flush of manhood. He was an accomplished plainsman, at home in a harsh and demanding environment. He had traveled the length and breadth of the central plains and knew its geography like the lines on the palm of his hand. He could read the changes of the weather and sense the direction of the buffalo herds. He was adept in dealing with a variety of people, Indians and whites alike, and could speak with many of them in their own languages.

Confident and independent, free as only a person can be who knows who he is, Left Hand entered adulthood just as the Southern Arapaho world was about to be caught up in the bitter conflict that would alter forever the identity of its people.

[33] Barclay was also the first to render Left Hand's Arapaho name as Namus. In subsequent years, Niwot would also be rendered Niwathit, Nawat, Nawatch, Norwatch, and Norwanche, according to the particular white man's spelling ability ("Alexander Barclay's Diary," microfilm, Colorado State Historical Society, Denver, Colo.).

2

. . . permit us to dwell for a long time
on these beautiful prairie lands.

Medicine Man [Roman Nose],
Northern Arapaho

In the 1840s the whites began to invade the central plains. The
Oregon Trail, which ran south of the Platte River, and the Santa
Fe Trail, paralleling the Arkansas, turned into busy highways
clogged with wagon trains as the white population shifted
westward toward the promise of Oregon and California. Immigrants, armies, exploration parties, all poured across Southern
Arapaho and Cheyenne lands, leaving a wake of destruction.
Buffalo carcasses littered the prairie, grass was trampled and
depleted, and the virgin timber was felled and burned.

The great westward migration began around 1843, when one
thousand people crossed the plains on their way to Oregon. The
number grew steadily, and in 1845, three thousand immigrants
came west. In 1849 and 1850, years of the California gold rush,
the steady torrent turned into a deluge, and forty thousand
whites swept through Indian country.[1]

In the same period, additional thousands were following
Brigham Young to Utah, traveling over the Mormon Trail, which
ran along the north side of the Platte. Earlier in the decade John
C. Frémont had led two exploration parties up and down the
plains, traversing the heart of the buffalo country.

United States troops also crossed the plains from time to time,
in a show of strength that they hoped would prevent Indian attacks on travelers along the Oregon Trail. The major troop movement came in 1846, however, when the Army of the West under
Col. Stephen Watts Kearny marched down the Santa Fe Trail
toward the arena of the Mexican War with 1,600 men, 1,556
wagons, and 20,000 oxen, mules, and horses.[2]

Never had the Southern Arapahos seen so many white men,

---

[1] Colin Taylor, *The Warriors of the Plains*, p. 86.
[2] LeRoy R. Hafen, *Broken Hand*, pp. 232, 262. The dates of Frémont's
three expeditions were 1842, 1843–44, and 1845–46.

and this at a time when their own population was only beginning to stabilize after a period of sharp decline. Within a twenty-year period disease and hardships had reduced the Arapaho tribe from an estimated ten thousand persons to three thousand, about equally divided between the southern and northern branches. This meant that the Southern Arapahos, counting men, women, and children, were about as numerous as the troops in Kearny's army, which constituted only a small part of the white invasion.[3]

Some of the warriors raged against that invasion. Led by Coho the Lame, they joined the Comanches in attacking immigrant trains along the Santa Fe Trail throughout 1846 and 1847.[4] Although Left Hand was one of the young warriors at this time, he stood with the tribe's responsible leaders who, aware of the hopelessness of contending against ever-increasing numbers of whites, urged restraint and cautioned their people to remain friendly. Left Hand always maintained that he had shown friendship to the white man, even during the most difficult periods.[5] Despite this attitude of restraint by the leaders, the growing hostility of most members of the plains tribes was clear to Indians and whites alike.

In 1846 the United States government attempted to defuse this explosive situation by creating the Upper Platte and Arkansas Indian Agency. The first agent appointed to the post was Thomas Fitzpatrick, a forty-five-year-old Irishman who had spent half his life on the plains. He was widely known and respected by both Indians and whites as an honest trader and a first-rate guide. It was none other than Fitzpatrick who had guided Frémont's expeditions and Kearny's troops through the region. He was still with the army, in fact, when he learned of his appointment on August 3, 1846.[6]

[3] Hugh L. Scott, "The Early History and Names of the Arapaho," *American Anthropologist* n. s., 9 (1907):551. Donald J. Berthrong, *The Southern Cheyennes*, p. 107, p. 108n.

[4] Berthrong, *Southern Cheyennes*, p. 108.

[5] U.S., Senate, *"Sand Creek Massacre"; Report of the Secretary of War*, Sen. Exec. Doc. 26, 39th Cong., 2d sess., 1867, p. 30 (hereafter cited as "Sand Creek Massacre").

[6] Benton to Medill, Commissioner of Indian Affairs, April 9, 1846, and Benton to Fitzpatrick, August 27, 1846, Letters Received, Upper Platte

Almost immediately Fitzpatrick began pressing for a treaty between the government and the plains tribes that would specify the rights and obligations of all people in the region. Superintendent of Indian Affairs Thomas Harvey, in St. Louis, also saw the importance of the government reaching some agreement with the Indians.[7] But to make treaties with other nations (the legal status of the tribes), required an authorization by Congress, the appointment of commissioners, and the appropriation of funds—all of which would consume five years.

In the meantime Fitzpatrick had immediate orders from the commissioner of Indian Affairs to visit all the tribes within his jurisdiction: the Kiowas, Kiowa-Apaches, and Comanches who lived south of the Arkansas; the Southern Arapahos and Cheyennes in the vicinity of Fort St. Vrain and the South Platte; and the Sioux near Fort Laramie. The new agent made his way across the plains, listened to complaints, urged the tribes to remain peaceful, assured them of the government's good will, and paved the way, he hoped, for a treaty council. It was the summer of 1848 before he had completed his first rounds.[8]

While Fitzpatrick went about his duties, Lt. Col. William Gilpin and a battalion of Missouri Volunteers moved down the Santa Fe Trail under orders from the War Department to protect immigrant trains from the raiding Comanches, whose ranks were sometimes augmented by Southern Arapahos. During the winter of 1848, Gilpin pushed south of the Arkansas toward the Canadian River, pillaging the land, killing game, destroying the grass, and, as Berthrong has noted, rendering the area temporarily unfit for human habitation.[9] Although the march did not directly affect the Southern Arapahos, the government's double-pronged tactic of sending an agent to talk peace while its troops

---

Agency, *OIA*, Record Group 75, Federal Archives and Record Center, Denver, Colo.

[7] U.S., Department of the Interior, Bureau of Indian Affairs, *Reports of the Commissioner of Indian Affairs* (hereafter cited as *BIA Reports*), Sen. Exec. Doc. 1, 30th Cong., 1st sess. (1847), p. 834.

[8] Benton to Fitzpatrick, "Instructions for Establishing Indian Agency," August 27, 1846, Letters Received, Upper Platte Agency, *OIA*, Record Group 75, Federal Archives and Records Center.

[9] Berthrong, *Southern Cheyennes*, p. 111–12.

despoiled the land did little to relieve the growing pressure felt by all the plains tribes.

That pressure reached near breaking point during the California gold rush. In addition to the trail of buffalo carcasses and devastated grazing lands, the goldseekers also left diseases to which the Plains Indians had little immunity. Cholera spread through the tribes during the spring and summer of 1849, and hundreds of men, women, and children died in agony. The number of Indian deaths resulting from the gold rush will never be known, but death stalked the tribes so relentlessly that year that the seasoned trader Ceran St. Vrain wrote that he had never seen a worse state of affairs on the plains.[10]

Although the cholera epidemic hit the Cheyennes and Pawnees especially hard, the Southern Arapahos did not escape it. Nine years later their agent reported that the tribe still suffered from the effects of cholera as well as other diseases brought by the whites.[11]

During these last years of the 1840s, years of hardship and sickness, Left Hand reached his late twenties, the marriageable age for Southern Arapaho men. Sometime around 1850 he married a fifteen- or sixteen-year-old girl whose name is unknown.[12] She had probably caught his eye when the tribe camped together for a major buffalo hunt or the Sun Dance. Since unmarried girls were closely chaperoned by their mothers and grandmothers, courting demanded patience, perseverance, and a great amount of ingenuity on the part of the young Southern Arapaho suitor. He would send one of his female relatives to her father with a marriage proposal. Although the father received the proposal, he usually left the final decision to his sons, who were of the same generation and presumably better able to judge the suitor's worthiness. If the girl's brothers gave their approval, her female

[10] Ibid., p. 114.

[11] LeRoy R. Hafen, *Relations with the Indians of the Plains*, vol. 9 in *The Far West and the Rockies Historical Series*, p. 168; *BIA Reports* (1849), Sen. Exec. Doc. 1, pt. 2, 31st Cong., 1st sess., p. 451.

[12] See Sister M. Inez Hilger, ''Arapaho Child Life and Its Cultural Background,'' Smithsonian Institution, Bureau of American Ethnology Bulletin no. 148 (1952), pp. 193–216, for explanation of Arapaho courtship and marriage customs; Virginia Cole Trenholm, *The Arapahoes, Our People*, pp. 57–58.

relatives built and furnished a new lodge for her. When it was complete, they sent for her prospective mate and his family.

At the moment the man stepped across the threshold into his bride's lodge, the couple was considered married. An older, respected man in the girl's family, probably her father, would greet the couple and, holding their hands in his own, pray for their health and happiness and advise them on their life together. After the ceremony, members of both families would feast and exchange gifts with one another.

Although it would seem that the Arapaho girl had little to say about her fate, this is not the case. Had Left Hand's bride raised a serious objection to marrying him—such as her love for another man—her brothers and father would not have forced her to do so. That she became Left Hand's wife meant that she found him acceptable as a husband and had no reservations about joining her life to his.

It is quite likely that both she and her family welcomed the match. Left Hand was a strikingly handsome man. Although no description of him exists from this period, an account written ten years later suggests the figure he must have presented as a young warrior. Julia Lambert, who followed her husband to the plains, called him

> the finest looking Indian I have ever seen. He was over six feet tall, of muscular build and much more intelligent than the average Indian . . . [He was] the only Indian I ever saw who did not braid his hair; it hung loosely over his shoulders. When wearing his war bonnet and full warrior's regalia, he looked every inch a chief. [13]

[13] Julia S. Lambert, "Plain Tales of the Plains," *The Trail* 9 (1916):20. Early comments by whites (i.e., "far more intelligent than the average Indian") often reflect the preponderant nineteenth-century view of Indians as an inferior people. They are quoted in this book as a reflection not, of course, on Indians but of the minds of the white population with whom Left Hand and others had to deal. Teresa Dean, for example, reporting for the *Chicago Herald* in 1891 from the Wounded Knee battle site, watched while a Sioux identified the bodies of his sister and her three children. She wrote that the man looked at her "with an expression that was unmistakeable agony and his lips quivered. For the first time, I realized that the soul of a Sioux might possibly in its primitive state have started out on the same road as . . . the soul of a white man" (quoted in James Murphy and Sharon Murphy, *Let My People Know: American Indian Journalism, 1828–1978*, p. 6).

No doubt the girl's brothers had also seen that aspect of him. Left Hand had already established a reputation as a brave warrior, a skillful hunter, and, more important, a man of generosity. With white men entering the plains, his ability to speak their language was becoming an increasingly valuable asset. He was a man one would notice in a crowd, and his new brothers-in-law had realized that such a man was destined for a position of importance in the tribe. Their own standing would not be damaged by a connection with him through marriage.

It is possible that in his later life Left Hand married other women, since polygamy was widely practiced among the Southern Arapahos. As a matter of practicality, it ensured that all women had husbands to provide for them in a society where work was divided along male-female lines: men were hunters; women were nurturers. A man might marry his wife's younger sisters, for example, to ensure their security. He was also obligated to marry his brother's widow, thus ensuring that she and her children would be protected and cared for, regardless of whether he already had a wife.

Apart from the security conferred upon women, polygamy also had special benefits for men. With several wives a man could count on having his food prepared, clothing washed and sewed, at least one lodge clean and comfortable, and his sexual appetite satisfied. If one wife did not welcome him, he could simply visit another.

Because of the many duties that went with their position, tribal leaders were especially likely to take several wives. The work involved in preparing feasts, entertaining visitors from other tribes, hosting tribal meetings, and in similar obligations of a leader could outdistance the best efforts of one woman. It was probably for this reason that Chief Little Raven eventually had seven wives.[14] Whether Left Hand also took additional wives is not known.

For Left Hand, as for other Southern Arapaho men, marriage marked another step toward maturity. His years of youthful strength had been given to his people, protecting the village from surprise attack, taking part in pony raids that increased the tribal wealth, hunting buffalo and other game. Now these duties were

[14] Carl Sweezy, *The Arapaho Way*, p. 23.

expanded to include personal responsibilities toward a wife, the children they would have, and his wife's family.[15]

Shortly before Left Hand was married, another important marriage took place in the tribe. In November, 1849, Agent Fitzpatrick, white-haired, fifty years old, and still a bachelor, married Margaret Poisal, the teen-aged daughter of John Poisal and MaHom. This was no light dalliance between a comely young half-blood Indian girl and an older white trader. Fitzpatrick took the marriage seriously, losing no time in writing a will that named Margaret and any children they should have as his sole heirs.[16]

Before his marriage into the Southern Arapaho tribe, Fitzpatrick had consistently demonstrated a tough-minded attitude toward the Plains Indians, advising the government to take a strong stand with them because, he claimed, "nothing short of an efficient military force" would keep the Indians quiet.[17]

Although Fitzpatrick trekked tirelessly back and forth across the plains, ferrying government gifts from St. Louis to the tribes as a sign of good will and keeping the hope for a treaty council alive, he himself harbored a deep skepticism about its value. In 1848 he wrote:

> There is not a single day in the whole year that I could not make a treaty with any of these Indian tribes if I happen to have sufficient merchandise on hand to make presents worthy of the inconvenience and trouble of assembling the nation; and let the stipulation of that treaty be whatever I might choose to propose, it would be solemnly and apparently in good faith ratified and agreed to, but not for one single moment longer than a favorable opportunity offers for its violation.[18]

That attitude underwent a change. Two years later, following his marriage to Margaret and a more intimate acquaintance with the Southern Arapahos and their customs, Fitzpatrick began

[15] See Hilger, "Arapaho Child Life," p. 198, for a description of the duties of young Arapaho men.
[16] Hafen, *Broken Hand,* pp. 308–309; "Dawson Scrapbooks," vol. 4, p. 141, Colorado State Historical Society, Denver, Colo.
[17] *BIA Reports* (1848), House Exec. Doc. 1, 30th Cong., 2d sess., p. 473.
[18] Trenholm, *Arapahoes,* p. 130.

serving as a kind of government conscience. In his official reports he wrote feelingly about the great injustices suffered by the plains tribes. "The immense emigration traveling through that country [over the Oregon Trail] for the past two years," he told the commissioner of Indian Affairs in 1850, "has desolated and impoverished it to an enormous extent."[19]

That kind of honesty and willingness to look squarely at situations and people won Fitzpatrick the respect and trust of the Southern Arapahos. They admired his straight-forwardness and devotion to duty. They always knew where they stood with this man, and, many years later, they would remember him as the fairest agent the government had ever sent them.[20]

In late summer of 1849, while Fitzpatrick was making his rounds to the tribal villages, Congress finally authorized a treaty council with the plains Indians. Fitzpatrick and D. D. Mitchell, who had replaced Harvey as superintendent of Indian Affairs in St. Louis, were named United States commissioners, with full authority to reach an agreement with the Indians over matters of importance on the plains. The only thing the commissioners lacked was the necessary funds to hold the council. They would wait two more years until Congress appropriated the necessary $100,000.

But at least the wheels were set in motion, and Fitzpatrick cast about for an appropriate council site. He had originally hoped to hold the council at Bent's Fort, established in the Indian mind as a place of peaceful mingling and trading. Before any arrangements could be made, however, William Bent destroyed the fort.

Unfortunately for Bent, the successful businessman-trader, now forty-one years old, the wheel of fortune had taken a downward turn. Years before, Bent had committed his life to the plains. He had married into the Cheyenne tribe twice, first to Owl Woman, who died in childbirth in 1847—leaving him with four young children—and then to her sister Yellow Woman, who bore him a fifth child.

As Bent's family grew, his fur-trading business declined. Fur

---

[19] BIA Reports (1850), Sen. Exec. Doc. 1, 31st Cong., 2d sess., p. 55
[20] Hafen, Broken Hand, p. 321.

hats had been replaced by high silk hats in the world of fashion, and beaver pelts were no longer in demand. Moreover, the mass migration of whites across the plains, increasing tension between the Indians and all white men, including traders, had not helped Bent's business.

Discouraged by these developments of the last few years, Bent offered the fort to the government as a military post for the price of $16,000. The government was interested, but only at the figure of $12,000, a counter offer that seemed to add an insult to his discouragement. About August 22, 1849, the trader settled the matter by rolling powder kegs into the fort's main room, torching the wooden beams, and blowing the adobe buildings sky high. He then moved his family thirty-five miles downstream to Big Timbers, a grove of cottonwoods about one mile wide that stretched for four miles along the Arkansas River.[21]

With Bent's Fort out of the picture, Fitzpatrick was pressed to find another suitable council site. He finally settled upon Fort Laramie, on the Platte River, which turned out to be a better choice since it was more conveniently located for both northern and southern tribes.

After Congress had appropriated the council funds, Fitzpatrick spent the spring and summer of 1851 traveling among the tribes and instructing them to meet at Fort Laramie in August. Superintendent Mitchell also sent runners up the Missouri, Arkansas, and Platte rivers with similar instructions. On July 25, Fitzpatrick arrived at the fort to find thousands of Indians waiting for the long-desired talks to begin.[22] There they remained for nearly six weeks, while Fitzpatrick sent additional runners to the bands that were still missing, urging them to come in. By September 1, when Mitchell arrived, the plains tribes were assembled.

It was an extraordinary sight. Lodges of ten thousand Indians—Arapahos, Cheyennes, Sioux, Assiniboines, Arikaras, Gros Ventres, Crows, and Shoshonis—were spread across the

[21] George E. Hyde, *Life of George Bent,* p. 83; David Lavender, *Bent's Fort,* pp. 313–16.

[22] *BIA Reports* (1851), Sen. Exec. Doc. 1, pt. 3, 32d Cong., 1st sess., pp. 288–90; Hafen, *Broken Hand,* p. 280; LeRoy R. Hafen, "Thomas Fitzpatrick and the First Indian Agency in Colorado," *Colorado Magazine* 6 (1929):59.

bluffs and bottomlands around Fort Laramie. Thousands and thousands of ponies were herded beyond the lodges, and about two hundred uniformed United States troops scouted the area, charged with keeping order.[23] Before the council convened, the Indian ponies had eaten all the available grass, and Fitzpatrick was forced to move the council site to an area of level, grassy fields near Horse Creek, thirty-seven miles below Fort Laramie.[24]

For eighteen days and nights the large Indian camp took on an air of a county fair, with music, games, dancing, and feasting around the clock. Tribes that had been enemies as long as anyone there could remember now camped side by side, visiting back and forth in one another's lodges, exchanging gifts, smoking together, and pledging peace.

One of the great spectacles of this spectacular assembly came when a thousand Sioux warriors, in a spendid display of horsemanship, rode down the Platte four abreast, in perfect cadence, shouting and singing. Filing across the top of a ridge where everyone could see them, they descended into the council area and reined their ponies in front of the commissioners' tents. Not to be outdone by this impressive sight, the Cheyennes immediately assembled their warriors and staged another show of horsemanship, much to the delight of the onlookers.[25]

Left Hand was certainly among them. His people were there in full force, and both Little Raven and Poisal, with whom he was closely associated, took an active part: Little Raven signed the treaty for the Southern Arapahos, and Poisal acted as interpreter. Left Hand's name does not appear in the council records only because he was not yet a tribal leader. There is no possibility that he would have missed this momentous event, which in large measure would determine his people's future. Nor would he and his wife have missed the opportunity to socialize with friends and relatives from the northern bands, visit with other tribes, display their first child, a daughter, and take part in the feasting and dancing.

When the council formally opened on September 8, 1851, the tribal chiefs assembled in a circle around the commissioners

[23] *BIA Reports* (1851), pp. 288–90.
[24] Hafen, *Broken Hand,* p. 290.
[25] Ibid.

under a huge canopy erected by the Indian women. Behind the chiefs stood their close advisers and other important men in each tribe. Left Hand probably was seated in a position behind Little Raven, in clear view of the proceedings.

Before the talks began, the commissioners and chiefs smoked the calumet, a large red pipe with a three-foot stem, decorated with colored beads and hair and filled with a mixture of plants, tobacco, and the bark of the red willow. As each chief accepted the pipe, he drew his hand from the bowl to his throat as a sign of the sincerity and truthfulness with which he would speak.[26]

Preliminaries over, Fitzpatrick and Mitchell immediately turned to the subjects of most concern. They acknowledged that the Indians' complaints about the destruction of buffalo herds and grazing lands were justified and offered the tribes payment of $50,000 in annuities for fifty years. They also promised government protection from further depredations by United States citizens.

Even more important was the acknowledgment of Indian ownership of the land. Each tribe was guaranteed the legal right to the area that it had traditionally claimed. Fitzpatrick, with the aid of Robert Campbell and Jim Bridger, two other traders familiar with the tribal grounds of the different tribes, wrote descriptions of the boundaries. Southern Arapaho and Cheyenne lands lay between the Platte and Arkansas rivers, from the Continental Divide eastward across the plains into central Kansas.

Satisfied with the government's acknowledgment of Indian land ownership and its offer of annuities, the chiefs gave the government permission to establish roads, military posts, and similar buildings on Indian lands. They also agreed to keep the peace among themselves and to remain at peace with the whites. On September 15, 1851, the Treaty of Fort Laramie, the first treaty between the United States and the Plains Indians, was signed.[27]

Optimism ruled the day. Indians and whites alike looked upon the treaty as an assurance of future peace on the plains. Rights

[26]*BIA Reports* (1851), pp. 288–90; Hafen, "Thomas Fitzpatrick," p. 59.
[27]Charles J. Kappler, *Indian Affairs: Laws and Treaties,* 2:55–60.

and obligations had been spelled out and agreed upon. The Indians had the right to the land; the government could move men and materials across the land and establish posts in the region. The Indians would refrain from attacks on whites; the government would recompense the tribes for past losses.

The commissioners swelled with pride. Fitzpatrick considered the treaty a job well done. As his biographer LeRoy Hafen wrote: "On the surface all that he had hoped and struggled for had been accomplished, and there was apparent promise of a lasting peace."[28]

Father Pierre-Jean De Smet, the Jesuit missionary who spent the eighteen days of the council baptizing Indian babies, including Fitzpatrick's son (Andrew Jackson Fitzpatrick), expressed the hope prevailing among the Indians: "It will be the commencement of a new era for the Indians—an era of peace," he wrote. "In future, peaceable citizens may cross the desert unmolested, and the Indian will have little to dread from the bad white man, for justice will be rendered to him."[29]

Several days after the signing of the treaty, supply wagons, tardy but welcome, arrived with the first $50,000 worth of annuity goods. Among the gifts parceled out were United States Army uniforms for the chiefs, complete with coats, pantaloons, sabers, and medals. Within moments the leaders of the Plains Indians, with moccasined feet, painted faces, and hair flowing over their shoulders, were parading proudly about in the white man's uniforms. It was, Hafen wrote, a sight "both ludicrous and pathetic."[30]

As Left Hand and his village moved downstream of the council site and toward the buffalo ranges with the other Southern Arapahos that September, 1851, there was much to reflect upon: the hope for the future, the mingling and socializing, the pageantry and festivities of the Plains Indians, the sense of pride in themselves.

There was also something else to reflect upon. In the midst of

[28] Hafen, *Broken Hand,* p. 300.
[29] Pierre-Jean De Smet, *Life, Letters and Travels of Father Pierre-Jean De Smet,* p. 684.
[30] Hafen, *Broken Hand,* p. 300.

the council's optimism, a discordant note had been heard. It was
an ominous note sounded by the different chiefs when, one by
one, they had spoken of the passing of the buffalo and the growing poverty of their villages. They had wondered aloud how their
people would live in the days to come.[31]

[31] Ibid., p. 296.

3

My friend, you are about to be
   made a chief.
After this you will no longer be a
   common man. . .
Walk straight ahead, and do your
   best for your people.

Carl Sweezy,
Southern Arapaho

The promise of Fort Laramie soon faded. The treaty notwith-standing, conditions on the central plains deteriorated steadily during the 1850s for the Southern Arapahos and Cheyennes. Immigrant trains, surveying parties, and troops continued to plow through the land, slaughtering game, dispersing buffalo herds, and cutting through the ranges of grass. The continuing devastation threw the tribes into panic and confusion. Poverty and hunger were now their constant companions.

During these years of devastation, Left Hand and his people roamed as usual over their lands between the Platte and Arkansas rivers, maintaining their trading business with other tribes and with whites when possible, and hunting buffalo wherever they could. Times were exceedingly hard. Thomas Fitzpatrick reported in 1853 that the Arapahos, Cheyennes, and Sioux were in a "starving state. They are in abject want of food half the year. . . their women are pinched with want and their children constantly crying out with hunger."[1]

The Northern Arapaho chief Medicine Man poignantly described the hardships suffered by both northern and southern tribes during this period when he said:

> We see the white men everywhere; their rifles kill some of the
> game, and the smoke of their campfires scares the rest away and
> we are no longer able to find any game; our little chilren are crying
> for food. . . . Our horses, too, are dying because we ride them so
> far to get a little game for our lodges.[2]

[1] *BIA Reports* (1853), Sen. Exec. Doc. 1, 33d Cong., 1st sess., p. 368.
[2] LeRoy R. Hafen, *Relations with the Indians of the Plains*, vol. 9 in *The Far West and the Rockies Historical Series*, p. 178.

As the hardships intensified, the Southern Arapahos and Cheyennes came to depend more and more upon the government annuities promised by the Fort Laramie Treaty. Flour, sugar, coffee, bolts of fabric, household utensils, and wool blankets were distributed each fall at the new stone fort William Bent built in 1853 on the north bank of the Arkansas River, near his ranch at Big Timbers.

For Bent, business was on the upswing due, in large measure, to the government contract he had received for hauling the annuity goods from St. Louis. Adding to his good fortune was the growing demand in the states for the luxurious buffalo robes that Bent obtained from the tribes, either through trade or by outright purchase. Wagons piled high with robes regularly rolled from Bent's Fort to the market in St. Louis and returned loaded with annuity goods. Because money earned from the government contract covered the cost of the robes, Bent was able to realize profits of 100 percent on their sale.[3]

Seeing how some of the white men were profiting from the shifting situation on the plains, many Southern Arapahos and Cheyennes began to look to them for help in overcoming the growing hardships. At Fort Laramie these Indians earned the name "Laramie Loafers," hanging around and begging for food or other handouts. At Bent's Fort they were considered nuisances, always in the way, looking for odd jobs or offering their wives in prostitution for a little money with which to buy the white man's food and whiskey. Now, along with smallpox and cholera, venereal disease and drunkenness began to demoralize both tribes.[4]

The dire effects of alcohol on the Plains Indians had long been recognized by the federal government, which had outlawed the trade of alcohol to Indians in 1834. Unscrupulous traders had continued to deal in it, however, making enormous profits by exchanging bottles of cheap, diluted whiskey for valuable beaver pelts or buffalo robes. Even Bent, St. Vrain and Company had traded whiskey during the 1840s, and not until smaller traders had begun to cut into their business did they stop handling alcohol and demand that the superintendent of Indian Affairs

[3] George Hyde, *Life of George Bent*, p. 95.
[4] David Lavender, *Bent's Fort*, p. 329.

enforce the law. The result, of course, was that smaller traders, whose main commodity was whiskey, were put out of business, leaving Bent's company to dominate trade on the plains.[5]

Although Bent was no longer in the whiskey business in the 1850s—circumstances were such that he did not need to be—there were always independent traders or other white men passing through the region and stopping at the forts who were eager to flaunt the law and exchange alcohol for buffalo robes or anything else of value. Among the Southern Arapaho and Cheyenne men, the demand for whiskey grew apace with the accumulating hardships.

At the same time the warriors refrained from attacking whites moving across the plains and, in fact, endeavored to stay out of their way. In 1852, the year following the Fort Laramie Treaty, Commissioner of Indian Affairs Luke Lea reported to Congress that the Plains Indians were making a conscientious effort to abide by the treaty, though they suffered greatly from the continuing white immigration.[6]

Despite this demonstration of good faith by the tribes, the Senate decided that the treaty terms were too generous and unilaterally cut the length of time that annuities would be distributed from fifty years to fifteen. Fitzpatrick was charged with the unpleasant task of notifying the Indians and obtaining their agreement.

With a heavy heart the agent once again made the rounds to the Indian villages, trying somehow to explain why the Senate found it necessary to reduce payments while the devastation on the plains mounted. He found the Southern Arapaho and Cheyenne villages near the crumbling adobe walls of now-abandoned Fort St. Vrain. To his surprise, the chiefs agreed to the treaty change and willingly placed their marks next to their names on the new document.

No doubt they saw the velvet hammer in the Senate's action. Their failure to agree would render the treaty null and void and, rather than receiving a reduced amount of annuities, their people would receive nothing at all from the government. It is also true

---

[5] Janet LeCompte, "The Hardscrabble Settlement: 1844–1848," *Colorado Magazine* 31 (1954):81–98.

[6] *BIA Reports* (1852), Sen. Exec. Doc. 1, 32d Cong. 2d sess., p. 299.

that the whole question of annuities—the amount and the number of distribution years—was second in importance to a far more threatening development. According to Fitzpatrick, the chiefs voiced stiff opposition to the movement of troops over the plains and told their agent that they were "strongly adverse to the establishment of military posts in their midst."[7] They had not understood the magnitude of the military presence on the plains when they agreed to the treaty, and now they were filled with deep concern for the safety of their villages. They were powerless, however, to negotiate any changes in the treaty, despite the Senate's unilateral action.

It was sometime during this period of growing concern over the direction of events that Left Hand became one of the Southern Arapaho chiefs, although no evidence exists to pinpoint the exact date. That he had not signed the Fort Laramie Treaty in 1851 indicates that he was not then one of the principal men. By 1858, however, he was a respected chief who held office with confidence, suggesting that he had been accustomed to a position of leadership for some time. Probably he had become a chief in the mid-1850s.

Until that time chiefs had traditionally been selected from one band, but the growing white traffic on the plains caused the Southern Arapahos to seek out leaders who could deal with white men.[8] Left Hand's command of English made him a valuable leader. That alone, however, would not have been sufficient to make him a chief. Only the most qualified young men, those who had proved themselves brave and trustworthy, who were unselfish in procuring food for others, and who had shown good sense and judgment in the past were considered eligible for the position. The male members of the tribe, guided by the wisdom and insight of the elders, made the final selection.[9]

The selection was a solemn undertaking, since the survival of the tribe, especially during these years of change, depended upon having outstanding leaders, men with vision who could

[7] Ibid, p. 363.
[8] Sister Inez M. Hilger, "Arapaho Child Life and Its Cultural Background," Smithsonian Institution, Bureau of American Ethnology Bulletin no. 148 (1952), p. 188.
[9] Ibid., p. 190.

guide their people toward the future, make wise decisions, and act with courage. For these reasons the office of chief was not hereditary.[10] There was no reason to believe that a chief's sons, because they were his sons, were qualified to lead. Nor was there room for petty politics, nepotism, or other political games that might result in placing unfit men in office. For the good of all, every effort was made to confer authority upon the best-qualified men in the tribe.

By the 1850s, Left Hand had already met the traditional tests of courage and resourcefulness demanded by a warrior society. For some time he had worked closely with Little Raven who, as white men continued to press upon Indian lands, probably depended upon him more and more as an interpreter and looked to him for advice. It was natural that Left Hand's expanding role in tribal affairs should be formalized with the title of chief.

Left Hand was probably installed in office during the Sun Dance, the usual occasion for conferring authority upon leaders. According to the Southern Arapaho Carl Sweezy, installation ceremonies, which were solemn and reverent, took place before the entire tribe. The head chief or other leading man faced the man who had been selected for office and said:

> My friend, you are about to be made a chief. After this you will no longer be a common man. You will stand in a high place where everyone can see you. Sometimes your people will praise you, and sometimes they will find fault with what you do. Do not be discouraged when they blame you, or ashamed when they laugh at you. Walk straight ahead, and do your best for your people.[11]

For Left Hand these words would prove prophetic. Although he would counsel with other principal men and seek advice from the elders, in the end he would walk alone. He would bear the responsibility for his decisions and would act upon them regardless of their popularity. His authority would always rest on the trust his people had willingly placed in him.

Left Hand would hold the office of chief for life. Scholars differ on whether any Southern Arapaho chief could actually be deposed, but it is clear that a poor leader who lost his people's faith

[10] Virginia Cole Trenholm, *The Araphoes, Our People*, p. 52.
[11] Carl Sweezy, *The Arapahoe Way*, pp. 18–19.

could be ignored. Not even the Spear Men age society would enforce a chief's rules if they did not respect him. Authority was
given by the people, and it could be recalled by the simple
method of refusing to obey leaders who were out of favor.[12]

Sweezy's descriptions of a chief's duties provide insight into
the wide scope of Left Hand's responsibilities. A chief's most important concern was for the safety of his people, Sweezy wrote.
He decided when his village would move to a new location and
which trail his people would follow. He sent out scouts to find the
buffalo herds that would guarantee successful hunts and decided
when raiding parties should be sent against other tribes. If his
village was in danger of attack, he was responsible for moving the
women and children to a safe place. He scheduled the dates of the
tribal religious ceremonies, including the Sun Dance, and
watched over the plans.

An assortment of mundane concerns vied for his attention, according to Sweezy. A chief knew all the families in his village and
took an interest in their welfare. When someone was ill, the chief
called the medicine man. If a family met with misfortune, he saw
that food, shelter, and clothing were provided. He was often
called upon for advice, which he gave as best he could. And he
kept the people informed of news by sending criers through the
village. "To be our kind of leader," Sweezy wrote, "[a chief] had
to spend much time talking and listening, and thinking and con-
templating. By these means he could look at things clearly and
fairly. He was what white people would call a statesman and a
philosopher."[13]

When Left Hand became a chief, Little Raven, a moon-faced,
muscular man in his mid-forties who had been a tribal leader
since 1840, was principal chief. Still other leaders included Big
Mouth, Storm, and Shave Head, each responsible for a band
which might increase or decrease as the people moved about.[14]
Together the chiefs formed the tribal council that made decisions

[12] Hilger, "Arapaho Child Life" p. 189, Sweezy, *Arapaho Way*, pp.
18–19.
[13] Sweezy, *Arapaho Way*, p. 19. Sweezy refers specifically to Little Raven,
but the description of a chief's duties applies to the office in general.
[14] These chiefs would sign the Fort Wise Treaty in 1861, indicating their
prominence during this period.

and regulations for the tribe as a whole and selected, from among themselves, the principal chief.

Throughout the 1850s the Southern Arapaho chiefs attempted to follow a course of restraint in the face of the white migration. Despite provocations by immigrants who wasted the buffalo and generally behaved as though the plains' resources were inexhaustible, the chiefs labored to keep the young warriors in check and prevent any actions that could bring the white man's military might against their villages. It was the steady influence of responsible leaders that accounted for the peace on the plains which Commissioner Lea had commented upon in 1852 and which continued until the latter part of the decade.

As they worked to prevent conflicts between their people and the whites, the Southern Arapaho chiefs gradually came to acknowledge that the continuing white migrations which had brought so many hardships were putting an end to the Indians' traditional way of life. Eventually, they realized, their people would be forced to find a new livelihood. As long as they had believed that they could continue to hunt the buffalo and roam about as usual, they had resisted the idea of change. But now change was being thrust upon them.

By the mid-1850s the chiefs had begun to talk about the possibility that their people could adapt to an agricultural life, given the proper tools and instruction. The idea that Plains Indians could become farmers was not new. It had emerged from time to time since the 1840s, but had always been discounted. In 1847, Fitzpatrick wrote that farming was "too laborious" for the Indians and that they could never adapt to such a life. At the Fort Laramie Treaty Council the chiefs themselves had referred to "this thing of farming, which the white man was always suggesting," and had protested that they knew nothing about it and did not see how they could be expected to make their living in this way.[15]

By 1852, Superintendent Mitchell had reported that the Indians were definitely opposed to learning agriculture because they believed that they would soon be driven into the mountains

[15] LeRoy R. Hafen, *Broken Hand,* p. 296; *BIA Reports* (1847), Sen. Exec. Doc. 1, 30th Cong., 1st sess., p. 242.

or out onto the driest part of the plains and that it would be impossible to farm in either place.[16]

As the 1850s wore on, however, and the realities of their situation became more apparent, the chiefs began to view farming as yet another accommodation to their own survival, one in a long series of adaptations that their people had made throughout history. They were, after all, experts at moving into new traditions without letting go of the old, and this ability to adapt had broadened and improved their lives. Pushed onto the plains by the migration of eastern tribes in the eighteenth century, they had found an excellent and seemingly inexhaustible food supply in the buffalo. After acquiring ponies from the Comanches, who had gotten them from the Spanish, they were able to follow the buffalo herds vast distances, thus ensuring their food supply. Rifles and gunpowder—bringing still further adaptations—made the kill easier and more certain. No longer did they have either to herd the buffalo and drive them off steep bluffs or to rely solely on the bow and arrow. This past history gave the chiefs hope that agriculture might bring their people a measure of safety and security that would improve their lives.

In the last half of the decade the necessity for further adaptation took on new urgency. In 1855 a surveying party traversed the central plains and mapped out a new wagon road through the heart of the buffalo range from the area of the Kansas, Solomon, and Smoky Hill rivers to Bent's Fort on the Arkansas. The following year countless immigrant trains moved over the new road, called the Smoky Hill Trail, which was a shorter route across the plains than either the Oregon or the Santa Fe Trail. In addition three different surveying parties had crossed the plains looking for the best route for the proposed transcontinental railroad. The Indians feared that it was only a matter of time before the white man's steel horse thundered through their lands, connecting the eastern states with the new state of California.[17]

To make matters worse, the Southern Arapahos lost the man they had come to depend upon as an honest and fair intermediary

[16] *BIA Reports* (1852), p. 356.
[17] Donald J. Berthrong, *The Southern Cheyennes*, pp. 132-33.

between them and the government, someone whose advice they could trust. Agent Fitzpatrick had been called to Washington to report on a treaty he had concluded with the Kiowas and Comanches, similar to the Fort Laramie Treaty, and, while ensconced in the comforts of the Brown Hotel, the rugged plainsman took suddenly ill and died on February 7, 1854.[18]

Given these developments, it was not surprising that the man who replaced Fitzpatrick, John W. Whitfield, reported that the Southern Arapahos and Cheyennes were "uncertain as to their position toward the United States." Whitfield viewed the situation on the plains in the simplest of terms. As he saw it, the government had three options in dealing with the Plains Indians: it could conduct a war of extermination against them; it could allow them to die natural deaths from famine and disease; or it could feed them until they could adjust to changes and care for themselves. The last option, he allowed, was the most humane—and probably should be adopted—but not until, as he put it, the tribes had been "whipped into submission."[19]

In 1857, the War Department laid plains to do just that. Gen. Persifer F. Smith, commanding the Department of the West, ordered Col. Edwin V. Sumner and Lt. Col. Albert Sidney Johnston to set out from Missouri "at the first springing of the grass" and "severely punish the Cheyennes."[20]

The order resulted from Cheyenne raids along the Oregon Trail—also called the Platte Road—in the late summer of 1856 in which several immigrants were killed and others taken prisoner. According to Thomas S. Twiss, agent to the Northern Arapahos and Cheyennes, the Cheyenne chiefs had done everything possible to prevent the raids, even organizing parties of their own relatives and friends who were sworn to kill any raiders leaving the villages. Still they had been unable to keep the young warriors from seeking vengeance against the whites who had driven off the game and invaded their lands.[21]

[18] Hafen, *Broken Hand,* p. 318.
[19] *BIA Reports* (1855), Sen. Exec. Doc. 1, 34th Cong., 1st and 2d sess., pp. 435–38.
[20] Hafen, *Relations,* p. 19.
[21] *BIA Reports* (1856), Sen. Exec. Doc. 5, 34th Cong., 3d sess., p. 638–45; see especially "Report of Agent Thomas Twiss."

Reaching the plains in the early summer of 1857, Col. Edwin Sumner divided his command, sending Maj. John Sedgwick with four companies of cavalry up the Arkansas River while he led two companies of cavalry and three of infantry along the Platte. Sedgwick circled the plains by turning north at present Pueblo and marching along the base of the foothills until he rendezvoused with Sumner east of present Greeley, Colorado. The entire force then drove toward the southeast directly into Indian country, where scouts found signs of Cheyenne camps. On July 29, 1857, Sumner spotted a group of Cheyenne warriors and hurled a surprise cavalry charge against them. The warriors quickly broke rank and fled, leaving four dead. Sumner's loss was two.

When the nearby village of Cheyennes got word that their warriors had been routed, the people fled in all directions. They left behind 171 lodges, fifteen to twenty thousand pounds of buffalo meat—their entire winter food supply—and all their equipment, robes, clothing, bedding, and utensils. Sumner marched into the abandoned village and burned it.

Still Sumner was not satisfied that the Cheyennes had been sufficiently punished. He continued his drive toward the Arkansas searching for the Indians, who by this time had scattered across the plains.[22]

The so-called war of 1857 was strictly a Cheyenne affair. Although the Southern Arapahos had camped near Cheyenne villages the previous summer, when warriors from that tribe were raiding white trains, they had not taken part. Nevertheless they suffered from Sumner's march, finding it impossible to send out hunting parties while troops patrolled the plains and rode through the buffalo ranges. As the Southern Arapahos knew, whites could not distinguish one Plains Indian tribe from another, and all were in danger while Sumner searched for Cheyennes.

On July 13, 1857, Robert C. Miller, the second agent to succeed Fitzpatrick in three years, came across a Southern Arapaho village on the Arkansas River. The people were starving, and

---

[22] Hafen, *Relations,* p. 19; Berthrong, *Southern Cheyennes,* p. 140.

Miller reported later that he immediately issued food and other annuities rather than compel them to travel to Bent's Fort, the customary distribution point. Terrified by Sumner's army, the Southern Arapahos assured Miller of their peaceful intentions and friendship for the whites. Little Raven, speaking with urgency, asked the agent to request the Great Chief to send them agricultural tools and white men to teach them how to farm. "The buffalo are disappearing," he said, "and our people will starve unless we learn to cultivate the soil."[23]

Miller continued to Bent's Fort where he met Sumner, who was still searching for Cheyennes. Not content with the destruction of a village and much of the tribe's winter food supply, Sumner ordered Miller to withhold Cheyenne annuitites as further punishment and to give all the goods to the Southern Arapahos and Apaches. Lead and flint, also earmarked for the Indians, were thrown into the Arkansas.[24]

Rather than "whipping the Cheyennes into submission," Sumner's actions that summer had only served to increase their hostility, causing them to adopt a more menacing attitude toward whites. In his September, 1857 report to the Headquarters of the Army, Sumner professed surprise that the Cheyennes now seemed "more hostile than they were before they were punished."[25]

But Sumner's march had left a deep impression on the Southern Arapahos, who were probably responsible for the assembly of Plains Indians—Cheyennes, Apaches, Kiowas, Comanches, and their own people—that waited at Pawnee Fork on the Arkansas for Agent Miller the following summer of 1858. As Miller approached the large Indian encampment, he was struck by the beautiful sight of fifteen hundred lodges, "snow white sides giving back the light of the sun," he rhapsodized, "numerous horses grazing quietly upon hill and dale, covering the whole face of the prairie like 'cattle upon a thousand hills'."[26]

The tribes, however, had no time for such rhapsodizing.

[23] Hafen, *Relations*, pp. 32–34.
[24] Ibid., pp. 38–39.
[15] Ibid., p. 47.
[26] Ibid., pp. 168–69.

Events on the plains began taking a dangerous course. Colonel Sumner was again on the march, this time searching for Kiowa villages south of the Arkansas. The chiefs told Miller that they had assembled to propose a new treaty, which they hoped would protect their people from such forays as Colonel Sumner's. They said that they fully recognized the uselessness of contending against the white man "who would soon occupy the whole prairie with his villages." "We have eyes," they continued, "and are not blind."[27]

Under the treaty proposed by the chiefs, the tribes would live upon certain lands and would take up farming, if the government would agree to provide them with the necessary instruction and tools. The government must also guarantee that whites would not encroach upon Indian lands. "They said they had often desired ploughs and hoes and wanted to learn to use them," Miller reported to the commissioner of Indian Affairs.[28] Unfortunately, the agent could only report the chief's proposal. Policy was made in Washington.

The proposal held a note of desperation, and Miller indicated as much to his superiors when he reported that the Southern Arapahos were still suffering from the effects of the great cholera epidemic of 1849 and 1850, which, he said, had "swept them off by the hundreds." Smallpox had also ravaged the tribe and "at this time, veneral [sic] is gradually but surely thinning them out.... Scarcely a family is not to a greater or less extent afflicted by this terrible disease."[29]

In the summer of 1858 the Southern Arapahos clearly were in no condition to stave off the white invasion or fight army troops. Their future depended upon finding a new way of life, and their leaders, along with the leaders of other tribes, were desperately casting about for the best possible way. The new treaty proposal, which was more realistic than the treaty they had concluded at Fort Laramie seven years before, shows the influence of more sophisticated leaders, men who were assessing events on the plains with a straighter eye. Most certainly Left Hand attended this meeting and had a hand in the proposal.

[27] Ibid.
[28] Ibid.
[29] Ibid.

While the chiefs sounded out the government agent about a new treaty, a party of prospectors from Georgia, led by William Green Russell, was working its way along the foothills, stopping to wash sand out of the streams, and hoping to spot the glint of gold. In a tributary of the South Platte known as Dry Creek, on the site of the Southern Arapaho winter campgrounds and the present site of Denver, their hopes were fulfilled.

News that gold had been discovered spread like prairie fire to the white settlements on the Missouri River and throughout the plains tribes. For the whites, the news brought a message of hope; for the Indians, despair. The gold discovery in California ten years before had caused most of the current hardships on the plains. This new discovery meant that the white hordes, similar to those who had crossed the plains throughout the decade, would now come to stay.

The times demanded bold action. Following the meeting with Agent Miller, Left Hand decided to travel across the plains to the white settlements on the Missouri to see for himself, as he put it later, "how the white man procured his subsistence from the soil."[30] By visiting farms and picking up jobs during the harvesting season, he hoped to get a feeling for what agriculture was all about and learn what kinds of tools his people were going to need.

There would be another benefit in such a trip, not overlooked by a man like Left Hand. With one of their chiefs traveling across the plains to the white man's territory, in a sense reversing the situation of nearly two decades, the Southern Arapahos would be able to see themselves once again taking control of their own future, rather than merely waiting for misfortune to pile upon misfortune.

Such a trip by a Plains Indian was unprecedented. Only a few Arapahos had visited the states, and they had been escorted by Fitzpatrick following the Fort Laramie Treaty Council. Other agents had taken Plains Indians to the states from time to time, usually to impress upon them the power of the United States

---

[30] Marshall Cook manuscript (early 1880s), pp. 148–49. Colorado State Historical Society, Denver, Colo.

government, but no record exists of any other Plains Indian making the trip on his own.[31]

To reach the white settlements on the Missouri, Left Hand decided to follow the Platte Road—the Oregon Trail—a familiar Indian trail before it was taken over by immigrants. He would have to travel through territory held by the Sioux, Pawnees, and Arikaras, the latter two tribes being traditional Southern Arapaho enemies. As he crossed present-day Nebraska, he would come dangerously close to Fort Kearny, where Sumner's troops wintered between expeditions against the plains tribes. He would continue to bear eastward, moving farther and farther away from his own people until he reached the Nebraska farming settlements and the teeming, raucous Missouri River towns.

Such a trip was filled with dangers. In view of Left Hand's responsibilities as a chief he would not have undertaken it without the consent of the tribe's other principal men. Details of the trip were probably discussed in council, where it was decided that he should neither travel alone nor with a group of warriors who could be mistaken as a raiding party by other tribes or by frightened whites along the road who might hastily reach for their rifles. Instead he would travel in a wagon that he had gotten in trade with white men and would take along his wife and their young children. The reasoning behind this was probably that an Indian family could more easily pass in peace among both Indians and whites.

The trip would take about ten to twelve weeks, allowing three to four weeks for each crossing. While Left Hand was gone, his village would remain at Beaver Creek, and his brother, Neva, would see to Left Hand's responsibilities.

[31] Trenholm, *Arapahoes,* pp. 131, 139; see also Katherine C. Turner, *Red Men Calling on the Great White Father.* Long Chin, a Brulé Sioux, said in 1857 that he had been down to the Missouri and had seen the white man's settlements, but he was probably escorted. (Hafen, *Relations,* pp. 18–19.)

My children, when at first I liked
   the whites
My children, when at first I liked
   the whites
I gave them fruits.
I gave them fruits.

4

Southern Arapaho song

Left Hand, his wife, and their young children set out for
Nebraska and Iowa in July or early August, 1858, following the
intertribal meeting with Agent Miller.[1] Either they left directly
from the Pawnee Fork campground, traveling north until they
picked up the Platte Road next to the South Platte River, or they
moved with their village to Beaver Creek before setting out for
the East. No matter; they were on their way as summer was drawing to a close.

The family traveled in a small wagon pulled by two ponies. A
third pony, a fine, spirited animal that Left Hand reserved for
hunting buffalo, trotted alongside.[2] His wife rode in the wagon
beside him on the hard wooden seat, while their children— their
daughter was now about eight years old and had one or two
younger siblings—rode behind. Stored under the seat, within
easy reach, was the single-shelled shotgun which Left Hand had
obtained in trade with whites, and he had a hunting knife
sheathed to his belt.

Pulling a wagon across the rough, arid plains was an exhausting
feat for horses, accounting for the fact that white immigrants
usually pressed into service the hardier oxen and mules. Left
Hand was a knowledgeable horseman, fully aware of his ponies'
limitations, and to spare their strength his family traveled lightly,

[1] The meeting with the plains tribes was held on July 19, 1858 (*BIA
Reports* [1858], Sen. Exec. Doc. 1, pt. 1, 35th Cong., 2d sess., p. 448. 52).
[2] Marshall Cook manuscript, pp. 148–49, 155–64, Colorado State
Historical Society, Denver, Colo. The information on Left Hand's trip to the
Missour River is based on Cook's unpublished manuscript and is not cor-
roborated by any other source. It was accepted at face value, however, by the
eminent historian LeRoy R. Hafen (LeRoy R. Hafen, ed., "George A.
Jackson's Diary, 1858–1859," *Colorado Magazine* 12 [1935]:208).

probably carrying only a few blankets for warmth at night and a
parfleche packed with dried food.

Details of Left Hand's trip to Nebraska, still a territory at the
time, and Iowa, which was a state, might have been lost to history
had it not been for a fortuitous circumstance. On his return to the
plains he happened to join a train of goldseekers led by C. W.
Fisk out of Rulo, Nebraska. When this train neared Fort Kearny
in south-central Nebraska on October 6, it met and joined
another train under Marshall Cook out of Doniphen, Kansas.
Cook later wrote of his trip across the plains and included a detailed account of his conversations with the Southern Arapaho
chief who was his traveling companion for nearly three weeks.

In fact it was Left Hand who hailed Cook when they met and
proposed that the two trains merge for mutual protection while
crossing Arikara and Pawnee land. "We readily granted his request," Cook wrote, "as he could speak not only English but
Sioux and Arapahoe and many other Indian languages which
made him a valuable acquisition as an interpreter and guide."[3]

In conversations with Left Hand, Cook was given enough information about the chief's trip to make it possible to plot his
itinerary. He and his family had followed the Platte Road, which
was in reality little more than wagon ruts meandering through
the flat valleys and sandy bluffs south of the river. They probably
made camp each night among the stands of cottonwoods, watering the ponies and turning them out to graze.

When they passed Fort Kearny, they crossed a symbolic di-
viding line. With the exception of Fort Laramie, Fort Kearny was
the farthest extension on the plains of the white man's military
power, an outpost of white civilization. Beyond it was territory
rapidly coming under the control of whites. The outreach of
Nebraska farming communities, for example, now extended
about one hundred miles west of the Missouri River.

With the help of a rope ferry there, Left Hand and his family
probably crossed the Platte near the village of Columbus and continued to bear eastward, stopping at farms where Left Hand took
on odd jobs. Pushing still more deeply into white areas, the family arrived in Omaha, where they took another ferry across the

[3] Marshall Cook manuscript, p. 148.

Missouri to Council Bluffs and again visited farms and asked for work.[4] It was not uncommon for farmers to take on itinerant farmhands for harvesting, and no doubt there were at least a few who welcomed the work of a strong, English-speaking Indian who was obviously eager to learn. That he was successful in finding work seems to be the case, because later he told Cook that his experiences had taught him a great deal about farming.

The Missouri River towns through which Left Hand passed that fall were teeming with excitement over the prospects of the Pikes Peak gold rush. On August 26, the *Kansas City Journal of Commerce* had heralded the gold discovery as the New Eldorado that promised instant wealth to those who were courageous enough to seek it. On September 4, the *Nebraska News* prophesized that a great many would find the courage and that a rush of humanity would head across the plains to the goldfields.

The prophecy was already coming true. The river towns had long served as supply centers for the immigrant trains, surveying parties, and military expeditions embarking across the plains, and now, with news from the South Platte, the towns surged with goldseekers. Farmers and storekeepers, riverboat hands, and drifters from up and down the Missouri poured into the towns, clogging streets with their wagons while they haggled over oxen and mules and purchased supplies for the trip to the Pikes Peak region. Left Hand could not have traveled through Omaha and Council Bluffs that fall without encountering the frenzied knots of whites preparing to depart for Indian lands and instant fortunes. It could only have filled him with dread.

During the same time that Left Hand was making his way through Nebraska, trying to gather as much information on agriculture as he could, another man—who would later cast his lot on the plains—was also traveling the area, but on a different mission. John Milton Chivington, Methodist minister and presiding elder of the Omaha District of the Methodist Kansas-Nebraska Conference, was making his circuit rounds, stopping in the towns and farming communities to preach righteousness and

---

[4] Council Bluffs, Iowa, *Bugle* and *Non Pareil*, September, October, 1858; a search of these two newspapers reveals no mention of Left Hand or any other visitor to Council Bluffs.

God-fearingness, and robustly condemning the vice, corruption, and greed which he found everywhere.[5]

Although chance had placed the two men in the same area at the same time—the one to learn, the other to instruct—they were, of course, unaware of each other's existence. Had Left Hand happened upon a church or tent where a barrel-chested, red-bearded preacher was holding forth in front of a crowd of whites, it is unlikely that he would have stopped, nor would the preacher have wasted more than the slightest glance on an Indian family passing by. Nevertheless, from this time forward, the lives of these two men would follow similar paths which eventually would converge.

Near the end of September, Left Hand and his family began the long journey home. There is no account of how they happened to join C. W. Fisk's train on the return trip, but probably they met along the Platte Road and decided to join forces for mutual protection, the reason Left Hand later gave for merging Fisk's train with Cook's.

Both trains were composed of a new kind of plains traveler. In the past, few of the white immigrants moving through Indian lands had had any intention of settling there, with the exception of the indomitable traders. The great immigrant trains that had destroyed countless buffalo and disrupted the Indian way of life were only passing through; the plains merely represented an obstacle which had to be overcome in order to reach the promise of Oregon, California, or Utah. But the destination of the plains travelers in the fall of 1858, estimated at several hundred men, was the South Platte, in the heart of Indian territory, and they meant to stay as long as it took to find their fortunes.

Soon after the two trains merged, Cook was elected captain. According to his memoirs, he relied strongly upon Left Hand as guide through the vast, inhospitable land and looked to him to select the best camping sites, find grass for the animals, and negotiate the treacherous and numerous quicksand traps near the Platte.

In the evenings, when the men had a chance to relax around the campfire, Cook and Left Hand engaged in long, friendly con-

---

[5] Reginald S. Craig, *The Fighting Parson,* pp. 40–45.

versation. The Southern Arapaho chief spoke movingly of his concern that the plains would be appropriated by the white man, regardless, as he put it, of "primitive heridiment,"[6] or the prior rights of his people. There was much change ahead, he told Cook, and he hoped to be able to reconcile the minds of his people to its inevitability.

Left Hand told Cook that, because these changes were upon them, he had decided to see for himself how white men worked their farms and what kinds of food they planted and harvested. The trip had taught him many things, he said, but the most important was that an agricultural life would never suit his people—he called it too sedentary and unnatural for people accustomed to following the buffalo across the plains.[7] Despite the growing hopes in recent years that the Southern Arapahos could adapt to farming, Left Hand told Cook that he would not recommend it.

What he would recommend, however, was another kind of occupation, one with which he had become familiar during his trip: cattle ranching. It would suit his people, Left Hand told Cook, because it was not unlike their traditional ways (one wonders if Left Hand had entertained the notion of buffalo ranching). In addition, the arid plains seemed far better for grazing cattle than for farming. Certainly the plains sustained great herds of buffalo, and there was every reason to believe that the land would be ideal for raising cattle. His hope now, he said, was that the Great Father would help his people get started in this new life.

The campfire conversations gave Cook an insight into Left Hand's hopes and plans, but his actions during the daylight hours while the train wound its way across the plains taught the white men something about the life of the Plains Indians. Near the California Crossing, at the present site of Julesburg on the Nebraska-Colorado line and not far from where the Platte forks into the north and south branches, a herd of buffalo lumbered

---

[6] *hereditament?* This term of property law refers to "lands, tenements, any property corporeal or incorporeal, real, personal, or mixed" that may descend to an heir (*Webster's New International Dictionary,* 3d ed., s.v. "hereditament"), and is an impressive display of Left Hand's grasp of both concept and usage. (Marshall Cook manuscript, p. 148.)

[7] Ibid.

into view. "Great excitement prevailed," Cook wrote, "since most in the party had not witnessed the sight of wild buffalo running at large in a wild state."[8] The captain halted the train, and the men scrambled onto the wagon seats, shading their eyes against the sun and stretching to see the herd of black beasts on the horizon.

Left Hand caught the excitement. According to Cook, he handed the reins to his wife, grabbed his shotgun, jumped from the wagon "as lightly as a boy in his teens," and, placing three fingers in his mouth, whistled for his buffalo pony. Holding the shotgun high overhead, he rode toward the herd, man and animal moving in unison, Cook said, with "Left Hand's feet keeping time with the motion of the pony."[9]

Coming alongside a fat cow, Left Hand leveled the shotgun and fired. Instantly the pony veered sideways, to keep from being gored by the wounded buffalo, and circled at a safe distance while Left Hand reloaded. Once again, sensing his rider's commands, the pony moved in close enough for Left Hand to fire a second shot, which brought the buffalo down.

Cook and his men watched in awe as Left Hand dismounted, straddled the fallen buffalo, and cut its throat. Slicing long strips from the hide, he bared the flesh and began cutting off pieces, which he strung on thongs and hung around the neck of the pony patiently standing nearby. The white men gathered close around, watching as Left Hand continued butchering the animal, until finally he signaled them to make themselves useful and lend a hand. Cook wrote that everyone enjoyed a feast later that evening and that the meat was excellent.

Still more excitement was ahead. Not long after the buffalo kill, a small band of Sioux appeared on a bluff and began firing on the train. Cook halted the wagons as the men scurried for safety and crouched behind the wheels. Left Hand immediately volunteered to ride out and meet with the Sioux. Taking along an unidentified man who represented Cook, he rode toward the band, which, according to Cook, was headed by Red Cloud, the notable Sioux chief. Seeing Left Hand approaching, Red Cloud told his warriors to hold their fire. The two Indian chiefs greeted

[8] Ibid., p. 155.
[9] Ibid., p. 156.

each other, and Left Hand asked why the train had been fired upon. Red Cloud answered that the whites would have to pay for the slain buffalo.

The Sioux band probably had been hunting and was stalking the buffalo herd when Left Hand rode out and killed the cow. Red Cloud made it clear that his hunters did not appreciate losing one of the herd to a train of whites, and for the moment Left Hand found himself allied with white men accused of destroying Indian game. Red Cloud's demand for payment was the same demand that Left Hand and the other leaders of the plains tribes had been making since the days of the Fort Laramie Treaty Council.

Left Hand returned to the train, explained the situation to Cook, and probably suggested that sugar, considered a delicacy by the Indians, would be an appropriate payment for the buffalo. Cook sent several cups of sugar to the waiting Sioux, who then vanished, leaving the train of goldseekers to continue its way along the South Platte.

Toward late October the train reached Beaver Creek, where Left Hand's village was camped among the cottonwoods waiting for his return. Other Southern Arapaho villages may have been in the vicinity, since Cook wrote that there were so many lodges scattered all about that it looked as if the entire tribe was there. Waving good-bye to Cook, Left Hand and his family pulled their wagon out of the train and started toward their village.

As they approached, Cook noted, the Southern Arapahos swarmed from their lodges, like bees from a hive, throwing their hands in the air and whooping at the tops of their voices. Left Hand and his family jumped down and waded into the crush of people, the men embracing Left Hand, the women hugging his wife, and the children scrambling about, squealing and tugging one another.[10]

Before leaving the wagon train, Left Hand had invited Cook and some of the others to a feast in his village that evening. After making camp a short distance down along the South Platte, Cook and his men rode back to the Southern Arapaho village. Bonfires licked the air, Cook wrote, dogs were yapping, and children were

[10] Ibid., p. 159.

playing and running about. Women hurried in and out of the
lodges, tending the fires and preparing food. An air of excitement and celebration filled the village.[11]

Left Hand welcomed Cook's party, invited them to join a
group of Southern Arapaho men lounging around a bonfire, and
introduced Cook as the "cap-i-tan" of the train, using the
Spanish pronunciation. Toasting his guests, Left Hand said:

> We are but sensible affected that we can offer you but a poor
> welcome compared with the reception common among your peo-
> ple. Be assured that the best feelings of respect are put toward you
> and all we can offer you at present are our hearty welcome to visit
> our village and pass unmolested through our country, and you
> will allow me to tender my thanks for the many favors rendered
> me on my return.[12]

Following Left Hand's toast, Cook rose and said that he found it
gratifying, indeed, to have such a welcome from the noble red
men of the plains. Left Hand interpreted his words to the other
Southern Arapahos.

Then it was Neva's turn. Also speaking in English, Neva proposed a toast to the health of the Great Father who, he said, was
the only one who knew what would happen next on the plains.
Only a few years before, Neva explained, the Mississippi had
been a formidable barrier between the states and the plains.
Then "the great steam horse came plowing up the old muddy
Missouri, creating new apprehensions among our people. The
next moment that shocked our minds was the continued string of
wagons and swarming multitudes of people going west in the
Prairie Schooner."[13]

Following each toast, according to Cook, everyone took a drink

[11] Ibid., pp. 159–60.

[12] Ibid., pp. 161.

[13] Ibid., p. 161–62. Neva could not have used the term "prairie
schooner," the wind wagon invented in 1859 for plains travel (and never successfully used). No doubt Neva was referring to the immigrant wagons crossing
the plains since 1842, and Cook later ascribed to him the words "prairie
schooner," which had become the popular but incorrect name for the Con-
estoga wagons adapted for plains travel. (Percy Stanley Fritz, *Colorado: The
Centennial State*, p. 108.)

of the "sparkling waters of the Platte." The genial round of speeches ended when the women appeared and quietly placed portions of steaming food before each man. Left Hand turned to his guests and invited them to begin eating. Some of Cook's men asked what it was they were eating and Left Hand explained that the meat was fattened dog, the traditional Arapaho delicacy prepared for special occasions. Cook caught the horrified look in his men's eyes and made the clumsy excuse that the lateness of the hour demanded that they return at once to camp.[14]

Thanking Left Hand for his hospitality, Cook and his men hastily left the Southern Arapaho village and rode through the darkness toward their own campsite. Long after most of the white goldseekers had found a wearied sleep, Cook wrote, Left Hand's village remained an oasis of light and festivity on the darkened plains, the sound of laughter and singing and the muffled roll of drums intermittently punctuating the night.

[14] Ibid., pp. 163–64. The Southern Arapahos were fully aware that white men were repulsed by dog meat, yet they frequently shared this feast with whites, or attempted to, and occasionally made a few converts. Father De Smet, who partook of a roasted dog at the Fort Laramie Treaty Council, found it rather tasty, similar in flavor and texture to pork. (Pierre-John De Smet, *Life, Letters, and Travels of Father Pierre-John De Smet*, 2:682)

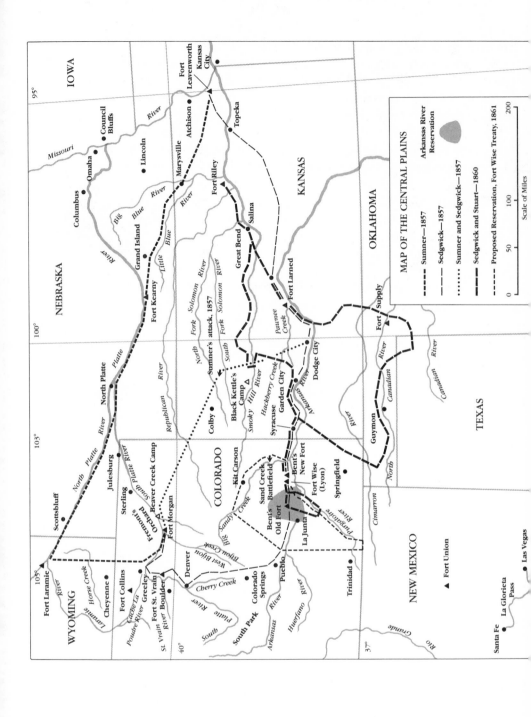

MAP OF THE CENTRAL PLAINS

- – – – Sumner—1857
- – – Sedgwick—1857
- · · · · · Sumner and Sedgwick—1857
- ▬ ▬ Sedgwick and Stuart—1860
- – – – Proposed Reservation, Fort Wise Treaty, 1861

Arkansas River Reservation

Scale of Miles

0   50   100   200

An Arapaho camp. *Courtesy of Smithsonian Institution, National Anthropological Archives, Washington, D.C.*

Arapaho women and children. *Courtesy of the Western History Division, Denver Public Library.*

Woman preparing a buffalo hide. *Courtesy of Smithsonian Institution, National Anthropological Archives.*

The Herd, 1860 drawing of buffalo on the central plains by M. S. Garretson.
Courtesy of the Kansas State Historical Society, Topeka.

An 1851 photo of Cheyenne chief White Antelope (left) made during a trip to Washington, D.C., with Agent Thomas Fitzpatrick following the Fort Laramie Treaty Council. Others shown here are Man on a Cloud, Cheyenne (center), and Little Chief, Sioux (right). *Courtesy of the Kansas State Historical Society.*

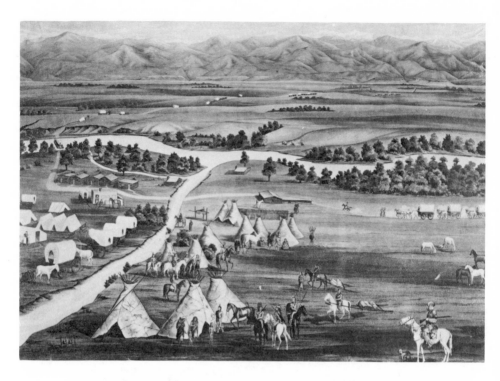

Denver in late 1858 was a mixture of goldseekers' shelters and Southern Arapaho lodges. This drawing may be the work of artist John Glendenin. *Courtesy of the Colorado State Historical Society, Denver.*

Goldseekers camping in Denver in the spring of 1859 are depicted in this engraving from *Frank Leslie's Illustrated Newspaper,* New York, April 30, 1859. *Courtesy of the Colorado State Historical Society.*

Apollo Hall, second from left, was situated on Larimer Street between Fourteenth and Fifteenth streets in Denver. Left Hand attended the play *Lady of Lyons* here. *Courtesy of the Colorado State Historical Society.*

Photograph of Denver in the early 1860s shows the offices of the *Rocky Mountain News* that Left Hand visited. *Courtesy of the Colorado State Historical Society.*

...the stars fell as thick
as the tears of our women shall fall
when you come to drive us away.''

5

Bear Head, Southern Arapaho

Left Hand reached his village at Beaver Creek about October 26, 1858, ahead of a severe storm that would blanket the plains with ten inches of snow by the end of the month. The storm abated as quickly as it had begun, however, giving way to open, sunny skies and exceptionally warm November days. Nevertheless, it warned of winter, and not long afterward Left Hand told his people to get ready to move to the winter campgrounds near the foothills in the high, lovely valley where Boulder, Colorado, is located today.

On the day of the move the women broke camp. Within two hours they had pulled down and folded the heavy lodge coverings, tied the poles into bundles, and loaded family belongings onto the travois support frames made of leather straps laced between two long poles; one end was hitched to the backs of dogs or ponies, while the other dragged the ground. Small items were stuffed into willow baskets that swung on the sides of the ponies. Puppies too young to scamper along also rode in the baskets, their heads bobbing in and out of view.

The move took place in the traditional manner. The people traveled in a long, irregular line with Left Hand and other prominent men riding in the front, followed by the old men, women, children, and pack animals, in that order. The village herd of ponies and mules, driven by several women, brought up the rear, while the young warriors rode back and forth along the column, aiding the herders and acting as lookouts. Large packs of dogs belonging to the village trailed behind.[1]

The trip from Beaver Creek to the base of the foothills required

[1] Few eyewitness accounts of a Southern Arapaho village move exist. Details presented here are drawn from Gen. George Armstrong Custer's account in *My Life on the Plains*, pp. 505–506.

three to four work-filled days for the women, who made temporary camp each evening, cooked, washed utensils and clothing as usual, and packed again each morning. The route lay along the South Platte to the mouth of St. Vrain Creek. Here the people crossed the larger river and continued along the St. Vrain into Boulder Valley. At the present site of Lyons they veered southward, moving along the foothills to Boulder Creek, where they stopped and set up winter camp. On the shoulder of the foothills to the west loomed the sheer, spectacular cliffs which white men would later call the Flatirons.

White men had to be a subject much on Left Hand's mind that November as he traveled with his people to their usual wintering area. There was no doubt that goldseekers were heading toward the plains—many had already arrived, including Marshall Cook's party—and the prospect of whites camping on Indian lands could only mean increased tension and conflict. Left Hand was certainly aware that difficult decisions lay ahead for the Indian leaders. Their people's safety and future would depend on how they met this new threat to Indian life. He was probably looking forward to spending the winter in Boulder Valley, thirty miles north of the gold discovery, and taking time to talk with his people, consider their views and concerns, and mull over the best future course.

Events were to deny him that time. His band had just set up their village on Boulder Creek when Left Hand learned that a white party was camped nearby, close to the prominent red sandstone outcroppings of the foothills. He was forced to deal immediately with this new vanguard of whites on Indian lands.

Like other goldseekers pushing into the Pikes Peak region that fall, the Boulder party had joined a larger train setting out from Omaha and Nebraska City and had followed the Platte Road west to St. Vrain Creek. Stopping to get their bearings, they had clambered up the ruined walls of Fort St. Vrain and surveyed the area: on the south lay the gold diggings at the confluence of the South Platte River and Cherry Creek; on the west stretched the mountains. Reasoning that gold found in the streams had probably washed out of the mountains, the Boulder party broke from the train and struck out on its own for the foothills.

Early histories list the following men in the party: Capt. Thomas Aikins; his son, S. J. Aikens; his nephew, A. A.

Brookfield; Charles Clauser; Captain Yount; Daniel Gordon and his brother; John Rothrock; Theodore Squires; Thomas Lorton; and two men named Moore and Dickens.[2]

These same histories are responsible for the legend surrounding Left Hand's first meeting with goldseekers in Boulder Valley. One account, attributed to Captain Aikens, has it that Left Hand hastened to the white camp, "full of apprehension, as if conscious of the impending fate of his tribe, and, assuming an air of authority, commanded: 'Go away; you come to kill our game, to burn our wood, and to destroy our grass'."[3] The account tells how the chief fully intended to drive off the white men, "but was caught by their guile. The crafty goldseekers affected to do obeisance to 'big Indian.' While being fed and flattered, in a gush of gratitude, the chief promised that the Indian and white man should live together in peace."[4] Another account adds that after the whites had fed Left Hand they offered him gold nuggets to pay for the land. He refused.[5]

Some of these accounts also include the story of a Southern Arapaho named Bear Head who challenged Left Hand's decision to allow the whites to remain and visited Aiken's camp himself. Pointing to the comet which was visible that November, he asked if the whites remembered when the stars had fallen. Indians and white men alike knew that he referred to the night of November 13, 1833, when ten thousand shooting stars had radiated out from the constellation Leo between midnight and dawn in one of history's most spectacular meteoric displays. Much later, William Bent's son George would comment that the Indians who had seen this spectacle never stopped talking about it.

To Bear Head the comet streaking across the sky was both an omen and a reminder of that other time, and he told Aikens that the stars had fallen "as thick as the tears of our women shall fall

---

[2] *History of Clear Creek and Boulder Valley, Colorado*, p. 379; Frank Hall, *History of the State of Colorado*, 1:225–26; Mary L. Geffs, *Under Ten Flags*, p. 235.

[3] *History of Clear Creek*, pp. 379–80.

[4] Ibid.

[5] Geffs, *Under Ten Flags*, p. 235. In fairness to the early historians, it must be understood that they were primarily interested in recounting the story of the goldseekers, not of the Indian chief whose land the whites had invaded.

when you come to drive us away."[6] Bear Head then threw down the gauntlet: Aikens and his men would leave Southern Arapaho lands within three days time or face an attack. During those days, dissension raged through the Indian village. Left Hand urged restraint; Many Whips, a Northern Arapaho, harangued the people about the necessity of driving off the whites; and the women mourned and wailed in fear.

On the morning of the third day Bear Head again appeared in the white camp and, to Aiken's surprise, announced that the whites need not fear attack. He had had a dream which had caused him to change his mind, he said.[7] In his dream the waters of Boulder Creek had risen until they flooded the land and washed away his people, and, when the flood subsided, only the white men remained.

These early accounts, written at some distance in time from the events, filled with hearsay and colored with nostalgia, told from the white man's point of view and probably incorporating a good deal of what the whites wished were true, are, nevertheless, the stuff of which legends are made. Left Hand appears the fool, the childlike buffoon easily beguiled and tricked by the crafty goldseekers into accepting the white camp near his winter campgrounds. There is a poignancy in the story of Bear Head that makes the legend all the more memorable and worth the retelling. Perhaps for this reason the legend has come to assume a truth of its own, wholly apart from what really happened.

What really happened is this: Left Hand reached Boulder Valley sometime in the early part of November, not in mid-October (in mid-October he was crossing the plains with Marshall Cook). By the time he arrived at Boulder Creek, Aiken's party had already constructed eleven crude log cabins. The presence of these whites some distance from their campsite threw Left Hand's people into an uproar, as it did other Arapahos, including a Northern Arapaho band which had also come into the area. Some of the young warriors immediately decided to force the whites off

---

[6] Frank Hall, *History of Colorado*, 1:225–26; *History of Clear Creek*, p. 379.

[7] Frank Hall, *History of Colorado*, 1:225.26; *History of Clear Creek*, p. 379.

the land. Eager to avoid conflict, Left Hand went to the white camp to learn about the goldseekers' plans.

He was the only man who could do this. During the following tension-filled days, he was the medium through which the Arapahos and white men communicated. Not only could Left Hand speak English, but he was also comfortable in dealing with whites. He had dealt with them all his life, and, as his recent trip to the white settlements proved, he did so with confidence and determination. Despite the legend's inference, he was no fool.

There are elements of the legend which are probably grounded in fact, however. No doubt Left Hand pointed out to Aikens, in strong language, that the party was on Southern Arapaho land and that the whites had already brought enough devastation to the plains. Certainly game had been killed, wood burned, and grass destroyed in the white migration.

Aikens assured Left Hand that his men intended to stay only through the winter and would move into the mountains to prospect in the spring. Like other early goldseekers, settling permanently on Indian land was, at this time, the farthest thing from their minds. They were consumed with the thought of finding fortunes and returning to their homes rich men. They were also determined. They had not endured the hardships of crossing the plains, living through a severe snowstorm, and finally reaching their destination full of high hope only to have a band of warriors frighten them away. Given these circumstances, Left Hand gave Aikens permission to stay through the winter. He may have accepted such gifts as sugar, coffee, and cigars—for which he had a great fondness. But the party could hardly have offered him gold nuggets since they had not yet found any.

It was not the gifts, however, which influenced Left Hand's decision to allow the party to stay. That decision was consistent with the course he and other responsible tribal chiefs had been following since the Fort Laramie Treaty Council. They had steadily worked to keep their young men from conflict with the whites, even as they watched whites bring unwanted changes to Indian life. There was no reason for Left Hand to have deviated from that policy when he met the goldseekers in his winter camping area.

The policy was based not on affection for whites, however, but rather on the ability of Left Hand and others chiefs to look at reality clear-eyed. As they had told Agent Miller the previous summer, any Indian attempt to drive whites from the plains would be useless, so great were their numbers in comparison to the population of the tribes.[8] The number of immigrants who had crossed the plains during the California gold rush, for example, exceeded the population of all the Plains Indian tribes, and the sheer weight of these numbers, as Neva had told Marshall Cook, had shocked the Indian mind. It was said that many Indians believed that all the white men in the world had passed over the plains.

Apart from this numerical superiority, white technology— the ability to manufacture arms and ammunition, to organize and transport large quantities of materials and hordes of men—gave whites an immense advantage over Indians and made them, in the minds of the chiefs, an insuperable force. The Indians had no way of acquiring arms except through trade with whites or by occasionally receiving them in their annuities. It was impossible for a nonindustrial society to wage war upon an industrial one— for warriors to contend against well-equipped troops who could be continually resupplied.

Nor was it likely that tribes which had long contended against one another could band together against a common foe. With the exception of the Southern Arapahos and Cheyennes, few of the plains tribes ever formed alliances for mutual aid.

Still another factor contributed to the chiefs' policy of restraint. Although not necessarily admiring the whites, many of the Indians—especially the practical, business-minded Southern Arapahos—had long admired white technology. Admiration was even implicit in the Arapaho word for white man, *niátha,* which means ''skillful'' or ''clever''. It also means ''spider,'' a creature the Arapahos believed was capable, like the white man, of wondrous and mysterious things.[9]

Many of the Indian leaders had come to view the white presence on the plains as double-edged. On the one hand whites brought destruction to the Indian way; on the other, they

[8] *BIA Reports* (1858), Sen. Exec. Doc. 1, pt. 1, 35th Cong., 2d sess., p. 450.

[9] James Mooney, ''The Ghost Dance Religion and the Sioux Outbreak of 1890,'' Smithsonian Institution, Bureau of American Ethnology Fourteenth Annual Report, no. 2 (1896), p. 978.

represented opportunities to learn white technology—especially that involved in farming and ranching—and to share in its benefits. This does not mean that these leaders had any intention of discarding their own customs or assuming those of whites. Their hope extended only to blending the practical aspects of one culture with the age-old traditions of the other.

Not all Plains Indians could appreciate those practical aspects, and not all agreed with the chiefs' policy of restraint. For this reason, the story of Bear Head has the ring of truth. It is likely that one or more of the young warriors from his village, outraged by the presence of whites near the winter campgrounds and bolstered by Northern Arapaho warriors in the area, defied Left Hand and threatened to attack Aikens's camp. It was Left Hand, of course, who told Aikens of the threat and made it clear that, because of his warriors' defiance, he could not guarantee the safety of the white camp—no more than the Cheyenne chiefs, two years before, had been able to prevent their young men from raiding the Platte Road.

During the three-day period following Bear Head's threat, Aikens's men prepared to defend themselves, while Left Hand met the insurrection in his village head on. By mustering support from the rest of his people, especially the elders and more mature men, he was able to force the young warriors to back down. He was also able in the same way to check the warriors from the other villages, including Many Whips, which gives some hint of his prestige in the tribe.

The crisis over, Left Hand returned to Aikens's camp with Bear Head and interpreted the warrior's poignant dream-story, a story also resounding with truth in its expression of the general feeling of hopelessness prevailing among the Arapahos. Thomas S. Twiss, agent to the Northern Arapahos and Cheyennes, described the feeling in his report to Washington that fall. The Arapahos believed, he wrote, that "when the white men come from towards the rising sun, [the Indians'] power and greatness must cease."[10]

The white men would come to Boulder Valley without fear. Left Hand had given his word to the goldseekers that they could

---

[10] *BIA Reports* (1858), p. 448.

remain in safety and had faced down his own warriors so that his word was not broken. He had met his first significant challenge as chief and had emerged with his authority intact—even strengthened. He had won the skirmish, but the major battles lay ahead.

"My wife will be a lady;
my children will be educated."

John Gregory,
upon discovering gold

6

It was an astonishing sight, never seen before on Indian lands. About 125 log cabins crowded the banks of the South Platte and Cherry Creek, and tents and makeshift shelters stretched in every direction. At least two hundred goldseekers had found their way to the gold diggings and another four hundred were camped up and down the South Platte. Each day brought a stream of newcomers, many in wagons and some carrying their possessions on their backs, having walked six hundred miles across the plains. All around was an air of purposeful activity: campfires burned steadily in the biting autumn chill, axes felled the cottonwood trees, and tents gave way to hastily built cabins.

Nearby, at the present site of Fifteenth and Blake streets in Denver, stood Little Raven's village of about twelve hundred persons, the entire Southern Arapaho tribe with the exception of Left Hand's band. The gold discovery had not deterred them from moving onto their winter campgrounds as usual. In fact, they had decided to make the best of the situation and, once settled, had launched a brisk trade with the goldseekers, hawking robes and skins for sugar, coffee, and flour.[1]

Sometime in late November or early December, Left Hand visited Little Raven's village. He probably left his own people in Boulder Valley, where they were settled for the winter, and, taking only the warriors closest to him, rode to Cherry Creek to see for himself the new developments. No doubt he also wanted to confer with Little Raven, whom he had not seen since his trip to the Missouri River.

The principal chief of the Southern Arapahos was then about forty-eight years old, with graying hair combed loosely over his

[1] Agnes Wright Spring, "Rush to the Rockies, 1859," *Colorado Magazine* 36 (1959):98–99; Jerome C. Smiley, *History of Denver*, p. 69.

broad shoulders. Like Left Hand he possessed a strong sense of responsibility toward his people and worried greatly about their future. The methods of the two leaders could not have been more dissimilar, yet, because of this, they complemented each other. Left Hand tended to act decisively, with confidence, as his trip to the Missouri River suggests. Little Raven liked to look at all sides of a question and consider every alternative before reaching a decision. He usually preferred a position in the middle of the road, rather than taking the chance of becoming entrenched on one side or the other. With whites swarming onto the winter campgrounds, Little Raven was probably most happy to see Left Hand, to exchange views with him, and to have his services as an interpreter. The two chiefs probably spent long hours talking and smoking together in Little Raven's lodge, within earshot of the goldseekers' increasingly frenzied activity.

The goldseekers were naturally eager to finish constructing their cabins before winter set in. With little concern over the scarcity of timber in the region, they waded into the cottonwood groves and felled many of the large old trees that had always provided shade and shelter to the Indians. One hurriedly constructed cabin turned out to look much like another, about fifteen feet square with a dirt floor, a single door, and no windows. Opposite the door was the only concession to comfort—a stone fireplace. Cracks between the logs were chinked with mortar made from riverbed clay and strengthened with saplings. Roofs were a combination of logs, thatch, and dirt which, according to contemporary accounts, acted like sponges, dripping water indoors for days following a rainstorm.

Unlike the Aikens party in Boulder Valley, some of these goldseekers had immediately seen the advantages of forming a permanent white settlement at the base of the foothills. The confluence of Cherry Creek and the South Platte was an ideal site, a natural hub around which prospecting and mining throughout the Pikes Peak region could turn. The mountains, which they hoped would disgorge riches, lay to the west; water was plentiful, and the South Platte provided the necessary lifeline to the Missouri River. They were not unaware that the land they camped on, and in which they hoped to find their fortunes, belonged to the Southern Arapahos and Cheyennes. Nevertheless, they moved swiftly to preempt Indian rights by establishing towns.

Under the Federal Townsites Act, settlers in border regions needed only to erect permanent dwellings and stake out 320 acres in order to form legal townships. Accordingly, the first town, Montana Town Company, was formed on September 7, 1858 (it would be deserted within a year). On September 24 the St. Charles Association laid out a town on the east bank of Cherry Creek; five weeks later, on October 20, Auraria was founded on the west bank; and on November 22 a party from LeCompton, Kansas Territory, jumped the St. Charles claim and founded Denver City Town Company.

Although towns were laid out, they had no legal basis. In the Fort Laramie Treaty, still in effect, the federal government had acknowledged Arapaho and Cheyenne ownership of the land bounded by the Platte and Arkansas rivers, and the Federal Townsites Act did not apply to Indian lands. In addition, Section Nineteen of the Organic Act of Kansas Territory, passed in 1854, had pointedly omitted all lands from territorial jurisdiction to which Indian rights had not been extinguished. Clearly there was no law, federal or territorial, under which the whites could claim title to any part of the central plains.

The Kansas Territorial Legislature had thought otherwise, however. On August 25, 1855, it had purposely ignored Section Nineteen and created Arapahoe County out of the area on the Kansas border west of the 103d meridian. With the discovery of gold the legislature saw additional reason to extend its influence into Indian lands; it authorized the LeCompton party to form Denver City Town, named, appropriately, after James W. Denver, the governor of Kansas Territory.

With the LeCompton party was an eager adventurer in his early twenties, Edward Wynkoop, who was appointed Arapahoe County sheriff and probate judge. Robust and darkly handsome, with a flowing handlebar mustache, Wynkoop had shunned the security offered by his middle-class Philadelphia family for the frontier excitement of Missouri and Kansas and, finally, the gold region. In his memoirs, written much later, he good-naturedly saw the irony of a man like him, who could feel at home in the finest Parisian salons, landing in the heart of Indian country and making do in a dirt-floored cabin. Like other whites coming into the region, Wynkoop traded with the Southern Arapahos when it served his purposes and thought of them, if at all, as wild savages and curiosities.[2] Later, however, he would cast his lot irrevocably with theirs.

In the last weeks of 1858, Wynkoop threw himself into the work at hand in the new towns, perhaps helping organize the settlement's first election on November 6, which named A. J. Smith to the Kansas Territorial Legislature. On December 5 he set out for Omaha, where he organized another train of hopeful goldseekers. These he guided across the plains to the fledgling towns in January.

The towns, by virtue of their existence, were beginning to take on an aura of legitimacy, at least in the view of the goldseekers. They held no legitimacy in the view of the Indians, however, whose fears grew apace with the numbers of goldseekers crowding the area. While the Southern Arapahos continued to mingle and trade with the newcomers, the Cheyennes disdainfully kept their distance, remaining in villages on the plains.

Not long after the new towns had been formed, however, both tribes sent messengers to William Bent, the old trader they had known for twenty-five years, who, following Fitzpatrick's death, was about the only white man on the plains they felt they could trust. Bent took up their cause in a series of letters to Superintendent of Indian Affairs A. M. Robinson, writing that the Cheyennes and Southern Arapahos were uneasy and restless, with "whites coming into [the region] making large and extensive settlements and laying off and building towns all over the best part of their country. This is their principle [sic] hunting grounds. They do not understand this. They have never been treated with for it." He also reiterated the Indians' desperate need to find a new way of life. "They are anxious to go to farming for a living," he wrote, but "they have not a single idea about what to commence at first."[3]

The Indians were caught in a tightening vise. Their traditional way of life had been under continual assault for nearly a decade, and now the goldseekers and their new settlements threatened to

[2] Percy Stanley Fritz, *Colorado: The Centennial State*, pp. 112–15; Edward W. Wynkoop manuscript, Colorado State Historical Society, Denver, Colo. (hereafter cited as Wynkoop manuscript), p. 27.

[3] LeRoy R. Hafen, *Relations with the Indians of the Plains*, vol. 9 in *The Far West and the Rockies Historical Series*, p. 173.

squeeze them out of existence. The Southern Arapahos were under no illusion about the consequences of the discovery of gold on their lands. During 1849 and 1850 they had seen the power gold exerted over white men, driving them to leave their homes and families, to travel long distances through the harshest kind of country, often without enough food or water, to endure disease and poverty, even to watch their children die. Such wondrous power was difficult for the Southern Arapahos to understand. Gold held no intrinsic value for them, although they occasionally obtained it in trade with the Mexicans, along with brass jewelry and items of silver. They liked to wear the brass bracelets and earrings, but they exchanged the gold and silver with other tribes, and with whites, for more practical goods.

For some time the Southern Arapahos and Cheyennes had lived in dread of whites learning about the gold on their lands. In 1850 a group of Cherokees bound for the California goldfields had found gold nuggets in Ralston Creek at the site of present-day Arvada, Colorado. Fortunately for the Plains Indians, the Cherokees continued to their original destination and the news of the discovery was lost in the rush to the Pacific Coast. The chiefs worried over the find, however, and from time to time expressed their fears to Agent Fitzpatrick. What if the goldseekers should return?

In his report of 1853, Fitzpatrick had made a startling prophecy of what would happen. Describing the South Platte, he wrote that

> mineral wealth likewise abounds in the sands of the water courses, and in the gorges and canons from which they issue; and should public attention ever be strongly directed to this section of our territory, and free access be obtained, the inducements which it holds will soon people it with thousands of citizens, and cause it to rise speedily into a flourishing mountain state.[4]

That, of course, was exactly what the Indians feared.

Those fears arose again for a brief time in the summer of 1857, when Fall Leaf, the Delaware scout guiding Sumner's troops in the campaign against the Cheyennes, discovered nuggets in a

---

[4] *BIA Reports* (1853), Sen. Exec. Doc. 1, 33d Cong., 1st sess., p. 366.

stream near present-day Denver. The discovery caused a flurry of excitement in the Missouri River towns, but it was not until the gold was washed out of Dry Creek by Russell's party, which included some of the Cherokees who had found the nuggets eight years earlier, that the dreaded white invasion got under way.

For the Southern Arapahos and Cheyennes there were two choices: they could accept the white settlements or they could attempt to force them off the land. Some of the young men advocated the latter, as Left Hand had discovered in Boulder Valley. They believed that they should act while they had a chance of succeeding, before the settlements became too strong and too numerous. It is true that the tribes numbered fifteen hundred persons each, and could field six hundred warriors armed with bows and arrows and an assortment of guns. No doubt this was a force strong enough to attack and overwhelm the groups of goldseekers arriving daily.

Still, the responsible men of the tribes, Left Hand among them, continued to speak for friendliness and restraint. The warriors might drive away some goldseekers, but the chiefs understood that others would come, probably bolstered by well-equipped army troops. Because they could not hope to succeed in any major conflict with the white men, they believed it best not to get involved in minor ones. There had to be other means of dealing with this latest threat to Indian lands, and, while the chiefs sought those means, they worked steadily to keep their warriors under control. In his letter to the superintendent, Bent noted that whites were able to pass through Indian lands unmolested, even though they stole horses from the Indians and antagonized them in other ways. Such was the influence of the chiefs.[5]

The policy of friendliness and restraint might not work, but it was all they had, and Left Hand was its strongest supporter. While staying in Little Raven's village, he made a point of getting to know the goldseekers, trading with them, and visiting their log cabins, generally demonstrating the policy he urged upon his people. Among the early goldseekers who became his friends were George Jackson, a prospector from Glasgow, Missouri, and Bob Hauck, whom he met later in Boulder Valley. Within a few

⁵ Hafen, *Relations*, p. 173.

weeks' time, the English-speaking Southern Arapaho chief had gained a reputation among the goldseekers as an intelligent, honest, and trustworthy man.[6]

He had also assessed their characters and found them very different from those of whites he had known in the past. Unlike the traders and trappers who lived on close terms with the plains environment, these newcomers arrived helpless and unprepared, lacking the most rudimentary understanding of the climate and land in which they hoped to thrive. They were accustomed to the rolling green hills and forests of the Middle West; the treeless, sandy bluffs of the plains, piling upon one another as far as the eye could see, seemed harsh and inhospitable. It was easy for them to become disoriented and lost in the bleak spaciousness. Distances were deceiving. The Rocky Mountains, which rose thirty miles west of the Cherry Creek settlements, appeared to be only a few hours' walk away. Everyone in the new towns had heard the story of the goldseeker who had left one morning to prospect in the mountains, expecting to return before dark, and had never been heard from again. No one doubted its truth.

Something else—an iron-clad determination—set these goldseekers apart from the traders and mountain men of previous years. Left Hand had encountered that determination in Aikens's party. It was a hard singlemindedness, a sense that the dice had been flung and everything rode on the outcome. It left little room for compromise.

There was good reason for it, however. The eastern and middle-western states were still reeling from the Panic of 1857, when banks closed, factories shut down, and thousands of people were thrown out of work. The gold discovery on the heels of this depression brought hope to those who had suffered the most— the unemployed factory workers, hod carriers, farmers, carpenters, street cleaners, and dock workers, as well as the

---

[6] Early accounts of relations between the whites and Southern Arapahos are replete with stories of Left Hand's friendliness. See: Jerome C. Smiley, *History of Denver;* Frank Hall, *History of the State of Colorado,* 1:225–26; Mary L. Geffs, *Under Ten Flags,* p. 239; Julia S. Lambert, "Plain Tales of the Plains," *The Trail* 9 (1916):20; and Lillian B. Shields, "The Arapahoe Indians," Master's thesis, University of Denver, 1929, Colorado State Historical Society, Denver.

drifters and roustabouts who had little hope of finding work in the best of times. These men had crossed the plains determined to strike it rich, no matter the cost in personal hardships or deprivation. They were men with everything to gain and nothing to lose.

It is true that some of the early goldseekers, after spending long days or weeks washing a pinch of gold dust out of the icy streams, gave up in disgust and returned home. Still, determination and forced optimism prevailed among those who remained and among the newcomers arriving daily.

As December waned, the new towns continued to grow. The hopefuls who came in outnumbered the discouraged who left. Provisions were dwindling, however, and many goldseekers were worried about whether they could hold out until spring. Most had received no news from home and had no idea how their wives and children fared while they tested their luck in the gold region. The occasional newspaper carried across the plains was two months old when it arrived, which increased the goldseekers' sense of having been cast adrift from civilization. To make matters worse, bitter cold had settled in, freezing the ground solid and threatening heavy snowstorms. Despite the increasingly bleak outlook, or perhaps because of it, the goldseekers were bent on having a rousing holiday celebration.

On Christmas Day, Left Hand and Little Raven got word that something unusual was taking place in the white towns. Along with some of their men, the two chiefs walked over to have a look and found the whites tending huge bonfires, roasting oxen over spits, and generally occupied in preparing a feast that included ox meat, venison, trout, dried fruits, coffee, whiskey, and the gritty bread made with flour from Mexico that was part flour, part sand.[7]

Sensing the lighthearted spirit among the whites, the chiefs offered to arrange a race between white and Indian ponies and mules. They also offered to wager 150 ponies that one of their trotting mules could outrun any mule in the white camp. With ponies worth about fifty dollars each, the goldseekers would have eagerly accepted the wager had they owned a fast trotter. Un-

    [7] LeRoy R. Hafen, ed., *Colorado Gold Rush: Contemporary Letters and Reports, 1858–1859,* vol. 10 in *The Southwest Historical Series,* p. 193.

fortunately, they did not. The chiefs then offered the same bet: 150 ponies on their fleetest pony against any horse in the white camp. Early accounts fail to note whether the race was actually held. The whites probably would have lost, since their animals were no match for the lightweight, strong Indian ponies ridden by expert Southern Arapaho horsemen.

The new year started off on the same friendly note. The Southern Arapahos made themselves at home in the white camp. They traded robes, moccasins, saddles, bridles, and softly tanned leather shirts for utensils, food, clothing, and whiskey. From time to time one of the white men would break out a fiddle and play a medley of familiar tunes while the whites and the Indians alike danced with the Southern Arapaho women. The only other woman was the Cheyenne who was married to John Smith. Smith, another quarter-century veteran trader on the plains, had built a small trading post on Cherry Creek in 1857. One of the dances ended in tragedy, however, when Smith found his wife dancing with one of the white men. He ordered her back to their cabin, where he beat her so viciously with a three-legged stool that he broke her back. This was too much, even for the rough-edged goldseekers, and they ordered Smith out of the settlement.[8]

Later that month, on January 27, the whites hosted Little Raven's village of about a thousand persons to a feast of oxen, gritty bread, and coffee. One goldseeker who was there, Rufus C. Cable, wrote later that he had never seen men eat as much as the Southern Arapahos. In fact, Cable was convinced that one warrior, Heap of Whips, could have eaten an entire ox by himself.[9]

Such occasions were not prompted by white charity. Recognizing that the Indians who camped nearby outnumbered them, and wary of depending solely upon the chiefs to keep their warriors friendly, the whites were eager to do everything possible to maintain peace. As one goldseeker explained in a letter home, "We fed the Indians all winter to keep them friendly."[10]

Left Hand did not take part in the January feast. At mid-

[8] Ibid., pp. 202, 208.
[9] Ibid., p. 219; Heap of Whips could have been the same man as Many Whips.
[10] Ibid., p. 341.

month he had become ill and had returned to his village in Boulder Valley, probably taking with him those of Little Raven's people who wanted to move away from the white towns. An entry in the diary kept by his friend George Jackson points to his departure and the reason for it. "January 23, 1859," Jackson wrote. "Staied [sic] all night at the mouth of Vasquez [present-day Clear Creek] with old Teboa and Neva. Niwot is sick, mountain fever, I think."[11]

What was known as mountain fever, which struck whites and Indians alike during the gold rush, was never more positively identified. One theory holds that it was Rocky Mountain tick fever, caused by the bite of a tick. Another theory, which seems more likely since the disease was so widespread, is that it was typhoid fever and resulted from drinking from streams which had been polluted by the goldseekers.[12] In either case its symptoms were high fever, chills, vomiting, and weakness.

Left Hand had moved back to Boulder Valley without knowing that, on January 7, Jackson had made a major gold discovery in Chicago Creek, a tributary of Clear Creek near present-day Idaho Springs, Colorado. The goldseeker kept his find a closely guarded secret until he was able to return to work it in the spring.[13]

There was still another discovery that month which was not kept secret and which Left Hand could not have missed hearing about. On January 16 six men from Aikens's party had taken advantage of the clear weather to move up Boulder canyon, prospecting along the way. Twelve miles from the mouth of the canyon, at Gold Run, their search was rewarded.[14]

Left Hand also got word that Aikens and his men, who had assured him that they meant to stay only through the winter, decided to follow the lead of the goldseekers at Cherry Creek and establish a town. Boulder City Town Company was formed on February 10, 1859, changing a crude, temporary winter camp

[11] LeRoy R. Haven, ed., "George A. Jackson's Diary, 1858–1859," *Colorado Magazine* 12 (1953):208.
[12] LeRoy R. Hafen, ed., *Reports from Colorado: The Wildman Letters, 1859–1865*, vol. 13 in *The Far West and the Rockies Historical Series*, p. 51n.; Henry Villard, *The Past and Present of the Pike's Peak Gold Regions*, p. 56.
[13] Hafen, "George A. Jackson's Diary," p. 203.
[14] Hall, *History of Colorado*, 1:178.

into a permanent white settlement on the winter campgrounds of Left Hand's people.

These new developments close upon one another were probably the reason why Left Hand decided to move his village out of the area. Another entry in Jackson's diary, for February 13, mentions that "Niwot has moved up on the South Fork of the St. Vrain.[15]

Three months after Left Hand's people had left Beaver Creek, they finally settled into a peaceful winter camp. This time they gave the whites a wide berth, moving fifteen miles north of the new Boulder town. Sick, and worried over events that now moved so fast that they swirled out of focus, Left Hand needed time to think about things ahead; he sought a place not overrun by whites.

[15] Hafen, "George A. Jackson's Diary," pp. 210-11.

7

A bigger army than Napoleon conquered half of Europe with is already equipping itself for its western march to despoil the plains of their gold.

Chicago Press and Tribune
February 4, 1859

On the chilly evening of March 4, 1859, George Jackson was cooking supper over a campfire near Table Mountain, a high, flat bluff on the edge of the foothills at the site of present-day Golden, Colorado. The sound of hooves beating the earth in the distance caught his attention, and, scanning the horizon, he fixed upon the approaching figures of a pony and rider. Squinting in the dusky light, he recognized his friend Left Hand.

Left Hand dismounted and greeted the prospector, saying that he had been on his way to Auraria to get medicine for his sick wife when he had spotted Jackson's camp. He was hopeful the prospector might have something that would help.

The white man invited the Indian to eat and spend the night. Left Hand, who had left his village on Bonita Fork of the St. Vrain early that morning and had ridden all day, gratefully accepted. He also accepted the bottle of Perry Davis's Pain Killer and a chunk of rhubarb root which Jackson assured him would help his wife. At dawn the following day, the white man's remedies packed in his leather pouch, Left Hand headed north toward his village.[1]

That Left Hand had sought help from the whites suggests the seriousness of his wife's illness, which had probably not responded to the medicine man's cures. Perhaps the mountain fever, which had struck him in January, had afflicted others in his village, including his wife. His search for help also suggests that the Plains Indians trusted the white man's knowledge.

Except for his trip to Jackson's camp, Left Hand spent the

[1] LeRoy R. Hafen, ed., "George A. Jackson's Diary, 1858-1859," *Colorado Magazine* 12 (1935):213.

spring of 1859 in his village near the St. Vrain, some distance away from both the white settlements, including Boulder City, and the heavily trafficked road along the South Platte. Those in the village who were ill could recuperate and regain their strength there, while the others could enjoy a certain peace and security. Without ranging too far afield, the warriors could find enough game to sustain the village, which probably numbered about three hundred. Elk, deer, antelope, and mountain sheep were still plentiful throughout Boulder Valley—one goldseeker that winter counted five hundred elk grazing on the bluff where the University of Colorado now stands.

The early months of 1859 were a time of calm for Left Hand's people, but not for the goldseekers, whose fortunes ebbed and flowed erratically. The discovery at Gold Run crowded Boulder Valley with two thousand eager whites who fanned out and opened the Boulder, Twelve Mile, Jefferson, and Greenhorn diggings. Within a few weeks Boulder City, the one-time camp of eleven cabins, expanded to seventy permanent dwellings spread along today's Pearl Street. [2]

Gold Run had infused new hope into the white settlements, but months passed without another discovery. Jackson's find, which was a major lode rather than loose nuggets, remained a secret. Most of the goldseekers found the going rough and the rewards small. One wrote home that he and a partner had worked steadily for three weeks to pan a total of nine dollars' worth of gold from the streams. [3]

It was becoming obvious that a man could starve while looking for gold dust and nuggets and that real fortunes could be made only by dislodging the veins of gold in the rockbeds. Few goldseekers—practically none—had enough mining experience to know how to do that, and all too many lacked the necessary tools even to start. Expecting to find chunks of gold lying at their feet, ready for the picking up, they had crossed the plains without so much as a pick or a shovel. Before long, some of the more enterprising goldseekers had decided that their path to wealth lay not in prospecting but in freighting necessary supplies from the

[2] *History of Clear Creek and Boulder Valley,* pp. 380–82.
[3] LeRoy R. Hafen, ed., *Reports from Colorado: The Wildman Letters,* 1859–1865, vol. 13 in *The Far West and the Rockies Historical Series,* p. 131.

Missouri River to the white settlements and selling them for outrageous profits.

Throughout the spring newcomers continued to crowd into the white settlements—Denver and Auraria now numbered two hundred log cabins in addition to tents scattered all about—although their prospects seemed bleak. On April 23, William Byers and Thomas Bigson published the first newspaper in the region, the *Rocky Mountain News,* dedicated in staunch optimism to the area's future. "The emigration is coming in at the rate of over 100 men each day, and constantly increasing," Byers enthusiastically noted. "Covered wagons are hourly passing in front of our office and canvas tents dot the valleys along the Platte River and Cherry Creek."[4]

Another reporter, Henry Villard, sent to the region by the *Cincinnati Daily Commercial,* was less enthusiastic. The goldseekers were discouraged, he wrote, and often talked about abandoning the area. Increasingly they had begun to see themselves as dupes of the promoters in the Missouri River towns whose economy had snapped out of the recent recession with the booming business of outfitting goldseekers. Each day more whites packed up what was left of their possessions and headed back across the plains in wearied disgust.

On May 8, Villard sat on a hard backless bench in the log-cabin offices of the Leavenworth and Pike's Peak Express Company, a stage and freighting business opened in February, discussing, as he put it, "the unpromising aspect of things," with Dr. J. M. Fox, company agent, and Joseph Heywood. In the midst of the conversation the door opened, and a short, slender, heavily bearded miner stepped inside, looking for his mail. He had been prospecting with John Gregory in the vicinity of Clear Creek, he said, and had not been in town for a while. Pulling a bottle from his pocket, he showed the results of his prospecting—about forty dollars' worth of gold dust. From another pocket he rolled out a handful of gold-bearing quartz. The other men jumped up for a closer look as Fox grabbed the quartz from the startled prospector and stepped outside to inspect it under a magnifying glass. The others followed, peering over his shoulder, waiting for the opin-

4 *Rocky Mountain News,* April 25, 1859.

ion of an experienced miner who had been in the California goldfields. At last Fox announced gleefully that it was "as fine a quartz as I've seen in the richest California mine."[5]

It was John Gregory's gold discovery, the first major find in four months, that set off the real Pikes Peak gold rush. Before Gregory's discovery, near present-day Black Hawk, only a trickle of goldseekers had come into the region. After the find came the deluge. An estimated 150,000 white men crossed the plains in the late spring and summer of 1859. One-third turned back before reaching the goldfields, finding themselves unable to endure the hardships of the bleak, sandy land, the relentless summer sun, and the scarcity of water. Still, 100,000 did complete the journey and poured into Auraria, Denver, Boulder City, and the mountain areas. Of these, between 25,000 and 35,000 would remain to become permanent settlers.[6]

Who were these goldseekers? Like their predecessors in the fall, most had been spewed forth by the Panic of 1857, the effects of which still cut through the country's economy. Many were honest, hardworking men with sound characters who had fallen upon hard times through no fault of their own. But the majority were adventurers, gamblers, desperadoes, and fugitives, the flotsam and jetsam of an unsteady society, men who sported three pistols in their belts and bowie knives in their boots.[7] Murders, robberies, and duels were common occurrences in the white towns; gambling and whiskey provided the favorite pastimes. Taos Lightning—obtained from Mexico traders who frequented the towns—and something known as tanglefoot whiskey sold for twenty-five cents a drink and, as one goldseeker noted, one drink was enough to "almost make a man shed his toenails."[8]

The swell of goldseekers in Denver and Auraria threatened to engulf Little Raven's village. Nevertheless, the chief stood his ground, refusing to move the village onto the plains, which also swarmed with whites. Hunting parties set out regularly in search

[5] Henry Villard, *The Past and Present of the Pike's Peak Gold Regions,* pp. 32, 35–36.

[6] William N. Byers Papers, Western History Division, University of Colorado Library, Boulder, Colo.

[7] Frank Hall, *History of Colorado,* 1:183.

[8] *Missouri Republican,* July 9, 1859.

of game to supply the village, and the Southern Arapahos expanded their trading business in the burgeoning towns. According to Villard, the Indians insisted upon closing each bargaining session by serenading the whites. Their singing sounded to him like "the growl of a bear, squeal of a pig, cry of a crow, and yelp of a frightened cur," he said. He also described them as peaceable and good-natured but, by his standards, rather squalid in appearance and habits. They "delight in indolence," he reported. "Happily, their wants are few."[9]

The Southern Arapaho hunting parties moving out onto the plains also demonstrated a peaceable and good-natured attitude toward the whites. One notable instance of this attitude was the way Southern Arapaho warriors treated a goldseeker by the name of Daniel Blue. They had come upon Blue wandering near the Smoky Hill Trail, alone, lost, and crazed from thirst and hunger. The Indians took him to their camp, fed him corn and gruel, and cared for him until he regained his strength. Blue then led the warriors to a grisly sight—the bodies of his brothers, Alexander and Charles, long strips of flesh cut from their legs and arms. No doubt the Southern Arapahos sized up the situation and understood what had happened.

The three brothers, like many goldseekers, had set out to find their fortunes unprepared for the arduous journey. Unfortunately, they had also chosen to take the Smoky Hill Trail, notorious for its dearth of water. Somehow they had lost their packhorses and provisions and, while trying to find them, had lost the trail. Tracing and retracing their steps around the sameness of the parched bluffs, they soon became too weak to go on. Alexander and Charles had died from starvation, and Daniel had survived by eating their flesh until he was found.

Had the Southern Arapahos wished to harass or kill white men, this crazed cannibal lost on the plains presented the ideal opportunity. Instead, the warriors helped him bury his brothers' remains and led him to a train of goldseekers, which he joined for the remainder of his journey.[10]

[9] Villard, *Past and Present*, p. 119.

[10] LeRoy R. Hafen, ed., *Overland Routes to the Gold Fields, 1859: From Contemporary Diaries*, vol. 11 in *The Southwest Historical Series*, pp. 271–75.

In the same spirit of friendly cooperation, Little Raven tried to bring about some kind of agreement between his people and the whites who had taken over parts of Indian land. On May 8, the day that the news of Gregory's discovery broke, the chief and a dozen warriors met with some goldseekers in the log-cabin office of Judge Smith. According to a correspondent from the *Missouri Democrat* who was there, the chief, whom he described as "dignified and Quaker-like," discussed the possibility of selling to the government the Indian lands occupied by whites and obtaining government aid to help the Southern Arapahos become "agricultural and civilized." "They are already about as civilized as the whites here," the correspondent observed, "and far more temperate; indeed, I've not seen an intoxicated Indian in the mining region."

The same could not be said for Little Raven's interpreter, Antoine Chet DuBray, a salty trader who had lived with the Southern Arapahos off and on for several years and had picked up their language. DuBray was so intoxicated, wrote the correspondent, that he fell off his seat, "rendering any attempt at a pow wow a farce. Consequently, the meeting was adjourned."[11]

On May 14, the *Rocky Mountain News* reported another meeting between Little Raven and his "escorts" and a large number of Denver and Auraria citizens. DuBray may have been sober enough to act as interpreter because, according to the newspaper account, the chief told the whites that he liked them well enough and was glad to see them get their gold but that the land belonged to the Indians and he hoped they would not stay around too long.[12]

Yet a third meeting was held the following week. On the evening of May 21, Little Raven and four other leading men of the tribe had dinner at the express office with several white men, including Dr. Fox and the journalist Villard. According to Villard's account, the chief pledged his word that his people would remain peaceful and friendly and that the leaders would do all they could to preserve order. "Raven is a very sensible and friendly disposed man," wrote Villard. "He handled knife and fork and smokes

---

[11] LeRoy R. Hafen, ed., *Colorado Gold Rush: Contemporary Letters and Reports, 1858*-1859, vol. 10 in *The Southwest Historical Series*, p. 349.
[12] *Rocky Mountain News*, May 14, 1859.

his cigars like a white man.'' After dinner Little Raven invited Dr. Fox to his lodge to reciprocate the hospitality, an invitation, Villard noted, ''not as heartily received as given.''[13]

It is unlikely that Left Hand was among the leading men with Little Raven on this occasion, since Villard makes no mention of an English-speaking chief. He was in the area not long after the series of meetings, however, having moved his village from the vicinity of the St. Vrain to the South Platte, close by Little Raven's. Much had happened in the time he had spent apart from the white settlements, and he was probably anxious to take stock of new developments. It is also likely that Little Raven, tired of trying to deal with whites through the drunken interpreter DuBray, had sent for him. At any rate, he was on hand in June, in time to serve as an interpreter for one of the period's most famous men, Horace Greeley.

Greeley, editor of the *New York Tribune,* had long been in the forefront of the movement to build a transcontinental railroad. In the spring of 1859 he decided to see for himself the Great American Desert and perilous Rocky Mountains which the railroad would traverse. At Leavenworth he boarded the Leavenworth and Pike's Peak Express stage for the trip to Auraria. With him was another journalist, Albert D. Richardson, correspondent for the *Boston Journal,* who was looking for some exciting, firsthand stories in the gold region. The two men arrived on June 7, having passed thousands of wagons carrying hopeful gold-seekers on the way. ''They will be dropping in on Denver at a rate of 100 a day,'' Greeley wrote in one of his first dispatches from the region.''[14]

Spotting the Southern Arapaho villages on the outskirts of the white settlements, the journalists inveigled some interviews from Little Raven, thinking that here was a subject certain to be of interest to their readers in the East. Richardson called the chief ''the nearest approximation to the ideal Indian I ever met, with fine manly form and human, trustworthy face.'' He also told his readers that Little Raven had seven wives and ten papooses, as well as many grown children.[15]

[13] Hafen, *Colorado Gold Rush,* p. 364.
[14] Horace Greeley, *An Overland Journey,* p. 113.
[15] Albert D. Richardson, *Beyond the Mississippi,* p. 175.

Each afternoon over a period of several days, Greeley and Richardson interviewed Little Raven in the Denver House, where the white men were lodged. They communicated through sign language, "but twice or thrice we became, as actors say, hopelessly stuck," explained Richardson. "Then my visitor sent for Left Hand, a linguist, for, as Day and Martin, the great blacking manufacturers kept a poet, so the chief of the Arapahos maintained an interpreter. Left Hand spoke English fluently, having acquired it from traders in boyhood, and soon extricated us from our conversational quagmire."[16]

Greeley sounded out the English-speaking chief on the subject of farming:

> I tried my powers of persuasion on Left Hand, the only Arapaho chief who speaks English—in favor of an Arapaho tribal farm—say of two hundred acres for a beginning to be broken and fenced by the common efforts of the tribe, and a patch therein allotted to each head of a family who would agree to plant and till it.[17]

His powers of persuasion met with little success. Left Hand had already concluded that his people would not adapt to what he termed a "sedentary and unnatural occupation"; he rebutted Greeley's ideas, causing the journalist to call him "shrewd and every whit as conservative as Boston's Beacon Street or our Fifth Avenue. He knows that there is a certain way in which his people have lived from time immemorial, and in which they are content still to live, knowing and seeking no better."[18]

Greeley did not say whether Left Hand told him of his trip to the Missouri River settlements which had shaped his opinion on farming. If he did, the information had no effect upon the journalist's conclusion that Left Hand disdained farming because he "may or may not have heard that it's the common lot of prophets to be stoned and of reformers to be crucified; but he probably comprehends that squaws cannot fence and plow, and that 'braves' are disinclined to any such steady, monotonous exercise of their muscles."

[16] Ibid., p. 190.
[17] Greeley, *Overland Journey,* pp. 149–50.
[18] Ibid., pp. 152–53.

During Greeley's visit that June, bands of warriors were continually leaving the Southern Arapaho villages for raids on Ute camps in the mountain canyons, a ridiculous expenditure of energy, in the *Tribune* editor's view. When he questioned Left Hand about the reason for such raids, the chief told him that Utes had always been Southern Arapaho enemies, that he could not remember a time when they were not. At this, Greeley jumped to another conclusion: the Southern Arapahos had deliberately set up their village close to the white settlements so that whites could protect the women and children while the warriors were off on "fighting, that is stealing—expeditions."[19]

A man whose own culture did not revolve around the horse naturally found pony raids purposelessly criminal. He did not understand that the Southern Arapahos contended with the Utes over land immediately east of the Continental Divide, including a major buffalo range in the South Park. With white traffic crisscrossing the buffalo ranges on the plains, scattering the herds and slaughtering growing numbers of animals, control of the mountain range was a matter of some importance. Moreover, the eastern journalist did not understand the psychological and social value of such raids.

Left Hand and Little Raven probably encouraged the raids throughout June. Not only did such forays allow the warriors to prove their mettle, count coups, and establish their reputations—the only means to do so in their society—they also helped to turn the warriors' attention from whites crowding upon their lands and reduce their growing discontent and smoldering resentment.

The Southern Arapahos also continued to wander among the log cabins and tents in the white towns, trading and begging. Whiskey was always flowing freely and many of the Indian men pestered the whites for it, although a vigilance committee had threatened death to anyone supplying whiskey to the Indians. Nevertheless, those who were unscrupulous and fearless enough traded bottles of cheap whiskey to Southern Arapaho men for the fine buffalo robes which their wives had spent long hours tanning.

[19] Ibid., p. 150.

One evening in mid-June several goldseekers were playing a game of whist in a log cabin when a man rushed in, shouting that two Indians had jumped him and that he had thrown a club at them and run. Within seconds the drunken Indians stumbled into the cabin, bent on punishing the white man. The others held them off while someone ran for the chief, who hurried to the cabin, threw out the Indians, and ordered them to go home. Instead, they stumbled back in, hot after revenge, whereupon the chief took a club and knocked them down. "He wanted to take a gun and shoot them" reported one onlooker, "but we would not let him." The chief was probably Little Raven, though he is not identified.[20]

The incident is important because it illustrates two growing problems facing the chiefs: the difficulty in controlling their warriors and the necessity of keeping whiskey out of their reach. The responsible men in both camps—Indian and white—understood that whiskey made the warriors as violent and irrational as it made the white men; its availability increased the likelihood of a serious confrontation between the two races.

As the hot summer days droned on, provisions in the Southern Arapaho villages grew more scarce. Although the warriors continually rode out in search of game, they often returned empty-handed. Buffalo herds were difficult to locate in the steady streams of white traffic, and the small game which the warriors found was not enough to sustain a large village of fifteen hundred persons. Sometime in July the Southern Arapahos packed up their lodges and belongings and moved eastward along the South Platte, searching for William Bent, who was due with annuity goods from St. Louis. Bent was returning to the plains after visiting Washington, where he had pleaded with government officials for a new treaty between the government and the Southern Arapahos and Cheyennes—a treaty that would show them some justice. While in the capital he had also arranged to sell his fort to the government for a military post.

In a letter dated July 23, 1859, Bent notified the superintendent of Indian Affairs that the Southern Arapahos had remained on the South Platte waiting for him until "they were in a starving

---

[20] Hafen, *Reports from Colorado,* p. 38.

state." Finally they were forced to travel to the vicinity of the Republican River and the Smoky Hill in a desperate search for buffalo. It was in this area that Bent caught up with them and distributed much-needed goods.[21]

Most of the tribe then moved south to the Arkansas River, an area not as inundated by whites as the South Platte and the Smoky Hill. A few of the leaders detoured back to Cherry Creek, where in September they held another meeting with the gold-seekers. Once again friendship and peace were pledged, and everyone took a turn smoking the peace pipe. The meeting was similar to those held in the past, in that nothing came of it.

About the same time, Left Hand and Little Raven were meet-ing with Bent at his fort on the Arkansas. Bent was now serving as acting agent to the Southern Arapahos and Cheyennes, although his appointment would not be confirmed by the Senate until April 27 of the following year. Also present were the Cheyenne brother-chiefs Black Kettle and White Antelope. It was White Antelope who had signed the Fort Laramie Treaty for his people.

Bent told the chiefs that the Department of Indian Affairs de-sired them "to assume a fixed residence, and occupy themselves with agriculture." The chiefs stated unanimously that they wished to do so, Bent reported to Washington, adding that he believed them worthy of the government's attention and aid. "They have scrupulously maintained peaceful relations with the whites and with other Indian tribes," he wrote, "notwithstand-ing the many causes of irritation growing out of the occupation of the gold region, and the emigration to it through their hunting grounds, which are no longer reliable as a certain source of food to them."[22]

Bent's report of this meeting concluded with a gloomy prophecy:

The Southern Arapahos and Cheyennes,...pressed upon all around by the Texans, by the settlers of the gold region, by the ad-vancing people of Kansas, and from the Platte, are already com-

[21] Bent to Robinson, July 23, 1859, Letters Sent, Upper Arkansas Agency, *OIA*, Record Group 75, Federal Archives and Records Center, Denver, Colo.
[22] *BIA Reports* (1859), Sen. Exec. Doc. 2, 36th Cong., 1st sess., pp. 137–39, Donald J. Berthrong, *The Southern Cheyennes*, p. 146.

pressed into a small circle of territory. A desperate war of starvation and extinction is therefore imminent and inevitable, unless prompt measures shall prevent.[23]

Prompt measures were out of the question; the bureaucratic wheels of Washington turned slowly. Nevertheless, Bent's pleas—the pleas of the Indians from the central plains—were finally heard, and, before the year ended, Washington moved toward initiating a new agreement with the Southern Arapahos and Cheyennes.

[23] *BIA Reports* (1859), pp. 137-39.

8

The Indian saw in the westward march
of civilization his rights diminishing;
the settlements along the streams
meant the loss of water. He saw his
hunting ground broken up and the
game going west before the white
man's advance. He is a reader of signs,
and in these signs he read "the beginning of the end."

Julia S. Lambert

In the spring of 1860, Left Hand's village returned to the high,
flat bluffs west of the South Platte overlooking Denver and
Auraria. Facing each other across the river, the two peoples, white
and Indian, awaited settlement of the land question. Both
understood that the land belonged to the Southern Arapahos
and Cheyennes. Both could see that it was occupied by whites.

Throughout 1859 the tribes had urged their acting agent,
William Bent, to arrange a treaty council with the government.
Bent in turn had fired off letter after letter to Washington detail-
ing the Indians' plight, warning of increasing tension on the
plains, and asking for a new treaty. The chiefs were willing to
meet with government officials during annuity distribution the
following summer, he reported, although they realized that a
new agreement would put an end to their old way of life.[1] For
some time they had seen this as inevitable.

Officials in Washington were also bowing to the inevitable.
Whites in the gold region, eager for clear title to the land they occupied, were forcing the government's hand. In the fall of 1859
the goldseekers had drafted a constitution for a proposed state, to
be named Jefferson. On September 5 an election was held to de-
cide whether to accept a state constitution or to establish a territory. A territorial status was favored by the voters, 2,007 to 649,

[1] *BIA Reports* (1859), Sen. Exec. Doc. 2, 36th Cong., 1st sess., pp.
137–39; Bent to Robinson, July 23, August 1, November 25, November 28,
and December 17, 1859, Letters Sent, Upper Arkansas Agency, *OIA*, Record
Group 75, Federal Archives and Records Center, Denver, Colo.

no doubt because the possibility of turning Indian land into a state seemed remote even to the most hopeful white settler. The voters had also drafted a petition to Congress praying that the new territory of Jefferson be accepted.[2]

Deep and sometimes paranoiac fears accompanied the gold-seekers' persistent efforts to bring some kind of government—and government protection—to the plains. In July, 1859, a band of Utes had attacked and killed several prospectors in the South Park area, setting off panic in the white population. At a general meeting prompted by the murders, the skittish settlers, who had traded every day for months with the Southern Arapahos, adopted a resolution asking Congress for a military force to protect them from Indian depredations.[3]

Although they now outnumbered the Indians, the goldseekers could never overlook their precarious position. They felt adrift in the heart of a hostile land, surrounded by "savages," far from the care or concerns of the federal government. Life on the plains, they realized, depended upon free, open commerce with the states. Food, clothing, tools, wagons, everything had to be freighted from the east. Settlers feared that the Indians, if they became hostile, would close off the roads and starve the settlements. With that possibility in mind, whites begged Congress to set up a territorial government and make a permanent land settlement with the tribes.

In January, 1860, the Senate finally authorized a new treaty with the Southern Arapahos and Cheyennes which would supersede the Fort Laramie Treaty. Its purpose was to legalize the status quo, that is, to remove Indian rights from land occupied by whites. The questions of where the treaty council would be held and who would act as government commissioner were still unclear, but Bent and the tribes were given reason to believe that it would take place in the coming summer.

There was nothing to do but wait. While they waited, Left Hand's people continued to ply their trading business in Denver and Auraria, exchanging Indian wares for the white man's goods

[2] Frank Hall, *History of Colorado*, 1:210, LeRoy R. Hafen, ed., *Reports from Colorado: The Wildman Letters, 1859–1865*, vol. 13 in *The Far West and the Rockies Historical Series*, p. 59.

[3] Hafen, *Reports from Colorado*, p. 65.

which appealed to them, especially sugar, flour, coffee, and tobacco. The men also began to trade for whiskey when they could, an inclination that cast increasingly dark shadows over tribal life. The warriors became insolent or impassive when they were drunk, adding to the heavy burdens borne by the other members of the tribe. Women, already worried about the growing impoverishment of their families, learned to keep themselves and their children out of the men's way when they returned to the lodges crazy and sick with alcohol.

Whites bided their time by strengthening their position. In March the two towns of Auraria and Denver were consolidated into Denver City, which was beginning to take on some of the airs of a thriving eastern metropolis. It numbered 2,000 permanent residents and served as the supply center and business mecca for 34,277 whites in the gold region.[4]

Goldseekers who had originally planned to make a fortune immediately and return to the East had discovered that, although fortunes eluded them, comfortable, promising livings could be made in the gold region. As a result, Denver City boasted twenty-seven retail stores selling groceries, clothing, liquor, hardware, drugs, boots, shoes, and crockery; eight hotels and seven boarding houses, two schools and two theaters, eleven restaurants and twenty-three bars, as well as billiard saloons, tenpin alleys, livery stables, and lumber yards. Goldseeking adventurers still trekked across the plains, but so did lawyers, physicians, contractors, realtors, carpenters, watchmakers, blacksmiths, tailors, and barbers—all the craftsmen and professionals necessary to keep the wheels of the new city turning smoothly.[5]

Nevertheless, Denver society could easily be characterized as rough and lawless. Streets were crowded with drunken goldseekers who spilled out of the saloons and gambling parlors. Duels and murders occurred so frequently that no one took much note, and one settler would recall later that the crack of pistols was heard day and night throughout the town.[6]

    [4] U.S. Census of 1860; Percy Stanley Fritz, *Colorado: The Centennial State*, p. 114.
    [5] Henry Villard, *The Past and Present of the Pike's Peak Gold Regions*, pp. 128–42.
    [6] Hall, *History of Colorado*, 1:236.

It was only a question of time until white lawlessness touched the nearby Southern Arapahos. On the night of April 14, 1860, while Left Hand and his warriors were absent from their village, a group of drunken white men invaded the lodges, dragged out the women and young girls, and raped them. "Age was not respected," reported the *Rocky Mountain News*. "The gray hairs of John Poisal's old Indian wife could not protect her. She was taken from her husband's side in bed. Crippled as he is, he compelled them by threats with his pistol to release her."[7]

The leader of this band was Charles Gardner, better known as Big Phil the Cannibal, one of the most depraved characters lurking around Denver's darker streets that spring. Big Phil, described by Edward Wynkoop as a man of "gigantic structure and repulsive aspect," had come to the West in 1844, an escapee from a Philadelphia prison. He had wandered aimlessly about the plains, and occasionally had pitched his tent in a Southern Arapaho village. Eventually he married two women of the tribe. One legend has it that, during a severe snowstorm one winter, he killed and ate one of the wives. The same fate is said to have befallen an Indian companion of his while the two men were traveling over the plains to Fort Laramie. An unknown Frenchman, probably a trader, was reportedly his third victim. Big Phil's evil reputation spread throughout the plains, among whites and Indians alike, all of whom strove to avoid him and knew, failing that, never to walk in front of him.[8]

So the assault on the women and girls in Left Hand's village was perfectly in keeping with Big Phil's character. Taking advantage of his familiarity with the tribe's habits, he had waited until the warriors were a safe distance away, either hunting or raiding the Utes, before leading to Left Hand's lodges a gang of men who observed no human laws or boundaries. Among their victims was

---

[7] *Rocky Mountain News*, April 18, 1860. Beckwourth had reported in his letter to the *Rocky Mountain News* that a band of Cheyenne and Apache Indians had visited Denver, called on him, and requested his help in finding a camping place. He invited them to stay and trade. He mistakenly labels the Southern Arapahos as "Apaches," although some Cheyenne and Apache warriors may have been visiting Left Hand's village at the time.

[8] LeRoy R. Hafen, "Charles Gardner: Big Phil," *Colorado Magazine* 13 (1936):53–58.

certainly Left Hand's sister, MaHom, and probably his wife and his ten-year-old daughter.[9]

Before Left Hand's return, however, Poisal, whose wife had been "dragged from his side," had sought the advice of Jim Beckwourth. The well-known Beckwourth, a mulatto from Virginia, had come to the plains in the 1820s and had spent most of his adult life trading and trapping (at one point he had been made an honorary Crow chief). Now living in a log cabin in Denver, Beckwourth was regarded by the Indians as an understanding and trustworthy outsider. The trader was outraged. He immediately wrote and delivered a letter to the *Rocky Mountain News* that described exactly what the "drunken devils and bummers" had done at the undefended Indian village. When it was published on April 18, responsible whites were shocked, and a series of public meetings was called.[10]

The meetings had already been scheduled by the time Left Hand returned, and, in view of this, Beckwourth prevailed upon him to abide by the public decisions concerning the guilty men and not to seek his own revenge. After all, public sentiment was on the side of the Indians.

In the end, Left Hand decided to accept Beckwourth's advice, but other factors also influenced him. If his warriors were to kill white men, even those so deserving of death as Gardner and his gang, it would alarm the settlers and could set them against his village. He had between sixty and one hundred warriors with him, no match for nearly two thousand white men, most of whom were armed to the hilt. But it was the upcoming treaty council that most influenced Left Hand's behavior: he had no intention of going to the council on anything but the friendliest of terms with whites.

As it turned out, nothing was done about Gardner and his men. The only concrete result of the public meetings was the appointment of Beckwourth as "local agent" to take charge of the tribes when they were in the area, transact business between whites and Indians, and note depredations on either side.[11]

---

[9] Stan Hoig, *The Sand Creek Massacre*, p. 6.
[10] *Rocky Mountain News*, April 18, 1860.
[11] James P. Beckwourth, *Life and Adventures of James P. Beckwourth*, p. 167.

Had white women been assaulted, there is no doubt that Gardner and his band of ruffians would have swung from the cottonwood trees, having been tried, sentenced, and executed within the hour. The People's Court and Vigilance Committee, formed to handle such matters, showed no squeamishness about dealing out harsh, swift punishment, and, on one occasion, the committee had not even waited for a crime to be committed: convinced that a certain man was dangerous and would eventually kill someone, the committee had lynched him, in advance, so to speak, to make sure that he would not. The affair came to be known as the "Precautionary Lynching."[12]

Despite the miscarriage of justice in the case of Gardner's men, Left Hand stood by his word to accept the public decision. That he did not take revenge on the guilty whites when the settlers refused to punish them, however, rankled his warriors, and within a short time the village left the Denver area and moved onto the plains.

Little Raven had kept his village near the Arkansas River that winter and spring. Why had Left Hand brought his village to the vicinity of the white settlement where the men could obtain whiskey and the women were liable to be insulted and degraded? The truth was that whether on the plains or near the burgeoning towns, there was no escape from the whites. In the month of May alone, for example, eleven thousand wagons filled with white families, eager for a new start and a better life, had crossed the plains and converged on Denver.[13]

When they were camping on the plains, it was hard for the young warriors—already restless and defensive—to ignore this steady stream of white traffic onto Indian land. The leaders were hard-pressed to keep the young men from attacking the wagons and thereby upsetting the prospects for a new treaty. It is just possible that Left Hand preferred to keep his band on the outskirts of Denver, in a confined area, where he could exert more control than he would have on the open plains.

Another danger also presented itself on the plains, as Little Raven discovered that spring. Kiowas and Comanches had re-

[12] Hafen, *Reports from Colorado*, p. 60.
[13] Hall, *History of Colorado*, 1:236.

volted against the white invasion the previous year and were still occasionally making raids up and down the Santa Fe Trail. Little Raven had his hands full trying to keep his warriors from joining them.

As the pressures from the white influx grew more severe, Left Hand turned his warriors increasingly toward their traditional foes, both to vent their anger and frustration and at the same time to allow them to gain some prestige within the tribe. Such recognition reinforced the crumbling Southern Arapaho social structure. Throughout May and June, Left Hand led his men on frequent raids against the Utes. Not only did the raids enlarge the Southern Arapaho pony herds and give the young men an opportunity to prove their courage, they also gave Left Hand the chance, in the aftermath of his decision concerning Gardner, to prove that he was still courageous, still worthy of leadership.

On May 17, Left Hand's village returned once again to the campgrounds on the South Platte next door to Denver, the warriors fresh from an expedition against the mountain tribe. The raid had been successful, netting several Ute ponies and four or five Ute scalps and prompting a victory celebration that enlivened the village throughout the night.[14]

The following day other bands joined Left Hand's village, bringing the total number in his camp to about a thousand persons, and three weeks later, on June 10, a large group of warriors set out on another raid. They followed the South Platte through the canyons into South Park where they surprised a Ute camp; several women and children were killed who had been caught in the sudden crossfire. The Utes rallied their forces and trailed the raiders down the South Platte, falling upon them in a surprise attack, killing six and wounding several others. When the warriors returned to their village on June 14, some still with arrows in their backs, gloom settled over the lodges, and, according to accounts of the white settlers, the women's lamentations for the dead pierced the air.[15]

Among the settlers arriving in Denver at this time was Marshall Silverthorne; his family had rented a four-room house at the

---

[14] Ibid.
[15] Ibid., 1:254.

corner of Fourteenth and Lawrence streets for eighty-five dollars a month. Drafty and bare, the house was constructed of the rough boards from Denver's new sawmill and featured muslin-covered window openings. As Mrs. Silverthorne unpacked the family's belongings that they had carted across the plains, and set about making the house as comfortable as possible, she noticed a dark-eyed Indian girl peering through a muslin window. She asked the girl to help with the tasks and to look after the young Silverthorne children. The girl seemed glad to help. Later the family discovered that their ten-year-old servant girl, who returned each day for a while to play with the white children and help their mother, was Left Hand's daughter.[16]

Another family among the settlers reaching Denver that May was that of John Milton Chivington. The newly appointed presiding elder of the Methodist Episcopal Church in the Rocky Mountain District, his wife, Martha, and their son and two daughters pulled into town on May 4, after a three-week trip from Omaha. They set up temporary lodgings in a tent on the east bank of Cherry Creek, near present-day Broadway Street, and from there, within a short time, they moved into one of Denver's first brick houses.[17]

The house was the closest thing to civilization Martha Chivington had found in the rough frontier settlement. During her twenty-year marriage, Martha had dutifully followed her preacher-husband around the frontier towns of the Missouri River, never losing faith that the Methodist church would one day see fit to post him in a civilized city in the East. His assignment to Omaha was a step forward from the smaller outposts of Illinois and Missouri, and she was convinced that the next post would be a city where her children could be properly educated. Instead, Chivington was ordered five hundred miles across the plains to the heart of Indian territory.

Despite Martha's keen disappointment, Chivington welcomed the order as the most stirring challenge of his career. And in truth he seemed a man who could measure up to most tasks: he

[16] Evelyn Bradley, "The Story of a Colorado Pioneer," *Colorado Magazine* 2 (1925):50.
[17] Reginald S. Craig, *The Fighting Parson,* p. 49.

was six feet, four and one-half inches tall and weighed 260 pounds. His hair was coarse and red and his black eyes were rather distinctive. He had long ago thrown his herculean strength on the side of goodness and decency, preaching, converting, building churches, and priding himself on always leaving a town better than he had found it. At times he had even visited the Missouri riverfronts to rid a town of outlaws and disreputable characters by personally seeing that some of them were shipped down river. "A leader in the fight for right and decency," his biographer has called him, "always righteous and intolerant."[18]

There is also no doubt that he was personally courageous, and unafraid to defend his principles. While preaching in Platte County, Missouri, in the 1850s, for example, he became embroiled in the controversy over whether Kansas should become a slave or a free state. In sermon after sermon Chivington took a strong stand against slavery. Finally, the proslavery faction had had enough and sent him a note threatening to tar and feather him if he preached in the area again. Chivington immediately sent back word that he would preach as usual on Sunday morning, and the following Sunday he entered the church as usual and marched to the pulpit. Placing the Bible on one side of it and two pistols on the other, he thundered at the congregation, some of whom had brought barrels of tar, "By the grace of God and these two revolvers, I am going to preach here today." He did.[19]

To Chivington, Denver was not unlike the other frontier towns where lawlessness made life unbearable for decent people like him and his family. He threw himself into the work as pastor of the First Methodist Church, begun as a mission the year before,[20] and tirelessly rode the circuit of mining camps, railing against the gambling, duels, drunkenness, and debauchery he found everywhere. Some of the settlers who met and became associated with Chivington at this time—including Irving Howbert, a teen-aged boy who, along with his father, helped the preacher minister to

---

[18] Ibid., p. 30.

[19] Ibid., p. 40

[20] The First Methodist Church building, which both Chivington and Gov. John Evans would later help to build, became an important Denver landmark.

the mining camps—were so impressed by his vigor and the seeming straightness of his intentions that, much later, they would become his staunch defenders.

Although Chivington's path again approached Left Hand's, as it had during the chief's trip to the Missouri River, the two men did not meet. Chivington arrived in Denver about the time Left Hand and his village moved onto the plains. When Left Hand returned, on May 17, the preacher was caught up in his work, probably away at the mines. In any case, faced with the formidable task of converting the white population, Chivington took no interest in the Southern Arapahos on the outskirts of town.

Throughout the spring of 1860 and into the first warm weeks of summer, most of the Southern Arapahos stayed in their village close by Denver. Raiding and hunting parties moved in and out at regular intervals and some times frequented the Boulder area. One of the settlers there, Alp Wright, wrote that they liked to hang around the claim he was working at the mouth of Boulder canyon, waiting for him to break out the frying pan at mealtime. As soon as bacon began sizzling over the fire, the Indians attempted to hook it out of the pan with their ramrods, but, said Wright, "they committed no more serious depredations than petty pilfering."[21]

One of the legends concerning Left Hand dates from this period. Supposedly he had some kind of misunderstanding with Jim Baker, another of the longtime mountain men who had come to the plains in the late 1820s and prided himself on having never been "broke by civilization." In the early 1860s, Baker was living in a log cabin on Clear Creek, and, although he was some distance from Left Hand's village, legend has it that he feared the Southern Arapahos were planning to attack him. Deciding to force the matter, he took rifle in hand and rode to Left Hand's camp, where he demanded to know whether the chief was a friend or an enemy. Left Hand replied angrily that the white man was no friend of the Arapahos and that he was not afraid of whites in general or of Baker in particular.

[21] *History of Clear Creek and Boulder Valley, Colorado*, p. 380.

Baker then challenged Left Hand to a duel, and the two men stepped off one hundred yards. Before either could fire a shot, however, the Indians, fearing that their chief would be killed, intervened. Baker returned to his cabin, confident that he had settled the matter in his favor without firing a shot, and he liked to boast that he was "never again molested by Left Hand."[22]

It is possible, of course, that Left Hand had some kind of conflict with Baker and that Baker challenged him to a duel, but no evidence exists to corroborate the mountain man's story. Had the challenge actually occurred, it is unlikely that Left Hand would have taken a chance on killing Baker at a time when he was counseling his warriors to remain peaceful and patient in anticipation of the long-awaited treaty council. It is likely that Left Hand tried to pass over Baker's challenge as not worth the trouble it could bring, hurried him out of the Southern Arapaho village, and made every effort from then on to stay out of his way.

To be sure, Left Hand had more important concerns at this time than a feisty old trapper. Some of his warriors were raiding along the Platte, running off cattle and otherwise stealing from whites whenever they could. On June 27, the *Rocky Mountain News* reported: "Daily we hear of petty depredations by the Indians. A war party on return from fighting Utes robbed several houses in Plum Creek settlement. Old Mister Steele, living about ten miles up Cherry Creek, has had three head of cattle killed by them, and one of his neighbors has lost four by the same means."[23]

The journalist Richardson, still in the region, reported: "Unless the Arapahos very soon abandon such proceedings, they will find a more formidable enemy in the field than the Utes," meaning, of course, that the white settlers were in no temper to disregard Indian thefts.[24]

Neither was Left Hand. The raiding had set him against his own warriors, growing numbers of whom were angry and frustrated by their chief's failure to act in the face of wrongs and

---

[22] "W. Ferril Scrapbook, 1887," pp. 73-74, Western History Division, Denver Public Library, Denver, Colo.

[23] *Rocky Mountain News,* June 27, 1860.

[24] *Lawrence Republican,* May 22 to August 15, 1860.

tired of placating the goldseekers who thronged over their lands. According to the historian Jerome Smiley, the warriors began to accuse Left Hand of being "too much under the white man's influence," and thereafter "his standing among them dropped."[25] dropped."[25]

Since the raids were in direct violation of his orders, Left Hand had no choice but to leave his village. The same *Rocky Mountain News* article that reported the problem also noted that, when Left Hand was appealed to "for redress, he informed the whites he had nothing to do with his village; he had withdrawn from it and could offer no satisfaction or assurances that such stealing would cease."[26]

It was easy for the young warriors to disagree with the chief's policies, of course, since they bore no responsibility for the outcome. They saw immediate wrongs and demanded immediate action. As whites usurped their lands and destroyed their resources, they felt justified in running off the whites' cattle and slaughtering it for food.

Left Hand and the other leaders, however, had to consider the welfare and safety of all the people, including the women, children, elders, and those who were helpless. The chiefs could not allow the actions of a few brash young men who were capable of protecting themselves to bring retaliation upon the others. At the same time, Left Hand was convinced that his people could obtain a fair settlement in the upcoming treaty negotiations only if they maintained an attitude of friendship and peace toward the white settlers. But the most important consideration was that troops were again on the march across the plains.

In May, Maj. John Sedgwick, the same cavalry officer who had campaigned with Colonel Sumner against the Cheyennes three years earlier, was ordered to "chastise" the Kiowas and Comanches for their ongoing raids along the Santa Fe Trail.[27] Even William Bent, their agent, had earlier reported to Washington that the southern tribes were "purtay saucy" and had exhibited

[25] Jerome C. Smiley, *History of Denver*, p. 71.

[26] *Rocky Mountain News*, June 27, 1860.

[27] LeRoy R. Hafen, ed., *Relations with the Indian of the Plains*, vol. 9 in *The Far West and the Rockies Historical Series*, p. 193.

so much hostility over the past year that he, for one, was making every effort to stay out of their way.[28]

Sedgwick embarked on what would prove to be a notably unsuccessful campaign, chasing hostiles across the southern plains all summer without finding them, while another command, under Capt. S. D. Sturgis, pressed northward from Texas with the same results. Troops sweeping part of the plains—news of them was carried swiftly from tribe to tribe—compelled Left Hand to adopt the strongest stand possible against his warriors' raids. He could not countenance any actions that might bring the troops north to the central plains. He therefore left his village.

Almost two years earlier, in Boulder Valley, Left Hand had faced a similar insurrection among his warriors. At that time he was able to gather enough support from the more mature men and the elders to force the young warriors to abide by his decisions. But this time the disagreement with his policies was so widespread that the support was not there when he called for it.

Left Hand's departure put the other men in a predicament. Either they could give the hot-headed young warriors free rein, and suffer the consequences, or they could recall their English-speaking chief and hope that in the treaty council he would be able to persuade the government to right the many wrongs. In the end they recalled Left Hand; they had no other choice.

On July 20, when the Southern Arapahos and Cheyennes arrived at Bent's Fort on the Arkansas for the annuity distribution, Left Hand was again with his village, again in authority.[29] He had laid down the terms on which he would return, and, clearly, they had been accepted. Bent reported to Washington that, although wagons of immigrants clogged the roads throughout July, the Southern Arapaho warriors had molested no one.[30]

Bent turned the wagon loads of annuities over to Left Hand and Little Raven, who saw that they were distributed in an orderly manner, first to the warriors seated in an inner circle and then to the women and children in an outer circle. Each family received its share of coffee, flour, bacon, dried apples, sugar, rice, and

[28] Donald J. Berthrong, *The Southern Cheyennes,* p. 146.

[29] Hafen, *Relations,* p. 207

[30] Ibid.; *BIA Reports* (1860), Sen. Exec. Doc. 1, 36th Cong., 2d sess. (see "Report from William Bent").

beans. Shirts, knives, hatchets, and some blankets were given to the men; the women received calico, blankets, coffee mills, and cooking utensils.[31]

After the distribution, Left Hand remained in the large village on the Arkansas—his and Little Raven's people were camped together—throughout the final weeks of summer. Only once did he and some of his warriors ride northward, and that was to warn a rancher on Cherry Creek, twenty miles from Denver, that Kiowas might launch an attack on outlying settlements. He told the rancher that he believed Denver itself would be spared because of the large number of men there.[32]

It was not out of any fondness for whites, or approval of their takeover of Indian lands, that Left Hand rode nearly two hundred miles to sound this warning. Should the hostile Kiowas carry out their plans, he wanted no misunderstanding about which tribe they belonged to. The earlier raids by knots of Southern Arapaho warriors had made the settlers jittery, and a rumor current at the time had it that two thousand Southern Arapahos and Cheyennes were moving up the South Platte with the object of attacking and burning Denver. The editor of the *Rocky Mountain News* reported Left Hand's visit to the ranch: "We have no doubt a large party is in the neighborhood, but have no idea they meditate any harm, other than their natural dispositions to beg and steal."[33] As it turned out, the hostiles stayed south of Denver and the rumor proved unfounded. No attack was launched by the Southern Arapahos and Cheyennes because none was planned.

As summer gave way to fall, Major Sedgwick received orders from the War Department to abandon his campaign, march to Bent's Fort, and construct a new military post. It was to be named Fort Wise after the governor of Virginia. The 350 troops in his command set up camp some distance from the large Southern Arapaho village and began constructing the post on the low, flat banks of the Arkansas, about a mile from Bent's New Fort. The fort itself, purchased by the government for $12,000, was turned into a commissary and storehouse.

Gradually, the buildings of the new post took shape, con-

---

[31] Julia S. Lambert, "Plain Tales of the Plains," *The Trail* 9 (1916):20.
[32] *Rocky Mountain News*, August 29, 1860.
[33] Ibid.

structed from the thick stone that was plentiful in the area and roofed with thatch and dirt. Beef hides stretched across rough frames served as doors and windows. Sedgwick's troops worked day and night to finish the task and ensure shelter for themselves before winter set in.

During the time he was building Fort Wise, Sedgwick took his own gauge of the white settlements on the plains. In a letter to his sister that September, he wrote:

> I hope there never was a viler set of men in the world than is congregated about these mines; no man's life is safe, and certainly not if he has fifty dollars to tempt one with. They have established a vigilance committee and it may get rid of some of the scoundrels, but it would depopulate the country to kill them all. Half the murders that are committed on the plains, and laid to the Indians, are committed by white men.[34]

Autumn days fell over the Arkansas River valley in a burst of sunshine and warmth, allaying Sedgwick's fears that winter would sweep in unexpectedly. But the nights turned ominously cool, spurring him and his men to complete their task. The major laid aside his work one day in early September, however, when a runner arrived from the Southern Arapaho village requesting that the chiefs be granted safety to approach the fort for a talk. Sedgwick agreed and, soon afterward, met with six or eight leading men who, he reported, were "suing for peace."[35] Although he did not name them, Left Hand was undoubtedly there. Since Sedgwick, a humane, well-intentioned man, had orders only to build a military post, not to treat with the Indians, the meeting, like so many others, served no purpose except that of assuring the commander of the troops that the nearby Indian village was friendly.

Not all the Southern Arapahos were friendly, however. Some of the warriors, chafing under the firm control of Left Hand and Little Raven and disagreeing with their policy of appeasement, had slipped away to join a Cheyenne war party. The result was a major battle against the Delawares and Potawatomis, one hun-

---

[34] Hafen, *Relations*, p. 271.
[35] Ibid., p. 276.

dred miles from Fort Riley in the eastern section of Kansas Territory, a battle that left three hundred warriors dead.[36] Once again, the frustrations caused by the white invasion had been turned against other tribes who, also under white pressure, had pushed into the traditional Southern Arapaho and Cheyenne buffalo ranges.

With the hostile warriors out of the village, tensions eased somewhat. There was food in the lodges from the annuity distribution and the summer hunts. The men could relax and lounge about, sleeping in the warm sunshine. The women tanned robes and prepared food for the winter while the children played at their feet. Left Hand and Little Raven had time to prepare for the treaty council while awaiting the arrival of the government commissioner, who, Bent had assured them, was expected at any moment.[37]

[36] Virginia Cole Trenholm, *The Arapahoes, Our People*, pp. 160–61.
[37] *Rocky Mountain News*, September 19, 1860.

9

It was the old, old story of the white man with plenty of fine presents and a paper which he wished the Indians to sign.

George Bent

From the half-built stone walls of Fort Wise, the wagon train could be seen clattering over the Sante Fe Trail, raising billows of dust on that hot, dry day of September 8, 1860. Major Sedgwick and some of his troops raced out to greet Commissioner of Indian Affairs Alfred B. Greenwood and his assistant and physician Dr. F. B. Culver, who had come to negotiate a new treaty with the Southern Arapahos and Cheyennes.[1]

Left Hand probably had observed the long-awaited train from his village nearby. During the distribution of annuities several weeks earlier, Bent had informed the chiefs that Congress had finally appropriated funds for a council and that the commissioners would be on their way. In August a lone army officer had ridden to Fort Wise with a message from Greenwood, instructing Bent to assemble the tribal chiefs. The agent had sent runners to the Cheyennes, who were camped about 250 miles away, asking them to come to the fort in September.

For Greenwood the trip had been long and arduous. He had left Washington on August 15, having received instructions only four days earlier from the Department of the Interior, Office of Indian Affairs. Traveling by train to St. Louis, he had purchased part of the gifts, clothing, food, and utensils which he intended to give the Indians after concluding a successful treaty. He stopped again at Kansas City, where he purchased additional gifts, and made up a wagon train to haul the supplies across the plains. All the treaty expenses, the commissioners' travel ex-

---

[1] *BIA Reports* (1860), Sen. Exec. Doc. 1, 36th Cong., 2d sess., pp. 452–54; Fort Wise Treaty, Record Group 75, Federal Archives and Records Center, Denver, Colo.; "Fort Wise Treaty" in Charles J. Kappler, *Indian Affairs: Laws and Treaties*, 2:807–11.

penses and the costs of Indian gifts, were paid from the congressional appropriation of $35,000.[2]

The last leg of the long journey, the six hundred miles from Kansas City to Fort Wise, gave the commissioner of Indian Affairs his first view of the increasingly unsettled conditions on the plains. It was a sobering view:

> On route I passed through the country claimed by the Kiowa Indians, who are known to be hostile, and whom, as well as the Comanches, the Secretary of War has ordered the army in the West to chastise, as the only means of compelling them to respect their engagements with the United States, and to stay their murderous hand. Citizens of the United States in advance of me as I went out were brutally murdered and scalped upon the road.[3]

In south-central Kansas Territory, Greenwood passed Fort Larned, which was also under construction that fall by the military, and noted that even the guns of Larned did not stop the hostiles. As he put it, "They cautiously approach the Santa Fe road, commit the most atrocious deeds, and flee to the plains."[4]

Reaching Fort Wise, Greenwood was annoyed to discover that the Cheyennes had not yet arrived, and he immediately sent runners to the bands. Eight days after his arrival, Black Kettle and White Antelope, the dignified brother-chiefs who were widely respected among the plains tribes, reached the fort, along with four or five other Cheyenne leaders. Like Left Hand and Little Raven, they were deeply concerned about the future. The commissioner then sent for Left Hand, Little Raven, Storm, and Shave Head and convened the council.

The council opened in a friendly enough manner, with Greenwood informing the chiefs that "the Great Father had heard with delight of their peaceful disposition, although they were almost in the midst of the hostile tribes." The chiefs, in turn, expressed pleasure that the Great Father had heard of their good conduct and wanted him to know they intended to conform to the wishes of the government.[5]

---

[2] U.S. *Statutes at Large*, vol. 12, p. 59.
[3] *BIA Reports* (1860), p. 452.
[4] Ibid., p. 452.
[5] Ibid.

When these preliminary exchanges were over, Greenwood got down to business. He laid out a map of Indian lands under the Fort Laramie Treaty and outlined the boundaries from the Platte River along the Continental Divide to the Arkansas, down that river to a point near the present site of Dodge City, Kansas, and north again to the Platte. Later Greenwood reported that the chiefs had understood the map perfectly and could locate significant geographical points, streams, and rock formations. "In fact," Greenwood wrote, "they exhibited a degree of intelligence seldom to be found among tribes, where no effort has heretofore been made to civilize them."[6]

The chiefs also understood the changes that had taken place since the Fort Laramie Treaty Council. At that time the white invasion of the plains was only beginning, and, with the exception of the Oregon and Santa Fe trails, the vast land belonging to the Southern Arapahos and Cheyennes stretched to the horizon, open and unmarked. Buffalo and wild game were still plentiful and the streams ran clear amid the stands of cottonwoods.

Now, in the wake of the gold rush, roads were always filled with white traffic, and white settlements pushed against the foothills and crowded into the mountains. The buffalo and other game were indiscriminately slaughtered in greater numbers than the Indians could have dreamed possible ten years before; many of the streams were polluted and much of the timber was destroyed. Faced with such changes, the chiefs looked to the commissioner for explanations and answers concerning the future of their peoples. Greenwood's response, and the response of the government, was an offer to further reduce the Indians' means of livelihood.

In place of the vast land between the rivers, Greenwood proposed that the tribes accept a small tract on either side of the Arkansas River: "I stated to them that it was the intention of their Great Father to reduce the area of their present reservation, and that they should settle down, and betake themselves to agriculture, and eventually abandon the chase as a means of support."[7] According to the commissioner, the chiefs were in full agreement:

[6] Ibid., p. 453.
[7] Ibid.

They informed me that such was their wish, and that they had been aware for some time that they would be compelled to do so; that game was growing [more] scarce every year, and that they had also noticed the approach of the whites, and felt that they must soon, in a great measure, conform to their habits.[8]

The reservation proposed by Greenwood formed an irregular triangle that dipped south of the Arkansas to the Purgatoire River and ran northward to the Huerfano River and Big Sandy Creek. Within this boundary lay some of the most arid, inhospitable land on the plains. The Southern Arapahos called it the "no-water land." Small game that had once maintained an uncertain existence in the area had long since been driven off by the traffic on the Santa Fe Trail, and no buffalo had been seen there in several years.[9]

To counter any objections the chiefs might have raised, Greenwood hurriedly explained his intention of allotting each person in the two tribes forty acres with water and timber, which, he allowed, was "exceeding scarce." The individual allotments were to extend along the Arkansas River since, according to Greenwood, this was the only land fit for cultivation within the reservation.

There was a problem with the proposed allotments, however. The War Department had already appropriated twenty-five miles of this land as a military reserve for Fort Wise, and the commissioner was not in a position to allot military land. He could only express his hopes—and he did so in the strongest of terms—that the military would relinquish part of the reserve because

it was so much larger than has been regarded usually as necessary for military purposes, contains more timber than any portion of that country visited by me, and might with propriety be reduced, at least one-half of its present extent, and still have sufficient timber for firewood and other ordinary demands.[10]

   [8] Ibid.
   [9] Author's interview of March 23, 1976, with Gus Yellowhair, Geary, Oklahoma, who described the proposed reservation as part of the "no-water land"; *BIA Reports* (1863), House Exec. Doc. 1, 38th Cong., lst sess., pp. 252–53 (Colley's statement to Evans was also applicable in 1860).
   [10] *BIA Reports* (1860), p. 453.

In return for relinquishing their Fort Laramie Treaty lands, Greenwood explained that the government was prepared to offer the tribes $450,000, to be paid in annuities over a fifteen-year period, and would also help the tribes set up farms and ranches by providing buildings, tools, seeds, and instructors.

Despite such seemingly generous terms, the chiefs refused to sign the agreement. Black Kettle and White Antelope told Greenwood that, to avoid future trouble among their people, they wished to consult the other leading men and warriors. Left Hand and Little Raven also refused to sign, although the leading men of the Southern Arapaho tribe were present; perhaps they wanted to await the Cheyennes and come to a joint decision. This initial refusal should have alerted Greenwood to the stumbling blocks inherent in the proposal. It did not.

The first stumbling block was the misunderstanding between the commissioner and the chiefs about who was to settle on the reservation. Greenwood had thought he was making a treaty with "the Cheyenne and Arrapahoe Indians, on the Upper Arkansas"—the southern tribes—but the chiefs insisted that the Northern Arapaho and Cheyennes also be asked if they wished to sign the treaty. If they did not, they could make separate arrangements with the government.

The biggest stumbling block, however, concerned the location of the proposed reservation. Greenwood was charged with the task of working out an agreement that would forestall future conflicts on the plains and meet the Indians' needs. That being the case, it would have made sense to let the tribes select their own reservation land. Had they been given that opportunity, they would have chosen an area in the vicinity of the Republican River where buffalo could still be found and where they could survive while they learned to farm or ranch. It was an area they later said they much preferred.[11]

Instead, Greenwood arbitrarily determined the reservation area before setting foot on the plains, giving no thought to the tribes' traditional way of life. To suppose that the Southern Arapahos and Cheyennes would abandon the buffalo ranges and move onto a gameless, parched tract of land, where their families

[11] *BIA Reports* (1863), p. 248.

were likely to starve while they learned to farm, was to take a long flight from reality. This the commissioner was prepared to do.

Greenwood's report to Washington was couched in optimism. Ignoring the difficulties, he wrote that the chiefs ''readily consented to the propositions I made to them, . . . notwithstanding they are fully aware of the rich mines discovered in their country, they are disposed to yield up their claims without any reluctance.'' On the question of whether the northern tribes were to be included in the treaty—a serious question for the chiefs—Greenwood blithely stated that the chiefs ''did not regard [the northern leaders'] assent to the proposed agreement as important.''[12]

Greenwood hurriedly closed the council, packed his bags, and on September 20, less than two weeks after his arrival, set out for Washington. He left Culver to meet with the chiefs after they had consulted the northern leaders. He promised to draw up a treaty based on the understanding that he believed had been reached and send it to the agent, who, along with Culver, would carry out the formality of obtaining the chiefs' signatures.

Evidently Culver was not pleased to be left on the plains, because the commissioner promised to relieve him as soon as possible—a promise he had no intention of keeping. A few days' distance from Fort Wise, Greenwood sent a messenger back to inform Culver that no one else was available and that he would have to stay on. With no place to live except the fort, and with no sure livelihood, the hapless physician then hired himself out as a freighter on wagons going between Fort Wise and Denver.[13]

It was clear that the proposal required further negotiations and more time than Greenwood was willing to admit. Unfortunately, Greenwood's behavior seems to have been characterized by a tendency to see things, not as they were, but as he would have liked them to be. Also, the prospect of being stranded on the plains through the winter (a fate that befell Culver), caused him great uneasiness. As soon as he arrived at Fort Wise he began making plans for his earliest possible return to the East. When

[12] *BIA Reports* (1860), p. 453.
[13] William Unrau, ''A Prelude to War,'' *Colorado Magazine* 41 (1964):304–305.

Black Kettle and White Antelope reached the fort, Greenwood, though he felt compelled to carry out his assignment, was not willing to spend the time necessary to produce a workable agreement or to change his plans for starting back home. The so-called council, in fact, was comprised of one meeting.

At its conclusion, William Bent, almost the last friend left to the Southern Arapahos and Cheyennes, resigned as their agent. Although he had kept up a prolific correspondence with the commissioner in the past, expressing his feelings and hopes about the situation on the plains, he remained strangely silent on his motives for resigning, leading historians to conclude that he did so out of disgust with the government's proposition.

Yet it is difficult to understand how Bent could have abandoned his wife's people at a time when they were in danger of losing most of their lands and desperately needed someone trustworthy to oversee their interests. Perhaps some personal reason, such as ill health, led the fifty-year-old plainsman to resign. The memoirs of his son George suggest that another possible motive was his need to focus his attention and energies on his own business interests—something that held top priority with Bent. It is certainly true that Bent's trading business for the last two years had met with stiff competition from the goldseekers and settlers for the dwindling supply of buffalo robes. As George Bent put it, the "great rush of men into the mountains upset everything and [his father] gave up the agency in the fall."[14]

Bent recommended another seasoned plainsman, A. G. Boone, as his successor. He believed that Boone, the grandson of Daniel Boone, would deal honestly with the tribes. Boone's appointment as special agent was swiftly confirmed by the Senate, and by December he was in Washington working out the treaty details with Greenwood.

Following Greenwood's departure, Left Hand and Little Raven moved their bands northeastward, to the vicinity of the Solomon and Republican rivers, in search of buffalo. The annuity goods received in July were rapidly diminishing. Even Greenwood had noticed that the Southern Arapahos were in great want when he issued a portion of the gifts he had brought.[15] If the tribe

---

[14] George Hyde, *Life of George Bent,* pp. 107–108.

was to survive the winter, it was necessary for the warriors to find game.

By November a furious winter storm descended upon the plains, bringing deep snows and bitter cold. Food was scarce, buffalo difficult to find. Their sheltered winter campgrounds near the foothills were now overrun by whites and closed to Indians. For several weeks the Southern Arapahos wandered the plains, cold and hungry, bitter and disillusioned.

In the early part of January, winter still whipping the plains, Left Hand finally brought his village to the familiar South Platte campgrounds near Denver, regardless of the entrenched settlers. Not only were the Southern Arapahos looking for a respite from the storms, they were also probably eager to augment their living by trading with the whites.

Shortly after their arrival, Left Hand learned that an election had been called for January 26. Elections were frequent occurrences in town as the whites tried to establish and maintain some kind of political order—no fewer than nine had been held in the fall of 1859. On the day of this particular election, Left Hand and one or two of his warriors strode into the cabin where the voting was taking place and announced their intention to vote. The startled whites who were overseeing the balloting refused permission. When Left Hand pressed them for a reason, they lamely replied that the Indians' property was not subject to taxation.[16]

Left Hand's attempt to vote was no lark. At this time he was weighed down with concern for the future. The government proposal had not resulted in the treaty he had longed for, and the Southern Arapahos were no closer to a new way of life. For the time being, it looked as though they would continue to spend at least part of each year in the vicinity of the white settlements, and, that being the case, Left Hand thought it was perfectly natural that he should express his views on how things were being run. That the white men refused to let Indians vote was an omen not lost on the Southern Arapahos; they knew that the whites had no intention of allowing the Indians a place in the new society developing on the plains.

---

[15] *BIA Reports* (1860), p. 454.
[16] *Rocky Mountain News,* January 30, 1861.

While Left Hand was in the vicinity of Denver, Boone arrived at Fort Wise with a copy of the proposed treaty. Convening the Indian leaders who were still in the area, the new agent held another council. Interpreters for the Cheyennes were John Smith, the trader whom the Indians had known and distrusted for twenty-five years—familiarly known as "Lying John," he had been run out of Denver and Auraria two years earlier for beating his wife—and Robert Bent, another of William's sons. Since Smith certainly could not speak Arapaho, and Bent probably could not, the Southern Arapahos had no interpreter. And yet Boone made no effort to inform Left Hand of the new council.[17]

The treaty terms were much the same as those proposed in the fall. The Southern Arapahos and Cheyennes would cede most of their land in exchange for the triangle of land skirting the Arkansas and $450,000 in annuities over fifteen years. No white men would be allowed to live on or travel within the reservation without permission of the superintendent of Indian Affairs or the agent. Costs of building homes and storehouses and of ploughing and fencing the land would come from the annuity money, but the government promised to spend another $5,000 each year for five years to provide a mill, mechanic shops with tools, homes for an interpreter, miller, and engineer, and all necessary provisions, stock, implements, lumber, and machinery. In short, the treaty, like other treaties with other tribes, promised to help the Indians become civilized. Should they fail to make "reasonable efforts to advance and improve their conditions," the annuities would be discontinued.[18]

The Boone treaty contained many of the same obstacles as its earlier version. Because of the chiefs' insistence that the northern tribes be included, Article Six called for the commissioner to notify the absent chiefs of the treaty benefits and to induce them to sign. Those who refused to sign within one year from the ratification date would forfeit all rights to the benefits. This crucial article put the entire treaty in abeyance; it could not take

---

[17] Smith could not speak Arapaho, according to his own testimony. See U.S., Congress, Senate, "The Chivington Massacre," *Reports of the Joint Special Committees on the Conditions of the Indian Tribes,* Sen. Report 156, 39th Cong., 2d sess., 1867, p. 41 (hereafter cited as "Chivington Massacre").

[18] Kappler, *Indian Affairs,* 2:807–11.

effect until all the Arapaho and Cheyenne chiefs, northern and southern, had signed. Other terms of the treaty also presented problems. Article Eleven, for example, read:

> In consideration of the kind treatment of the Arapahos and Cheyennes by the citizens of Denver City and the adjacent towns, they respectfully request that the proprietors of said city and adjacent towns be permitted by the United States government to enter a sufficient quantity of land to include said city and towns at a minimum price of one dollar and twenty-five cents per acre.

What this article intended is unclear. Historians have interpreted it in various ways. Some believe it would have allowed developers to purchase reservation land in order to build new towns. Others interpret its meaning to be that whites living in already settled towns, such as Denver, could purchase the land they occupied, whether or not the full slate of northern and southern chiefs agreed to relinquish other land. Whatever the article intended, however, it would have benefited white settlers at the expense of the Indians, and the United States Senate, seeing the ruse, later disallowed it. Another last-minute addition to the treaty called for Jack Smith, the son of the interpreter, and Robert Bent to receive 640 acres of reservation land each "as a gift from the nation."

Both Article Eleven and the gift provision bear the unmistakable imprint of the two interpreters, if not of Boone himself.[19] Smith and Bent lived with the Indians and could not have been unaware of the chiefs' dissatisfaction with the location of the reservation. Yet every effort was used to induce them to sign the treaty. They may even have told the chiefs that the reservation would be on the Republican River; the Cheyenne chiefs later complained bitterly that that is what they had been led to believe.[20]

In fact, the two interpreters had seen the opportunity to enrich themselves (or, in Smith's case, his son) and had taken it. Ceded Indian lands would be opened to white settlement, as they knew,

---

[19] See Unrau, "Prelude to War," p. 304ff. for full discussion of the duplicity surrounding this treaty.
[20] *BIA Reports* (1863), p. 248.

and they would be on hand to snap up the choicest areas. They gave away their game by deeding themselves 640 acres and attempting to include Article Eleven, which would have put them and other like-minded whites and half-bloods in the position of acquiring still more land at advantageous prices.

Boone himself was not averse to deceiving the chiefs in order to ratify the treaty. At the time, he was building a ranch at the mouth of the Huerfano River, on a section of Indian land he had already usurped. The treaty would legitimate his claim and, at the same time, provide an opportunity of expanding his holdings onto the ceded lands.[21]

Left Hand's absence from the council suited Boone and the "interpreters." Left Hand was the only man who was able to speak Arapaho, Cheyenne, and English and was, therefore, the only man who could have ensured a measure of honesty in the proceedings. Even if his absence had not suited them, however, it is unlikely that Boone would have summoned him from Denver. There simply was not enough time.

That Boone was under the most stringent orders from Greenwood to conclude the treaty in all possible haste is clear. The commissioner had told him to invite all the Cheyenne and Arapaho leaders to sign the treaty and, if they refused, "to make it over their heads."[22] Political developments had made it necessary for the government to obtain clear title to the Southern Arapaho and Cheyenne lands. Under consideration in Congress was the bill to create a new territory on the plains, and it would hardly do to carve that territory out of land to which the government had no legal right.

It was for this reason that Boone had crossed the snowbound plains in the middle of a severe winter, taking the chiefs by surprise. It is unlikely that they expected him before spring. If Left Hand had had any idea that Boone planned to return in February, he certainly would have remained on the Arkansas, just as he had waited there nearly two months for Greenwood.

On February 18, 1861, the Fort Wise Treaty was signed by the

[21] Unrau, "Prelude to War," p. 304.

[22] Boone to Evans, January 16, 1863, Letters Sent, Upper Arkansas Agency, *OIA,* Record Group 75, Federal Archives and Records Center, Denver, Colo.

Arapaho chiefs Little Raven, Storm, Shave Head, and Big Mouth and the Cheyenne chiefs Black Kettle, White Antelope, Lean Bear, Little Wolf, Tall Bear, and Left Hand (Namos).[23] Following the signing, Boone distributed food and other gifts, which were happily and thankfully received by the Indians in their mid-winter need. He also passed out cavalry uniforms, complete with epaulettes and medals. Once again, leaders of the Plains Indians donned the white man's uniforms and paraded about, reminiscent of another treaty council ten years before. On February 28, ten days after the signing, Congress passed the Organic Act of Colorado Territory, placing under United States jurisdiction most of the land ceded by the two tribes.[24]

Rather than settling matters on the plains, the Fort Wise Treaty hopelessly entangled them. Within a short time the tribes came to believe that they had been duped by fast-talking white men who, for their own reasons, had lied to them. When Left Hand learned of the treaty, he strongly repudiated it, claiming that the council had been hastily called while he was away and that the other chiefs had been tricked into signing what they did not understand. Little Raven expressed the same opinion when he said later that "Boone came out and got [the chiefs] to sign a paper, but [they] did not know what it meant. The Cheyennes signed it first; then I; but we did not know what it was."[25]

Later, the Cheyenne chiefs went so far as to deny that they had signed the treaty.[26] They meant that they had not signed what they thought they had signed. The reservation was not where

[23] This Cheyenne by the name of Left Hand is the same man Lt. James Abert met at Bent's Fort in 1848 (J. W. Abert, *Western America in 1846-1847*, the Original Travel Diary of Lt. J. W. Abert, pp. 18-23).

[24] The Organic Act specifically excluded those lands not yet relinquished by the Indians in a treaty.

[25] *BIA Reports* (1865), House Exec. Doc. 1, 39th Cong., 1st sess., pp. 66-103, 517-27; Colley to Commissioner of Indian Affairs, September 30, 1863, Letters Received, Upper Arkansas Agency, *OIA*, Record Group 75, National Archives, Washington, D.C.; Donald J. Berthrong, *The Southern Cheyennes*, p. 160; Saville to Holloway, April 15, 1863, Letters Sent, Upper Arkansas Agency, *OIA*, Record Group 75, National Archives.

[26] *BIA Reports* (1865), p. 248; Colley to Commissioner of Indian Affairs, September 30, 1863, Letters Received, Upper Arkansas Agency, *OIA*, Record Group 75, National Archives.

they had supposed it would be, and, when they and their warriors learned the truth, they repudiated the agreement.

Thus it came about that the treaty—which Left Hand and the other chiefs had long hoped would end the injustices of the white immigrations and allow their people to pursue quiet lives on their own lands—only would increase the severe tensions between Indians and whites, harry the Southern Arapahos and Cheyennes from one end of the plains to the other, and, at last, ignite the flames of war.

The Years
of Hunger

As you come here hunting for gold,
then hunt after the gold and let the
Indians alone.

10

Left Hand, Southern Arapaho

Within weeks of the signing of the Fort Wise Treaty, a dark and disturbing thunderhead began building on the plains. Small bands of embittered Cheyenne warriors had not only repudiated it but had also showed their disdain for the government-proposed reservation by attacking isolated ranches, stealing cattle, and burning buildings.[1]

The attacks increased the anxiety of Plains Indians and white settlers alike. Left Hand, who remained with his village on the sandy bluffs near Denver, and the other peacefully disposed chiefs feared that the outbursts could bring army troops against their people. Their fears were justified. Major Sedgwick's seasoned troops, who had campaigned against the Cheyennes in 1857 and had scoured the southern plains three years later looking for hostile Kiowas and Comanches, were still at Fort Wise ready to move against the Cheyennes—or the Southern Arapahos—if ordered to do so. Other army troops were garrisoned at newly constructed Fort Larned in the heart of the buffalo range in south-central Kansas.

Despite the presence of these troops on the plains, white settlers reacted to the Cheyenne raids with a clamor for a territorial militia or some other local protective force. Since the summer of 1859, when the Utes had murdered several goldseekers, whites had made several attempts to raise such a force and had finally organized two militia companies under the spurious authority of a short-lived Jefferson Territory. When the Territory of Colorado was formed, both of the companies, ill-trained, unequipped, and ineffective, were disbanded. Now the settlers believed they were virtually defenseless, and, from their viewpoint, the moment could not have been worse.

[1] Boone to Robinson, April 25, 1861, Letters Sent, Upper Arkansas Agency, *OIA*, Record Group 75, Federal Archives and Records Center, Denver, Colo.

The Cheyenne raids that spring were not the only dark cumuli moving across the plains and causing anxiety in the white settlements. Halfway across the country, on the Eastern Seaboard, events were unfolding that would splinter the union, lead to a long and life-draining war, and deeply affect the plains. On April 12, 1861, Confederate artillery opened fire on Union troops at Fort Sumter, and that volley ushered in the Civil War. The news did not reach the plains until nearly two weeks later. The *Rocky Mountain News* carried the story on April 24, and that same day secessionist sympathizers raised a Confederate flag over Wallingford and Murphy's store on Larimer Street, Denver's main street. Union sympathizers brought the flag down almost before it had unfurled in the breeze, but the affair focused attention on the strong sympathy for the South in Colorado Territory and emphasized the need for a militia to preserve order. Given these developments, Denver townspeople greeted the appointment of a military leader, William Gilpin, as Colorado's first territorial governor with a sense of relief and a conviction that some kind of a territorial army would become a reality.

The governor did not disappoint them. A West Point graduate, Gilpin was familiar with the plains, having commanded the Missouri Volunteers in a campaign against the Kiowas and Comanches in 1847, which had left the southern edge of the plains devastated and, in the words of Berthrong, "unfit for human habitation."[2] Gilpin arrived in Denver on May 27 to assume the uncharted duties of office and, recognizing the need for discipline and order in the territory, immediately laid plans to organize a standing army: he would ensure peace by having the means to wage war.

That spring Left Hand was actively pursuing the same objective of peace, but by different means. Toward the end of April, Left Hand visited William Byers, the editor of the *Rocky Mountain News,* to ask him to inform his white readers that the Southern Arapahos were friendly toward them and meant no harm. At this time the newspaper offices were on the second floor of a rather unsturdy building constructed of roughhewn lumber that stood in the dry bed of Cherry Creek at Thirteenth and Welton streets.

---

[2] Donald J. Berthrong, *The Southernn Cheyennes,* pp. 111–12.

A banner proclaiming "Rocky Mountain News" in large block letters stretched across the peaked roof, and the word "printing" was splashed over the door. To reach the office, it was necessary to cross a plankway from the river bank to the second-story door.

Byers managed a casual office, open to anyone who wanted to come in, pull up a chair, push aside piles of papers, prop his feet on the desk, and talk over local events. Two years before, the editor had offered part of his premises to the journalist Henry Villard, who dispatched his "Reports from the Gold Region" as Indians and goldseekers wandered in and out of the office. In one article Villard mentioned that as he was writing, a Southern Arapaho warrior, wrapped in a buffalo robe, and several women and babies were sitting on the floor together, "chuckling over and diving into" a cup of sugar. Meanwhile, according to Villard, the proprietor, Byers, was busy kneading bread.[3]

On the day of Left Hand's visit Byers's attention, like that of most people in town, was fixed on two topics: the Civil War and the recent Cheyenne attacks. He was glad to see the chief, whom he called "the most influential chief in the Arapaho tribe," and to get his views on "the position of Indian affairs as far as [the Southern Arapaho] tribe is concerned." With Left Hand were his brother-in-law John Poisal and two warriors.[4]

Left Hand told Byers, and the editor so informed his readers, that the Southern Arapahos still retained "the usual, long-standing friendship for the whites, and...under no circumstances will they injure or molest the whites." Left Hand said he could not speak for the Cheyennes, however, and that he feared difficulties with them. He was greatly concerned that should the Cheyennes cause trouble, the whites would retaliate against his people, "since whites can't distinguish between them."[5]

It was Left Hand's opinion that the fears of the settlers were

---

[3] LeRoy R. Hafen, *Reports from Colorado: The Wildman Letters, 1859–1865*, vol. 13 in *The Far West and the Rockies Historical Series*, p. 354–55.

[4] *Rocky Mountain News*, May 1, 1861. Although the article ran on May 1, the visit had taken place several days earlier, since Little Raven was already in Denver by May 1.

[5] Ibid.

based on misunderstanding and ignorance of Plains Indians. On his part Left Hand promised to control his warriors and to prevent them from accepting or buying whiskey. He also promised that any of his men who committed offenses would be punished. In return he asked that white settlers refrain from insulting and wronging his people and that they show "forebearance and conciliation and effort to restrain impulsive citizens from taking action."[6]

Byers then asked Left Hand about the current rumors that a hundred whites had been killed on the Arkansas River below Fort Wise and that Comanches were moving toward Denver. The chief replied that he had heard that Comanches were on the way but that they meant no harm, and he discounted the report of whites having been killed, using it as an example of the outright lies that had led to the present misunderstanding and consequent tension.

Before leaving the office Left Hand mentioned that he expected Little Raven in five or six days and that the two chiefs hoped to hold a talk with the white leaders in town. "He is very anxious that the present ill feeling be repressed and will use every effort to bring about that result," Byers reported. "We hope such good feeling will be fully reciprocated by our citizens."[7]

The same issue of the *Rocky Mountain News* carried another story calling for restraint. Special Agent Boone had visited the newspaper office at about the same time as Left Hand to express his regrets over the "disposition to inflame feeling against the Indians." Boone's visit was prompted by his concern that a few headstrong whites in Denver would attack Indian camps, even though such action would endanger ranches, settlers, and roads across the plains. "It would be disastrous," the agent warned. "Shall the folly and rashness of a few inconsiderate persons, who wish to gain a little personal notoriety, be allowed to embroil us in a war with the Indians? We trust not."[8] Byers added his own appeal for calmness, writing that

reports are reaching us of depredations and thefts by Indians.

[6] Ibid.
[7] Ibid.
[8] Ibid.

They have turned out to be false or greatly exaggerated. We hope nothing will be done toward avenging these until peaceful efforts prove unavailing. The leading men of the tribes around us are in favor of peace, and have promised to do all in their power to promote it.[9]

The following week, on Monday, April 29, the meeting mentioned by Left Hand took place in Boone's office. Left Hand, Little Raven, Storm, Shave Head, and fifteen warriors were there, which suggests that most of the Southern Arapahos had moved to the area.[10] With Left Hand acting as interpreter, Little Raven lodged a strong protest with Boone that the white settlers who occupied Indian land had destroyed the timber and impoverished his people. Game was scarce, he said, and "we are compelled to ask for food." He added that he expected his people to be paid for their land. As for the Fort Wise Treaty, he saw no signs of the houses, buildings, tools, and instructors the government had promised.[11] In this as in their past meetings with white officials, the chiefs had hoped to prod the government into honoring its promises and bringing a measure of justice to their people. Instead, the meeting accomplished nothing more than an opportunity for the chiefs to repeat their timeworn complaints.

On the following evening, April 30, Left Hand took ten warriors to the Apollo Theater, which was on the second floor of a small building on Larimer Street between D and E streets (present-day Fourteenth and Fifteenth streets). They strode through the first-floor saloon and climbed the rickety wooden stairway to an open room that was filled with rows of hard, backless benches. Across one end was a narrow stage, and to its side stood a smoldering potbellied stove. A makeshift wooden frame with a dozen flickering candles hung like a chandelier from the rafters overhead, and other candles edged the stage as footlights. Seated on one of the benches, Left Hand strained to catch the words of the play *Lady of Lyons* above the boisterous laughter and the sound of smashing glass from the saloon below. As soon as the play ended, Left Hand bounded up onto the

[9] Ibid.
[10] *Rocky Mountain News,* April 30, 1861.
[11] Ibid.

stage, and, before the audience could join the crowd downstairs, he held up his hands for attention and began to speak. "The Arapaho chief makes a handsome speech," reported Byers, who happened to be in the audience. According to Byers, whose report appeared the following day in the *Rocky Mountain News*, Left Hand told the white audience that he wished that his "white brethren would stop talking about fighting his people." His people had no enmity against them, he said, but looked on them as brothers. "As you have come here hunting for gold," he reminded his listeners, "then hunt after the gold and let the Indians alone." The speech concluded on a conciliatory note, with Left Hand pointing out that the white settlers, who had "intruded on [their] antelope and buffalo grounds," had brought great hardships to his people but that as long as there was peace the Indians would be able to find the buffalo.[12]

The message was the same plea for peace Left Hand had given Byers several days before, but there was now an added sense of urgency. Not only was he trying to discredit rumors and appeal for understanding but he was also trying to stop the increasing assaults on persons from his village.[13] A warrior bringing buffalo robes into town took the chance of being attacked from behind and relieved of his robes by force. Women were in continual danger of being dragged behind buildings and raped. Such senseless attacks—the "insults and wrongs" he had mentioned to Byers—invited some of Left Hand's warriors to seek revenge on isolated white ranches and wagon trains. They were the sure guarantees of serious conflict ahead, a conflict Left Hand was trying desperately to avoid.

Later that same month, on Sunday, May 21, Left Hand and Little Raven temporarily set aside these concerns to spend a sunny afternoon racing their ponies at the Denver track. Surrounding the track were the men, women, and children from both bands, shouting and betting on their favorite horses. It was a pleasant relief from the tension-filled days, but, shortly afterward, two Southern Arapaho warriors got into a fight on the streets of

---

[12] Ibid., May 1, 1861; Stanley Zamonski and Teddy Keller, *The Fifty-Niners*, p. 51.

[13] White attacks on Indians were frequent in Denver. See Frank Hall, *History of the State of Colorado*, 1:324.

Denver, a fight that left one of them seriously injured. Three Mexican traders were later arrested for selling whiskey to the two Indians.[14]

During the first days of June, Left Hand led his warriors into the mountains for another raid on a Ute camp, and on their return an incident occurred that found its way into the *Rocky Mountain News* on June 12. According to the newspaper, a settler named A. B. Adams, who kept a ranch twenty-five miles west of Denver, claimed that 160 Cheyennes and Arapahos had come to his house begging for whiskey, which he had refused them. Peering through the opened door, he reported, they saw some clothing hanging on wall hooks and pushed their way inside, demanding the articles. Adams said he gave the clothing to them, since they obviously intended to take it, but, still dissatisfied, one warrior stole into the attic and began taking everything he saw. When Adams tried to stop him, the Indian pulled a knife, and, at that point, Adams said, he picked up a stick, clubbed the Indian, and drove the rest from the house. Within a short time, Adams continued, Left Hand was at the door, asking to be admitted, and assuring him no harm would be done. The moment Adams drew the lock, however, the door burst open and the house again filled with Indians, who stole food, clothing, and a rifle. Byers, who had regarded Left Hand as a trustworthy leader, concluded the report by saying: "We are surprised at the part Left Hand seems to have taken in this affair."[5]

A week later, on June 19, Byers was even more surprised when an indignant Left Hand appeared in the *Rocky Mountain News* office and demanded that he publish a retraction. Poisal probably had shown him the article, and some of the men whom Left Hand had come to know in Denver had probably asked him about the incident. He was eager to set the record straight, and the account he gave Byers, which ran the same day, was markedly different from Adam's story.[16]

According to Left Hand, he and his party had stopped near a ranch to rest in the shade, out of the hot noon sun, when Adams appeared in an upper-story window of the ranchhouse, beckon-

[14] *Rocky Mountain News,* May 22, 1861.
[15] Ibid., June 12, 1861.
[16] Ibid., June 19, 1861.

ing an Indian boy to come to him. The boy, curious, wandered over to an outside stairway and climbed to where the man stood. As the boy approached, Adams suddenly raised a club he had been holding behind him and struck the boy, knocking him down. Then he stood over the boy, striking him again and again until he lost consciousness. "It is thought he will not live," Left Hand told Byers.[17]

Someone in Left Hand's party caught sight of the commotion and alerted the chief, who raced to the stairway and found the unconscious boy. Incensed by the attack on one of his people, Left Hand pounded on Adams's door, shouting his name and demanding to speak to the rancher. Adams, in the meantime, was cowering in the attic, leaving his wife to deal with the angry Indians. When she opened the door, Left Hand and some of his warriors stepped inside, and the chief told her that Indian custom required that some retribution be made for the injury inflicted upon the boy.

It was Adams's wife, Left Hand told Byers, who gave them a half sack of flour, an old gun, and several articles of clothing. The Indians then left the area without killing any of the ranch animals or committing any outrage. "These facts we learn from Left Hand himself through Poisal, interpreter," Byers reported.[18] Left Hand had brought Poisal along for the interview, obviously taking no chance that what he had to say would be misunderstood or misinterpreted. The old white trader also served as a witness, ensuring that Byers would truthfully report Left Hand's account. As it turned out, Poisal's presence was probably not necessary, because Byers's comments on "these facts" indicate that he accepted Left Hand's version of the incident. Certainly the incident was consistent with other wanton attacks on the Southern Arapahos by individual white settlers at this time.

In the same issue Byers ran the story, also attributed to Left Hand, of the Southern Arapaho raid against the Utes. He and his warriors had followed the South Platte into the mountains. As they neared South Park, they came upon five lodges of Utes at the mouth of Punch Creek. Hiding among trees and shrubbery, they

[17] Ibid.
[18] Ibid.

waited quietly through the night until daybreak, when they charged the village, killing six Utes and taking two prisoners—one of whom was killed on the way back to Denver—and stole thirty ponies as well as other property.[19] The raiders paid a tragic price, however. Left Hand told Byers that his adopted son, whom he described as "one of the finest Southern Arapaho warriors," had been killed. The youth's death was a severe blow to the chief, who had assumed a special responsibility for him.

Left Hand and his wife may have adopted the warrior when he was a young boy because he had been orphaned. Or they may have adopted him according to a unique Southern Arapaho custom: if Left Hand had noticed the boy's agility on horseback or his skill at hunting small game, if he had observed some special talent that he believed he could encourage, he and his wife might have approached the boy's parents, asking permission to make him their son. The parents would have been flattered by the interest shown to their son by one of the tribe's leading men, and would have happily given their assent. Following this arrangement, the boy would continue to live with his natural parents as before, but his life would have changed in that he had acquired a tutor, an adopted father who would oversee his education and teach him skills which his natural father perhaps was unable to teach, and would generally look out for his welfare, as he did for that of his own children. Left Hand's relationship to the young warrior would have been much like his own to Poisal.[20] The warrior may have been Left Hand's only son. The sketchy evidence of his natural children shows that he had at least three, but the sex of only one of them, his daughter, is known. The loss of the young man whom he had taught and helped rear to manhood, and whom he had grown to love as a son, weighed heavily on him.

After telling of the youth's death, Left Hand informed Byers that his village would leave Denver within four or five days for the Arkansas River and the buffalo ranges and that, because food supplies were low, his village "would welcome any provisions the citizens of Denver could spare before starting out."

[19] Ibid.

[20] See Sister Inez M. Hilger, "Arapaho Child Life and Its Cultural Background," Smithsonian Institution, Bureau of American Ethnology Bulletin no. 148 (1952), pp. 51–52 for Arapaho adoption customs.

The Southern Arapahos had no choice but to leave the vicinity of Denver. White attacks on individual Indians, such as Adams's attack on the boy, had become so frequent and vicious that the chiefs were forced to move their people to a safe distance and to keep them there.[21]

Little Raven, Shave Head, and Storm had already moved their bands onto the plains; Left Hand's village was the last to leave. In mid-June the women hauled down the skin lodges and poles, rolled and packed them with the household goods, and moved the band toward the plains in a long, irregular line, heading south. Young boys drove along the herd of ponies and mules, while packs of dogs, running and yapping, trailed behind. It was the last time that a Southern Arapaho village would be seen near Denver.

When Left Hand moved toward the Arkansas with his people, his brother-in-law, friend, and tutor decided to remain. It is quite likely that Poisal, ill and crippled, could no longer follow the nomadic Indian life. He moved his wife and the children who were still living with them into a log cabin behind the Denver House. Within a short time—the exact date is unknown—the old trader and friend of the Southern Arapahos was dead. After his death, MaHom and her daughter Mary, whose skin and hair were so fair that she often provoked comments by whites to the effect that she could pass for one of them, rejoined Left Hand's village.[22]

No mention of white attacks on Indians was made in Governor Gilpin's first report to the new commissioner of Indian Affairs, William P. Dole. "No trouble was expected from the tribes," he assured the commissioner, adding that Boone had received and stored provisions for the Southern Arapahos and Cheyennes at Fort Wise and that he planned to distribute them in the fall to keep the Indians from becoming "destitute and importunate in the winter." Gilpin also mentioned those chiefs who had not signed the Fort Wise Treaty, saying they led twelve distinct bands, were dependent on the chase, and were unrestricted to any locality. In an ominous note, he added: "[They are] hemmed

[21] Hall, *History of Colorado,* 1:324.

[22] Janet LeCompte, "John Poisal," vol. 6 of LeRoy R. Hafen, ed., *The Mountain Men and the Fur Trade of the Far West,* p. 354.

in by roads and lines of settlements and are menaced by fears," a situation he called "a prelude to despair and desperation."[23]

Gilpin was aware that such despair could lead to trouble, and much of the time his energies were spent organizing a territorial army. He began by buying arms and ammunition from the white settlers, although in doing this he faced stiff competition from the Confederate sympathizers—estimated to be one-third of the total population—who were secretly buying arms at higher prices and storing them near Pueblo, close to Boone's ranch.[24]

By late summer the First Regiment of Colorado—made up of miners, farmers, and storekeepers, along with a share of adventurers and desperadoes—was undergoing training at a hastily constructed camp on the high, sprawling bluffs flanking the South Platte, two miles southwest of Denver at present-day Eighth and Vallejo streets. The camp was named Camp Weld after the territory's secretary, Lewis Ludyard Weld.

Officers of the new regiment included some disappointed goldseekers happy to trade a pickax for the prestige and, they hoped, regular salary of the army. Among them was Edward Wynkoop, who became captain of Company A. A young lawyer, Jacob Downing, was named captain of Company D, and Scott J. Anthony, a cousin to Susan B. Anthony and a shopkeeper in Leadville, Colorado, became captain of Company E. The position of colonel went to a prominent Denver attorney, John P. Slough, and an erstwhile correspondent for the *New York Tribune* and *Boston Atlas,* Samuel F. Tappan, was named lieutenant colonel. The post of regiment chaplain was offered to the Methodist preacher John Chivington, who firmly declined, saying he preferred a "fighting position." He was made a major.[25]

By fall of 1861, the First Colorado was fully organized, and three companies under Lieutenant Colonel Tappan were ordered two hundred miles south to garrison Fort Wise. The other com-

---

[23] *BIA Reports* (1861), Sen. Exec. Doc. 1, 37th Cong., 2d sess., pp. 99–101.

[24] William Clark Whitford, *Colorado Volunteers in the Civil War,* pp. 40–41. Whitford gives the census of 1861 as: white males, 18,136; white males under twenty-one, 2,622; women, 4,484; Negroes, 89.

[25] Ibid., p. 47.

panies remained at Camp Weld under Major Chivington's direct command.

Within four months of his arrival in Denver, Gilpin had an army. But the problem of paying for it remained, since the territory did not have enough funds to meet the regiment's expenses. Assuming that the Civil War and the territory's isolated position justified emergency measures, Gilpin issued negotiable drafts on the United States Treasury for a total of $375,000, $40,000 of which was to pay for the construction of Camp Weld and the rest to equip and supply the regiment.

When Gilpin's "drafts" floated into Washington for payment, Salmon P. Chase, the United States treasurer, reacted in astonishment and fury. The treasury was having difficulty meeting the expenses of the Civil War without attempting to pay unauthorized drafts, and Chase refused to honor them. Consequently, merchants, freighters, and other businessmen in the territory were left holding worthless paper in exchange for services and goods. Naturally they held Gilpin personally responsible, and, according to one contemporary report, he was assailed on every hand by exasperated holders of the drafts.

One historian explained that

> as an old army officer, he was held to have known the government's rigid financial methods, and it was principally because of his presumed knowledge of such matters that the people had unquestioningly accepted his irregular and illegal orders upon the national treasury.[26]

Although Gilpin eventually traveled to Washington to explain his position, the treasurer remained adamant in his refusal, resulting in Gilpin's removal from office. In time, holders of Gilpin's drafts who could supply proof of money due them were repaid by the treasury.

In addition to the confusion caused by his bills of exchange, Gilpin also managed to increase the confusion about Indian affairs during his short term. In June he appointed Boone as agent to the Kiowas, Comanches, Cheyennes, and Southern Arapahos; in the following month, Commissioner Dole announced the ap-

[26] Ibid., p. 53.

pointment of his cousin, Samuel G. Colley, as agent to the tribes.[27] Colley's appointment was confirmed by the Senate on August 26, though he did not arrive on the plains until November. In the meantime, Boone, believing he had a permanent position, went about the duties of agent. For a time the tribes were not sure who had been authorized to deal with them. By October 8, when the Southern Arapahos and Cheyennes assembled at Fort Wise to receive their annuities, white troops encircled their lands from Denver to the Arkansas River and from Fort Kearny to Fort Larned. Living near the white settlements had become impossible, and they had at last abandoned their winter campgrounds. They believed Boone was their agent, but they had heard he was to be replaced by another, who was on the way. It is no wonder that Boone described the tribes as "restless" in his report. Boone also wrote that the Southern Arapahos had been pleased to sign an amendment to the Fort Wise Treaty, whereas, in fact, he had insisted upon their signatures before he would distribute their goods. Left Hand did not sign.[28]

Boone's report also hinted of new trouble on the plains. The Confederate states had sent a commissioner, Albert Pike, to negotiate a treaty with the Comanches. The treaty promised to settle the Comanches between the Canadian and Red rivers on the southern plains in Indian Territory in return for the tribe's support. Believing they were dealing with a United States commissioner, the Comanches had signed the agreement. When they learned the truth, however, they repudiated it and turned it over to Boone.

The treaty marked the first attempt of either the Confederates or the Unionists to extend the Civil War to the plains. It would not, however, be the last.

[27]. William Unrau, "A Prelude to War," *Colorado Magazine* 41 (1964):304–305.
[28] *BIA Reports* (1861), p. 105.

Crossing the plains in 1862. *Courtesy of the Colorado State Historical Society.*

Little Raven, principal chief of the Southern Arapahos. This photograph was taken during his visit to New York and other eastern cities in 1871. *Courtesy of the Trustees of the British Museum, London.*

John Evans at about the time he was appointed governor of the Territory of Colorado. *Courtesy of the Colorado State Historical Society.*

Colonel John M. Chivington about 1863. *Courtesy of the Colorado State Historical Society.*

Major Edward W. Wynkoop. *Courtesy of the Colorado State Historical Society.*

Major Scott J. Anthony. *Courtesy of the Colorado State Historical Society.*

Agent Samuel Colley is shown with three of the Indians he escorted to Washington, D.C., in 1863. The man next to Colley may be the Cheyenne chief Lean Bear, who was spokesman for the Indian delegation. *Courtesy of the Trustees of the British Museum.*

Following a meeting with President Lincoln, part of the Indian delegation adjourned to the garden room to be photographed with Mrs. Lincoln, standing right. Lean Bear may be the man seated in front center. Standing on the left are John Smith and Samuel Colley. *Courtesy of Smithsonian Institution, National Anthropological Archives.*

Fort Larned. *Courtesy of the Kansas State Historical Society.*

Fort Lyon, on the banks of the Arkansas River, is shown here with what probably were Southern Arapaho lodges nearby. It was here that the Fort Wise Treaty was signed in 1861, and it was from here that Chivington's troops departed for Sand Creek in November, 1864. *Courtesy of the Western History Division, Denver Public Library.*

With a pistol in each hand and one or two under his arms, he galloped through a storm of bullets, like a mad bull.

11

William Clark Whitford on
Major John Chivington

No other land offers such opportunities for the vast accumulation of wealth.

Governor John Evans on
Colorado Territory

After receiving annuities at Fort Wise in October, 1861, Left Hand's people and the other Southern Arapahos scattered in a wide arc across the plains between Forts Wise and Larned in an effort to avoid the white settlements and traffic. Whites were difficult to avoid, however. Ranches, trading posts, freight and stage stations crowded the South Platte both north and south of Denver—from Pueblo, on the Arkansas River, to present-day Fort Collins on the Cache La Poudre. Wagon trains and stagecoaches continually plowed not only the Platte River Road, the main supply route to the territory, but the Santa Fe and Smoky Hill trails as well, stopping to resupply at the white outposts along the way. The Pike's Peak and Leavenworth Express Company had established no fewer than twenty-seven stage stations on the Smoky Hill Trail alone.

With the white invasion the buffalo ranges that flanked the South Platte had been virtually trafficked out of existence, and the herds were dispersed to far-flung sections of the plains. The only dependable range that remained was in the vicinity of the Solomon and Republican rivers in west-central Kansas, near the Smoky Hill Trail, and hunting parties now had to ride great distances to find food. It was this reality that had led Medicine Man, the chief of the Northern Arapahos, to say earlier, "Our horses, too, are dying because we ride them so far to get a little game for our lodges."[1]

Not only had the ranges been broken up but the animals themselves were being destroyed at an alarming rate. In fact, 1862 marked the middle of a fifty-year frenzy of destruction. In the early 1840s an estimated thirty million buffalo had thundered across the plains between Texas and Canada; by the late 1860s that number had dropped below fifteen million; and by 1890 the animal was all but extinct—only five hundred buffalo were then in existence.[2] The year 1862 followed a twenty-year period of indiscriminate slaughter of the buffalo by whites; remains of slain animals, carcasses with rotting flesh, littered the central plains. Irving Howbert, who settled near present-day Colorado Springs that year, wrote that everywhere he looked the brown bluffs were strewn with white buffalo skulls glistening in the sun.[3]

This on-going destruction of their primary resource forced an immense change in the Southern Arapaho's social existence. No longer was it possible to camp in large villages alongside the Cheyennes, as in the past, with the warriors riding out in large hunting parties and returning triumphantly with a six-month supply of meat. Instead, the villages broke into small, isolated bands, usually family groups of ten or twelve lodges, which could be moved swiftly across the plains following the game. The vast country swallowed up the Indian families, overwhelming them with isolation. Apart from the large villages, there was no stabilizing community life: there were no councils around the campfires, no celebrations when the warriors returned from hunting, no religious dances or ceremonies. Women, accustomed to working together, chatting and gossiping and looking after one another's children, went about their chores alone, in bitter silence. Men, accustomed to sharing with other hunters the

[1] LeRoy R. Hafen, ed., *Relations with the Indians of the Plains*, vol. 9 in *The Far West and the Rockies Historical Series*, p. 158.

[2] See David A. Dary, *The Buffalo Book.* The University of Colorado's Henderson Museum provides the estimate that sixty million buffalo populated the plains in the early 1800s.

[3] Irving Howbert, *Memories of a Lifetime in the Pike's Peak Region*, p. 77.

burden of providing food, now bore it alone, aware that each failure might mean that their families would starve.

The most serious result of this isolation, of course, was the gradual breakdown in tribal authority. Such peace-minded, responsible leaders as Left Hand and Little Raven, men who were able to view the changing situation in a wider frame of reference, could keep the young warriors under control and enforce regulations in the villages only with the support of all the people. Wandering in small bands, the warriors answered only to themselves.[4] During the previous summer, for example, several warriors led by Big Mouth, one of the Southern Arapaho leaders who had signed the Fort Wise Treaty, robbed a Mexican train thirteen miles west of Fort Larned and stole two and one-half barrels of whiskey. Only a short time before, Little Raven's band had passed the same train without incident. Had the two bands been traveling together, Little Raven's influence might have prevented Big Mouth's actions.[5]

Except for this minor attack by Big Mouth, the Southern Arapaho warriors, although dispersed in -small groups, remained peaceful throughout the final weeks of 1861 and the long winter months of 1862. Their main concern was to feed their families, and to do this they traversed the area between the Republican and Arkansas rivers along the western boundary of Kansas, which had become a state in late 1861.

By spring the tribe faced another problem: a severe outbreak of smallpox. Little Raven, afraid that the disease would cause as many deaths among his people as it had among the Kiowas and Comanches, rode to Fort Wise to ask Samuel Colley, the new agent, when his village could move onto the reservation. Colley assured the chief that work was under way but that the reservation was not yet ready for the Indians. He told them that since there was no game in the area they would have to remain elsewhere.[6]

[4] *BIA Reports* (1863), House Exec. Doc. 1, 38th Cong., 1st sess., p. 239. In this report Governor Evans speaks of the necessity of the tribes to break into small groups in order to survive.

[5] Hayden to Boone, Fort Larned, August 3, September 1, 1861, Letters Received, Upper Arkansas Agency, OIA, Record Group 75, National Archives, Washington, D.C.

[6] Virginia Cole Trenholm, *The Arapahoes, Our People*, p. 166.

Although they were pressed with problems, with no relief in sight, the Southern Arapahos and Cheyennes still held to a peaceful course. There were reasons for this: their search for food kept the Indians apart from the roads filled with white traffic; it also kept them apart from the temptations and harassment of the white settlements. And the white settlers were concerned at this time with a threat more imminent than that represented by the Indians: the Civil War had come to the Southwest.

Before 1862, Confederate troops had begun moving from Texas along the Río Grande to Santa Fe with orders to capture Fort Union, northeast of the old city. This thrust into the Southwest was part of a wider Confederate plan aimed at capturing New Mexico Territory, which included the present state of Arizona, and opening a corridor to the Pacific, thereby defeating the Union blockade of the South. The Confederates hoped to gain control of the gold regions of Colorado and California at the same time, a move that would deprive the Union of gold while enhancing the Confederate treasury and providing much-needed collateral for foreign loans. To accomplish this, the Confederates hoped to win the loyalty and support of the plains tribes with promises that the hated ''blues''—the army troops—would be run from the region.[7] No mention was ever made, of course, of the ''grays'' that would then replace them.

In December, 1861, Col. Edward R. S. Canby, commander of the Union troops in New Mexico, sent an urgent request to Governor Gilpin for reinforcements to block the Confederate drive; soon afterward, two volunteer companies of infantry— independent of Gilpin's First Regiment of Colorado Volunteers—left for New Mexico. By February, 1862, another call for reinforcements came from Canby. Maj. Gen. David Hunter, commanding the Department of Kansas, which included Colorado Territory, telegraphed Gilpin to send additional troops. The governor was at that time in Washington explaining his drafts, but the acting governor, Secretary of State Weld, ordered the First to New Mexico.[8]

---

[7] William Clark Whitford, *Colorado Volunteers in the Civil War*, pp. 10–12.

[8] Ibid., p. 75.

According to the regiment's historian, William Clark Whitford, the First pulled out of Camp Weld on February 22 and marched south to the Purgatoire River, to present-day Trinidad, where they rendezvoused with the three companies from Fort Wise. Colonel Slough was in command of the entire regiment, with Lieutenant Colonel Tappan and Major Chivington serving directly under him.

The companies had hardly reached the Purgatoire when a messenger arrived from Canby with the news that the Confederates had routed Union forces in a battle at Valverde and were now moving unchecked toward Santa Fe and Fort Union. The First set out immediately in a race against the advancing enemy. They discarded unnecessary packs and marched day and night over the rugged, mountainous terrain, at times pushing through snow two feet deep. At most only two companies were mounted; the rest were on foot. During one stretch of the way they covered ninety-two miles in thirty-six hours. The officers drove the men and the animals mercilessly. Many of the horses died in harness.

Reaching Fort Union on March 10, the First waited twelve days for a Confederate attack, and, when none came, Colonel Slough decided to march across La Glorieta Pass towards Santa Fe to search out the enemy.[9] When the regiment reached Kozlowski's Ranch, (a freighting and stage stop on the Santa Fe Trail at the eastern mouth of the pass), Chivington took a detachment of 418 men, including the companies under Wynkoop, Downing, and Anthony, and moved ahead on a reconnaissance mission.

On March 26, the detachment stopped at Pigeon's Ranch, another stage stop, and Chivington sent out an advance guard that happened upon thirty Confederate scouts, whom they swiftly captured. Chivington learned from the scouts that a detachment of Confederate troops was ahead, camped at the western end of La Glorieta Pass. On hearing the news one of the men whooped: "We got them corralled this time."[10] Chivington could scarcely believe his good fortune. The detachment of Confederates, six hundred strong, was about the same size as

[9] Ibid., p. 81.
[10] Ibid., p. 87.

his own; he held the distinct advantage, however, because the enemy had no knowledge of any Union troops in the vicinity. Chivington, leading the way, ordered his men to follow with cautious, deliberate speed until they reached the place where the trail opened into a low, wide park called Apache Canyon. Ahead, filing into the canyon from the west, came the unsuspecting Confederates. Chivington's men swooped down upon them.

The Southern troops stopped, formed battle lines, and began firing at the advancing men of the First, causing some to break formation and dive for shelter. At this reaction from men who had never been under fire before, and who had received only the most elementary military training at Camp Weld—to call it "basic" was to stretch the facts—Chivington became livid with anger, shouting at the men to get back in formation.[11]

The surprise attack momentarily confused the Confederates but it did not bring them to their knees. Chivington, looking for another way to seize the advantage, ordered Wynkoop and Anthony to take their companies and scale a steep ridge on the left; Downing's company was ordered atop a ridge on the right. Once in position, the three companies overlooked and outflanked the enemy, scattering a devastating volley of fire over the canyon floor, which caused the Confederates to break and retreat down the pass.

Chivington followed. Using the same successful strategy, he sent Wynkoop and Anthony's men up a left ridge while Downing's climbed the right. According to Whitford, Chivington led the rest of the troops in a frontal attack, "giving orders with great energy." "With a pistol in each hand and one or two under his arms, he galloped through a storm of bullets," Whitford wrote, "like a mad bull." Three times Chivington charged the Confederate center, "forward and back through the fleeing and crowded ranks of Texans, running over them, trampling them down, and scattering them in every direction."[12]

From his ridgetop position Downing kept up such a barrage of fire that some Confederates were driven up the left side into the arms of Wynkoop and Anthony's companies, who took fifty pri-

[11] Ibid.
[12] Ibid., p. 90–91.

soners. At last the battle ended with a rout of the Confederate detachment as the terrified troops deserted their positions and fled down La Glorieta Pass, leaving behind thirty-two dead, forty-three wounded, and seventy-one captured.[13]

The battle for New Mexico, however, was not over. During the engagement at Apache Canyon the Confederate commander had sent a runner to Lt. Col. William R. Scurry, begging him to "hasten to his relief."[14] Scurry, then camped at Galisteo with eleven hundred troops, left immediately, camping overnight on March 27 at Johnson's Ranch on the western edge of La Glorieta Pass. Early on the morning of March 28, he moved up the pass in search of Union troops, leaving his supply train at the ranch under a small guard. At about the same time, Colonel Slough was moving up the pass from the opposite direction with seven hundred men from the Colorado First. When he reached Pigeon's Ranch, Scurry's troops had already arrived, and, from their hiding places among the trees, they opened fire.

Scurry assumed that the entire Union force was pinned down in front of him, an assumption that would undo his plans. What he did not know was that Colonel Slough had ordered Chivington to take 430 men and cross the pass by a different route. The detachment had moved through a mountainous area—picking a path over rocks and through dense thickets of cedar bushes and scrub piñons—outflanking Scurry's command. After a five-hour march, Chivington's men stopped at a point overlooking Johnson's Ranch a thousand feet below. An officer whispered to Chivington, "You are right on top of them."[15]

From a captured Confederate guard Chivington had learned that what he was right on top of was the Confederate supply train, horses, and pack animals, guarded by about 250 troops and a few teamsters. Most of the troops, as Chivington surmised from the sound of artillery in the distance, were engaged in a battle with Slough's forces at Pigeon's Ranch, eight miles away. For nearly an

[13] Ibid., pp. 85–97 (Battle of Apache Cañon casualties, p. 124); Frank Hall, *History of the State of Colorado*, 1:278; Reginald S. Craig, *The Fighting Parson*, pp. 89–100.

[14] Whitford, *Colorado Volunteers*, p. 98.

[15] Ibid., p. 116.

hour Chivington studied the situation. An unsuspecting enemy lay ahead—in this case, below—and that enemy was smaller in number than his command. Once again the element of surprise was on his side, but success would depend upon quick, decisive action while Scurry's troops were held down at Pigeon's Ranch.

Chivington gave the order to descend the steep precipice into the Confederate camp. The men quietly began lowering one another with leather straps, sometimes using rifles for drop ropes. When they had descended about 250 feet, crashing rocks alerted the Confederate guards. The Southerners began firing on Chivington's men, who were flattened against the sheer rocks of the canyon wall. Unflinchingly, Chivington moved downward, shouting to his men to do the same.[16]

As the First dropped into the camp, many of the terrified teamsters and guards threw down their guns and ran. Still other guards, Chivington learned later, had left earlier to join the main force at Pigeon's Ranch, so that fewer than 250 Confederates were actually in camp. Nevertheless, some of the outnumbered guards waged a stiff defense, forcing Chivington to put into operation the same plan that had worked successfully at Apache Canyon. Wynkoop was ordered to take thirty men to the top of a ridge and destroy a gun emplacement, and other companies were ordered up the opposite ridge. Chivington himself led the main charge against the handful of guards defending the wagon train, and, within a short time, the train was his.

Seventy-three wagons, loaded with food, ammunition, clothing, blankets, medical supplies, and forage—Scurry's total supplies for eleven hundred troops—made up the train. One by one, the loaded wagons were torched, sending billows of black smoke into the sky, and, when the flames died, all that remained was a pile of iron frames and spokes, twisted into grotesque shapes. Chivington then turned his attention to the corral located in a ravine about a half mile away. In the corral stood five or six hundred horses and mules, the transport and pack animals for the Confederate troops. Chivington ordered them bayoneted.[17]

---

[16] Ibid., p. 118.

[17] Hall, *History of Colorado*, 1:280; Craig, *Fighting Parson*, pp. 123–24; Whitford, *Colorado Volunteers*, p. 115.

While Chivington's troops were destroying Scurry's camp, the Confederates were on the verge of handing Slough a sound defeat. Outnumbered by four hundred men, Slough's troops had mounted a fierce defense for seven hours without rest, food, or drink. With his men stalemated and exhausted, the dying and the wounded littering the field, Slough finally called a retreat. Just as he did so, a Confederate ambulance, flying a white flag, approached the Union lines, and, to Slough's astonishment, the messenger brought Scurry's request for an armistice.[18]

While winning a battle Scurry had, in fact, lost the New Mexico war. A guard from Johnson's Ranch had rushed up to the Confederate commander, in the flush of victory, and informed him that all wagons, supplies, and horses had been destroyed. Scurry had no choice but to request a truce and fall back to Santa Fe in an attempt to find food and blankets for his men. The two battles at La Glorieta Pass blocked the Confederate drive in the Southwest. Confederate Brig. Gen. Henry H. Sibley, faced with the impossibility of salvaging the New Mexico campaign, ordered the ragtag army, battle-fatigued and on foot, back to Texas. After a few minor skirmishes to cover their retreat, the Confederates left New Mexico to the Union.

The toll of La Glorieta Pass was great, however. Both the Confederate and Union commands lost one-fourth of their forces. But the victory for Chivington and the First Regiment was sweet. In April, following Colonel Slough's resignation, Lieutenant Colonel Tappan presented a petition to General Canby requesting that Chivington be appointed colonel of the regiment over Tappan himself. Every officer in the regiment had signed the petition, testifying to the esteem in which Chivington was held by his men. On April 14, Canby made the appointment and ordered the new colonel to take command of Fort Craig on the Río Grande in south-central New Mexico.[19]

Chivington's daring exploits, decisive action, and bold victory had made him the man of the hour, a hero in the eyes of the troops who had followed him into battle and a hero to white set-

[18] See Whitford, *Colorado Volunteers*, pp. 98–127, for information on Johnson's Ranch and the battle at Pigeon's Ranch.

[19] Ibid., p. 130.

tlers from the Río Grande to the Platte. Tried in battle, he emerged as an important leader on the plains, a man henceforth to be watched and reckoned with.

The same week that Chivington and his soldiers won the decisive Civil War battle of the Southwest, another important white leader emerged on the plains. John Evans, a prominent Illinois businessman and physician, was appointed territorial governor of Colorado and ex-officio superintendent of Indian Affairs by his friend President Lincoln, who had only recently removed Gilpin from the post. Together the new governor and the preacher-turned-military-leader would hold the reins of power in the territory, never relaxing their grip until the question of who owned the land, whites or Indians, had been decisively resolved.

Like Chivington, the forty-eight-year-old Evans was a man shaped by the American frontier. He had been born on a farm near Waynesville, Ohio, and had lived in a series of rugged outposts of white civilization in the border region of Ohio and Indiana. The two men also shared something else: when they were quite young, they had both been influenced by fundamentalist frontier preachers who had converted them to a rigid Methodism and carved their attitudes into ones of uncompromising self-righteousness.

Evans was handsome, tall, and broad-shouldered, with attractive blue eyes and a jaw set in determination. In his early youth he had decided that, whatever else he did in life, he would surpass the humble circumstances into which he had been born. His two goals were to become a practicing physician and to amass a great fortune. He would accomplish both, although in time his desire to be a physician would be superceded by a drive for wealth.[20]

Evans completed the two-year course at Lynn Medical College in Cincinnati—a compact course of technical, practical information—and, taking his sole possession, a black mule, he moved to Indiana because, he said later, the "commercial opportunities

    [20] Edgar Carlisle McMechen, *The Life of Governor Evans;* Hubert Howe Bancroft, "Interview with John Evans," Western History Division, University of Colorado Library, Boulder, Colo.

there appeared more promising'' than in Ohio.[21] In 1848 he made another move, this time to Chicago—with a population of 12,000 the largest frontier town in the border region—where commercial opportunities were still more promising. For eleven years he taught obstetrics and gynecology at Rush Medical College while he judiciously invested in land, always following the iron-clad rule to "buy cheap and sell dear.'' As his land speculations began to pay off, Evans started investing in railroads and eventually became a director of the corporation formed to build the Fort Wayne and Chicago Railroad, connecting those two cities. After the railroad was built, land along its pathway, which Evans happened to own, jumped enormously in value.

In 1850, Evans was among the nine prominent Chicago businessmen who founded Northwestern University, and the board of directors voted to name the town just outside Chicago, where the school was to be located, after him. During the same period he served a term as a Chicago alderman, and by 1855 he stopped practicing medicine altogether to devote full attention to his growing interests in real estate and railroad construction.

While Evans's public life was soon to make him a millionaire, his private life was filled with loss. His first wife Hannah P. Canby had died, along with three of their four children, of tuberculosis. From 1850 to 1853 he lived with Josephine, his only surviving child. In 1853 he married a refined woman from a prominent Chicago family, Margaret Patten Gray. Of their four children, three would survive: William, Evan, and Anne.

Evans's support of Lincoln at the Illinois Republican Convention in 1860 marked the beginning of a political friendship between the two men, and at least once, during a campaign trip, Lincoln stayed at Evans's substantial home on the shores of Lake Michigan. Following Lincoln's election the president asked his friend to name his reward, and Evans, who by now had realized most of his life's goals, replied that he would "like to be called Governor.''[22] The first post Lincoln offered Evans was governorship of the Territory of Washington. This Evans declined, because it was too far away from his Chicago business interests.

[21] Olga Curtis, "The Evans Dynasty: A Century of Power,'' Empire Magazine, *Denver Post*, February 23, 1969, pp. 8–120.
[22] Ibid.

Since Nebraska, Evans's preference, had already been promised to another Republican loyalist, Lincoln offered him the governorship of Colorado.

By 1862, Evans was a millionaire, a founder of a university, a railroad builder, and a land and real estate developer. His spacious and well-appointed residence, over which Margaret presided with genteel charm, was the center of Chicago's social life. That he chose to exchange the comfortable life of a respected businessman for the uncertain future offered by a half-civilized territory still claimed by the Plains Indians has led historians as well as Evans's biographer to conclude that he unselfishly wished to devote the last years of his life to public service. But his subsequent actions call this appraisal into serious doubt.

The appointment came when Evans stood at the pinnacle, searching for new challenges. Before accepting it, he made a trip across the plains to survey the new territory with its towns and possibilities. What he saw excited his imagination. In his view, Denver was not a crude log-cabin town but the Chicago of the West, the main commercial center of a region comprising rich gold mines and vast expanses of land waiting for development. Most of all, it was the natural hub of the proposed transcontinental railroad which would link the Atlantic and Pacific coasts and, at this time, the railroad was much on Evans's mind.

Congress was then considering the Pacific Railway Act, following years of studies, surveys, and proposals. The act, which became law July 1, 1862, chartered a corporation to build the railroad. In 1853, Congress had appropriated funds for a survey of the most practical, economical route, and when it was completed, three years later, it named five possible routes. Included among them was the "Buffalo Trail," along the Smoky Hill road, that ran straight through central Kansas and Colorado Territory.

The act of 1862 also included an important section on land grants, not overlooked by an astute businessman like Evans. The government would extinguish Indian rights to provide the Union Pacific Railroad with a right-of-way two hundred feet wide through new territories, including Colorado. The railroad company would then receive ten square miles adjoining the track, or 6,400 acres, for each mile of track that was built. Obviously there were fortunes to be made in railroad building—through construction contracts, land grants, and business enterprises generated by the completed lines. Congress also appointed a board of 162 commissioners of the railroad company to raise money through the sale of stocks and bonds in order to finance construction. These commissioners comprised a blue-ribbon group of industrialists and businessmen from across the nation, and Evans was one of them.[23]

On May 17, 1862, while the act was pending, Evans arrived in Denver to take up his duties as governor and ex-officio superintendent of Indian affairs and delivered his first public speech. He remarked upon the area's brilliant future and promised Denver's citizens that the transcontinental railroad would soon connect their town to the rest of the nation. About the same time, Lt. Edward L. Berthoud was surveying a possible railroad route over the mountain pass which subsequently bore his name, and the new governor would lose no time in attempting to fulfill the promise of his inaugural speech by urging the other Union Pacific commissioners to adopt this route.[24]

Later Evans himself summarized his opinion of Colorado Territory and his motivation for accepting the governorship. In a letter written to the *Chicago Tribune,* his optimism concerning the future of the plains was boundless: "No other land offers such opportunities for the vast accumulation of wealth."[25] Within six months the Governor had gauged the magnitude of the problems to be overcome if the transcontinental railroad was to be built and wealth accumulated. First and foremost, it would be impossible to build the railroad through lands that belonged to the Indians, and yet all the land, including the settled towns, gold-mining camps, and open plains, was legally owned by the Southern Arapahos and Cheyennes. The Organic Act creating Colorado Territory, like the Kansas Act, had specifically excluded those lands not ceded by the tribes from territorial jurisdiction.

The government had hoped to get the tribes to cede the land

[23] McMechen, *Life of Evans,* p. 145. Samuel R. Curtis, Congressman from Iowa who would later play a role on the plains, was also a commissioner.

[24] Ibid; Thomas J. Noel, "All Hail the Denver Pacific," *Colorado Magazine* 50 (1973): 91–116.

[25] *Chicago Tribune,* June 27, 1864.

by the Fort Wise Treaty. Unfortunately, the treaty had a number of complications. To begin with, the northern chiefs had not signed it, and Article Six had the effect of rendering the treaty ineffectual until they had signed. And, as if this obstacle were not enough, those southern chiefs who had signed now repudiated the treaty.

Such a situation was intolerable to the governor, a man eager to move into promising new ventures. Many years later he recounted to the historian Hubert Howe Bancroft his frustration at having to deal with Indian rights to land:

> The idea that this country belonged to [the Indians] gets its most ridiculous aspect from the proposition that a country a thousand miles long and five hundred miles wide, one of the most fertile in the world, should belong to a few bands of roving Indians, nomadic tribes, in fee as their own property . . . [and] that we had to buy it of them by treaty or purchase, instead of teaching them what was the proper doctrine . . . [that is,] that they had a right to hunt on the land, but that [their] right must be subject to the higher occupation of the land, for a larger population and for civilization.[26]

Evans attempted to gain title to the land through legal means and remove the tribes to the Arkansas River reservation. "Whatever way this difficulty is to be adjudicated," he wrote in his first official report to Washington, "I would urge its immediate settlement, by negotiating with the disaffected bands who frequent the Platte River country, that the title to the settled portion of Colorado Territory may be perfected."[27]

For the most part the "disaffected bands" included the Northern Arapahos and Cheyennes, but Left Hand's band was also among them. When Evans visited Fort Wise shortly after his arrival in Denver, Left Hand sent Neva to meet with him and explain that the Southern Arapahos had been treated badly by the treaty and that "Lying" John Smith had deceived them.[28] But

---

[26] Bancroft, "Interview with John Evans," pp. 19–20.

[27] *BIA Reports* (1862), House Exec. Doc. 1, pt. 2, 37th Cong., 3d sess., p. 375.

[28] John J. Saville Report, April 15, 1863, Letters Received, Upper Arkansas Agency, *OIA*, Record Group 75, National Archives.

Evans ignored Neva's complaint, and its implicit warning of future problems, and clung to the belief that the reservation could be turned into satisfactory ranches and farmland for the Indians. It is true that, at this time, Agent Colley was busy surveying the reservation and preparing to allot individual tracts and construct necessary buildings as soon as the treaty took effect. Colley assured his new superior that

> from the care these Indians take of their horses, which are kept in large droves, I am confident that they would soon learn to herd cattle and sheep, so as to fully sustain themselves if not to become wealthy from the increase of their flocks and herds.[29]

With work underway at the reservation, Evans saw no obstacle to settling the matter by obtaining the signatures of the northern chiefs and negotiating with those southern chiefs who had repudiated the treaty. He was unaware, however, of the obstacles Colley himself was placing before his plan. Colley's son Dexter had become John Smith's partner in the trading business, and sometime later the Southern Arapahos and Cheyennes accused them of having traded their annuity goods for buffalo robes. The chiefs, including Left Hand, even complained to Bent that they had no confidence in Colley because he swindled them out of their annuities. Julia Lambert, whose husband was the station-master at Fort Wise, reported that "Agent Colley's son would take Indian goods furnished his father by the government and go to Indian camps to trade them for robes, furs and tanned skins." In addition, Colley's wife held forth as proprietor of the sutler's store at the fort where, the Indians said, she sold them their annuity goods.[30]

In the late summer and fall of 1862, Evans's determination to settle the land question assumed sharp urgency. On August 18 a large band of Sioux warriors launched a series of attacks on white settlements around New Ulm, Minnesota. Within three weeks, seven hundred whites were slaughtered, an estimated thirty thousand people fled their homes, and a tract of land fifty-nine

---

[29] *BIA Reports* (1862), p. 375.
[30] "Chivington Massacre" pp. 34, 68, 94, 95; Julia S. Lambert, "Plain Tales of the Plains," *The Trail* 9 (1916):17.

miles wide and two hundred miles long, once filled with prosperous farms, was left totally depopulated. Army troops halted the attacks by driving most of the hostiles into the Dakotas, but some moved southward toward Nebraska, Kansas, and Colorado.[31]

The New Ulm Uprising reverberated like a cannon shot across the plains. Settlers from the Missouri to the Rocky Mountains, from Minnesota to New Mexico, were terrorized by stories of Indian atrocities and a hardly controllable panic set in everywhere. When a band of Sioux later attacked a Pawnee camp in Nebraska, white settlers in nearby Columbus fled from their homes.[32]

Although they did not continue their attacks on whites as they moved southward, the Sioux presented an ominous threat and were considered a dangerous influence on the other plains tribes. Evans, in a letter to Commissioner Dole, reported that Oglala and Brulé Sioux bands were present on the Platte in late summer, frightening immigrant trains.[33]

Despite the Sioux uprising, the other plains tribes remained peaceful. Had the Southern Arapahos and Cheyennes wished to follow the Sioux example and rise against whites on the central plains, the summer and fall of 1862 presented the ideal opportunity. The First Colorado Regiment had not yet returned to Colorado Territory from New Mexico, and no more than a handful of regular troops—three hundred—were garrisoned at Forts Laramie, Larned, Kearny, and Wise. Acting in concert the tribes could have cut the major arteries across the plains between the white settlements and the east and perhaps succeeded in driving whites out of the region. They did not, for the same reasons they had refrained from launching such attacks in the past. Although their warriors outnumbered white troops, white settlers vastly outnumbered the Indians (according to the census, there were thirty thousand whites in the territory in 1862, compared to fifteen hundred Southern Arapahos, sixteen hundred Southern Cheyennes, and eighteen hundred each of Kiowas and Comanches).[34] The tribes still had no hope of stockpiling enough arms

[31] Ralph K. Andrist, *The Long Death: The Last Days of the Plains Indians,* pp. 66–67.
[32] George B. Grinnell, *The Fighting Cheyennes,* p. 129.
[33] *BIA Reports* (1862), p. 375.
[34] Grinnell, *Fighting Cheyennes,* p. 130; 1862 U.S. Census.

and ammunition to stage a successful uprising but, most important, the chiefs continued to counsel restraint, hoping that some acceptable settlement of the land question could be made with the government.

The year ended on the same note of peace with which it had begun. Agent Colley reported to Evans that the tribes had come to Fort Wise to receive their annuities—he refrained from mentioning his own underhanded dealings—and then had left for the buffalo ranges near the Republican River.[35]

In January, 1863, Chivington and the Colorado First returned to Denver following the colonel's unsuccessful attempt to have the regiment transferred to the Army of the Potomac. He had wangled permission from the War Department to have the men mounted, however, and shortly after their return the First received horses, new equipment, and new arms.

Colonel Chivington, the one-time preacher, was now commander of the Military District of Colorado. His men, seasoned by war, were now mounted and fully supplied, ready for the next battle. Although the Southern Arapahos and Cheyennes were friendly and peaceable and had remained so throughout the past year, Chivington posted various companies from the First Colorado along the South Platte in order, as one contemporary historian noted, "to hold in check the hostile Indians."[36]

[35] Colley to Evans, December 31, 1862, Letters Sent, Upper Arkansas Agency, OIA, Record Group 75, Federal Archives and Records Center, Denver, Colo.

[36] Hall, *History of Colorado,* 1:286–87.

12

Our little children are crying for food...

Medicine Man [Roman Nose],
Northern Arapaho

1863. The Southern Arapahos would remember that year as the blackest in a long, black period. They called it "the year of hunger."[1]

Left Hand stayed close to his band on the parched, monotonous bluffs between the Arkansas and Smoky Hill rivers, his energies consumed by the problems besetting his people. With buffalo hard to find and food growing continually more scarce, small, isolated Indian families wandered about the central plains hoping to find enough game to survive. Famine and disease were widespread; whooping cough and diarrhea struck almost every family, killing many children. Bitter restlessness overtook the young warriors as they realized that the chiefs, taxed with meeting simple daily needs, had no long-range solutions.

An uneasiness also prevailed in the white settlements. Following the New Ulm Uprising, settlers pressed the territorial officials, especially Evans and Chivington, to remove the danger of a local Indian outbreak by settling the land question with the tribes and placing them on the reservation where they could be controlled. Early in 1863, Agent Colley hit on a plan that he believed would influence the chiefs to accept the Fort Wise Treaty. On January 25 he wrote Commissioner Dole suggesting that a delegation of chiefs be brought to Washington for a visit, thus impressing upon them the great numbers and superior technology of the white man. The visit, in Colley's view, would also serve to cement the tribes' traditional friendship with the Union and block any further Confederate attempt to win their loyalties.[2]

---

[1] Virginia Cole Trenholm, *The Arapahoes, Our People*, p. 170.

[2] *BIA Reports* (1863), House Exec. Doc. 1, 38th. Cong., 1st sess., p. 253. For a discussion of white motives in bringing Indian delegations to Washington, see Katherine C. Turner, *Red Men Calling on the Great White Father*.

The proposal was not without risks, however. The chiefs Colley proposed to take were the same men who were trying to cope with the problem of holding young warriors in check and preventing conflicts with the white settlers. Although both white and Indian leaders recognized the danger in removing these men, they reacted enthusiastically to the agent's plan. Left Hand viewed the trip as a chance to go over the heads of local officials and talk to the Great Father himself, explaining the Indians' plight and dissatisfaction with the Fort Wise Treaty.[3]

Colley set a date in early February when the wagon train would depart on the first leg of the journey to Washington. Leading men from the Cheyenne, Southern Arapaho, Comanche, Kiowa, and Caddo tribes were to meet at Fort Wise (which had recently been renamed Fort Lyon in honor of Nathaniel Lyon, the first Union general killed in the Civil War).[4]

Left Hand arrived at the fort several days before the departure date to find that Colley had already left. Angry and disappointed, he told the post surgeon, Dr. John J. Saville, that John Smith, now working regularly for white officials as a Cheyenne interpreter, had goaded the agent into leaving him behind "because he [Left Hand] could speak English and Smith could not tell his lies."[5] There is no doubt that Smith had reason to fear that Left Hand would inform officials of how he had lied to the chiefs at the Fort Wise Treaty Council and, along with Colley's son Dexter, had engaged in shady business dealings with the tribes. Without Left Hand, Smith and Colley were free to paint any picture of the plains they pleased.

Little Raven, who had also been looking forward to the trip, happened to reach Fort Lyon before the wagon train departed, but, when he learned that Colley meant to leave Left Hand behind, he refused to go.[6] Obviously he had had enough talks

[3] John J. Saville Report, April 15, 1863, Letters Sent, Upper Arkansas Agency, *OIA*, Record Group 75, National Archives, Washington, D.C.

[4] Lyon was killed in the battle of Wilson's Creek, the same battle in which George Bent, son of William, and Chivington's brother, Lewis, fought on the Confederate side. Lewis Chivington was also killed there.

[5] John J. Saville Report, April 15, 1863, Letters Sent, Upper Arkansas Agency, *OIA*, Record Group 75, National Archives.

[6] Ibid.; Stan Hoig, *The Western Odyssey of John Simpson Smith*, p. 126.

with white men without the benefit of the only interpreter he could trust.

Although Left Hand had been deliberately slighted, his brother Neva and Spotted Wolf accompanied Colley, representing the Southern Arapahos. Lean Bear, War Bonnet, and Standing in the Water represented the Cheyennes. In addition, Colley took five Kiowa chiefs, two Comanches, one Apache, and one Caddo.[7]

Although Neva also spoke English, he was not as adept in the language as Left Hand, nor would it have been consistent with his personality to draw attention to himself by attempting to explain the situation on the plains. Neva was a self-effacing man, content to work quietly in the background as an adviser and messenger for Left Hand and Little Raven. Smith, who had known the Southern Arapaho brothers most of their lives, understood the difference between the two. It was safe to take one to Washington, but not the other.

Neva performed a valuable service to his people while he was in Washington, however. Listening carefully to conversations between Colley, Smith, and government officials, he later reported these conversations in detail to Left Hand. That Smith was duplicitous and unworthy of trust was clear, as far as the Southern Arapahos were concerned, when Neva reported that Smith had downgraded Left Hand, whose reputation as a peaceable, fair-minded chief had reached Washington, by claiming that Left Hand was a minor chief of no importance.[8]

A meeting on March 27, 1863, with President Lincoln in the East Room of the White House was the highlight of the chiefs' visit to Washington. When Lincoln entered, he found his guests seated on the carpet. They were dressed in buffalo robes, beaded skin shirts and leggings, and feathered headdresses. Their faces were painted. Smith introduced the chiefs who, one by one, arose and shook hands with the president. Everyone then turned to Lean Bear, who had been chosen as spokesman, and the Cheyenne chief asked for a chair to sit in, saying he was too nervous to speak while standing. Once seated, Lean Bear told Lincoln they

[7] Hoig, *Western Odyssey*, p. 126.
[8] John J. Saville Report, April 15, 1863, Letters Sent, Upper Arkansas

had come a long way for his advice and counsel. Great numbers of whites had come to the plains, he said, and many did not want peace with the Indians. But the Indians wanted only peace and they did not know what to do. He concluded by saying that he hoped peace would last as long as he lived.[9]

Following Lean Bear's speech, which Smith interpreted, Lincoln said a few words to the effect that he saw no way for the Indians to become as prosperous and numerous as the whites unless they began to live as whites lived, by cultivating the earth. He also assured the chiefs that the government's goal was peace with the plains tribes, and that the government would observe the treaties made with them. On those words of promise, the meeting ended and the chiefs adjourned to a garden room where their photograph was taken with Mrs. Lincoln and the wives or daughters of foreign diplomats.[10]

Before leaving Washington, and after a sightseeing trip to the Army of the Potomac (with special attention called to the army's latest artillery), the chiefs received an invitation from P. T. Barnum to visit his museum in New York and view the curiosities there. Colley and Smith eagerly accepted the invitation, and the delegation arrived in New York on April 8, heralded by the *New York Times:* "If paint and feathers, wampum and war-hoops, tomahawks and terrible fighters are sufficient to form an attraction, New York certainly has one now... The chiefs will hold a grand pow-wow, with all who please to go and see them at the Museum today."[11] The chiefs were not aware that they, too, were to be considered curiosities, and although they repeatedly asked Colley and Smith to return them to the plains, the white men, who were amply rewarded by Barnum, put them off, assuring them they would leave soon. Meanwhile, week after week droned on.

While words of peace and conciliation had been exchanged in Washington, back home on the plains Evans and Chivington had reached a tacit understanding that the first hint of Indian hostil-

Agency, *OIA*, Record Group 75, National Archives.
  [9] Hoig, *Western Odyssey*, pp. 127–32; *Washington Daily National Intelligencer*, March 28, 1863.
  [10] Ibid.
  [11] *New York Times*, April 8, 1863.

ity would be met with immediate and harsh response. In March, while the delegation of chiefs was still in the East, a group of Cheyennes, returning from a raid on the Utes, robbed some ranches near the Cache La Poudre, making off with food and other provisions. Chivington immediately ordered a detachment of the First to find and arrest the raiders.

In a letter written later to Commissioner Dole, Evans explained why this order met with his full approval: "My judgment is that it would be better to arrest under our laws against theft and robbery such Indians as can be proven guilty rather than let them commit such depredations with impunity."[12]

Lt. George W. Hawkins led the detachment in pursuit of the offenders, moving southeast from the mouth of the Cache La Poudre near present-day Greeley, to Bijou Basin, a plains oasis of timbered bluffs close to the South Platte and today's Colorado Springs. There Hawkins overtook a Cheyenne band of twenty-one lodges and, marching peacefully into the camp, he indicated that he wished to meet with the leaders. Through sign language Hawkins managed to learn that this band had nothing to do with the raid; in fact, it had no knowledge of it. He also learned something else which he passed on to Evans: "They talk very bitterly of the whites," he reported, "[and] say they have stolen their ponies, and abused their women, taken their hunting grounds, and that they expected they would have to fight for their rights."[13]

Nothing came of Hawkins's expedition except that Evans and Chivington had been made aware of the tribe's bitter feelings toward whites. Evans seized upon the report as an excuse to write Gen. John M. Schofield, commandant of the Department of the Missouri, demanding additional troops to reinforce those in the territory since "the tribes are ready to drive settlers away from the South Platte."[14]

This letter marked the first of an increasingly hysterical barrage of letters, messages, and telegrams from Evans to military offi-

[12] Evans to Dole, November 4, 1863, "John Evans Collection: Indian Affairs," Colorado State Archives, Denver, Colo. (hereafter cited as Evans Letters, CSA.)
[13] *BIA Reports* (1863), pp. 239-40.

cials during 1863 and 1864, requesting troops against a possible Indian uprising which the governor insisted was ready to break out at any moment. Since all available troops, every available man, in fact, was urgently required by the Union armies to meet the Confederate drive, pleas for troops against a possible uprising fell upon deaf ears. Evans, aware of this official indifference, consistently exaggerated the gravity of the situation on the plains, maintaining that isolated cases of theft by the Indians were part of a well-conceived and orchestrated plan to run whites out of the region.

Shortly after the Cache La Poudre raid, Evans got word from Maj. John Loree, agent to the Northern Arapahos, Cheyennes, and Sioux, that Sioux warriors had moved south and held a council with both Northern and Southern Arapahos and Cheyennes.[15] Nothing was more certain to alarm the governor, of course, than the thought of New Ulm veterans influencing local Indians, and he immediately sent messengers to different Arapaho camps scattered along the South Platte, about seventy-five miles north of Denver, asking the chiefs to come to Denver for a talk.[16]

Left Hand happened to be in the vicinity and he was among the chiefs who arrived at Evans's office on the second floor of a brick building on Larimer Street. The chiefs readily admitted that a council of Arapaho, Cheyenne, and Sioux warriors had been held "to discuss the matter of war," and that the Northern Arapahos Friday and Many Whips had attended. Left Hand made it clear to Evans, however, that the Arapahos had refused the war pipe and that he and the other chiefs strongly opposed war, although some of the other tribes favored driving whites off the land. Another meeting of the tribes was set for May 1 at Horse Creek, site of the Fort Laramie Treaty Council.[17]

The information confirmed Evans's worst fears. A few Arapaho bands may want peace, he concluded, but the majority of

[14] Evans to Schofield, May 30, 1863, Evans Letters, CSA.
[15] United States War Department, *The War of the Rebellion: A Compilation of the Official Records of the Union and Confederate Armies,* (hereafter cited as *WRR*), Evans to Schofield, May 27, 1863, series 1, vol. 22, pt. 2, p. 294; *BIA Reports* (1863), p. 240.
[16] *BIA Reports* (1863), p. 240.
[17] Ibid.

the Plains Indians wanted war. The impending council at Horse Creek was especially worrisome and the governor mulled over the best way to meet the threat. Several weeks after their first meeting, he again sent for the Arapaho chiefs. There is no evidence that Left Hand made a second visit to his office, but those who did received a dressing down: "I told them," Evans wrote later, "that a war would mean extinction for them."[18]

While Evans worried over an alliance among the tribes, the land question came close to a settlement—in favor of the Indians. In the early part of 1863 a conscientious U. S. Attorney in Denver, S. E. Browne, innocently wrote the secretary of the Interior for a clarification of which lands, if any, had been ceded by the Indians under the Fort Wise Treaty. The secretary, probably realizing he had been tossed a can of worms, ignored the request.

Browne then took the matter into his own hands, and, as official representative of the federal government in Colorado Territory, rendered his own interpretation. Since the chiefs who had signed the treaty lived south of the South Platte, he concluded that only their lands had been ceded. All lands north and west of the South Platte still belonged to the nonsigning chiefs. Browne dispatched a letter to Commissioner Dole informing him that these lands, which included Denver and the rich goldmining districts, were off limits to whites.[19]

When Evans learned of Browne's action, he sent a hasty follow-up letter to Dole, insisting that Browne's interpretation was unreasonable and without basis. The commissioner, however, sensed that it had a chance of being upheld by a federal court, should the question ever reach the courts, and he ordered Evans to straighten out the tangled land question immediately. "You must go ahead with a council," he wrote, "and get the rest of the chiefs to agree to the treaty of 1861."[20]

Evans had already decided upon that course and had been merely awaiting official authorization. In June, Major Loree returned from Washington with the authority to hold another

[18] "Chivington Massacre," p. 45; *BIA Reports* (1863), p. 240.
[19] William Unrau, "Prelude to War," *Colorado Magazine* 41 (1964):311.
[20] Ibid.

treaty council with the plains tribes. Evans, Loree, and Colley were designated United States commissioners, empowered to reach an agreement on behalf of the government.[21]

By this time Evans was under pressure from various factions. To be sure, the settlers throughout Colorado Territory wanted clear title to the land they were living on, and they looked to Evans to obtain it for them. In addition, town developers in Iowa were waiting impatiently to move into the territory as soon as the Indians relinquished their land, and they were not the only ones to see the possibilities in this vast, undeveloped region. At least one historian has suggested that even Commissioner Dole had appointed Colley, his cousin, as agent to the Upper Arkansas tribes in order to have his own man in position to acquire valuable tracts of land the moment legalities were settled.[22]

Chivington also had his eye set on the financial rewards promised by the territory: "Colorado in my judgment," he wrote at the time, "is not of second importance to any State or Territory to the General Government. If protected and kept quiet she will yield twenty millions of gold this year, and double yearly in years to come..."[23] It was the military commander's view that the territory needed to be protected from the Southern Arapahos and Cheyennes.

Evans himself had accepted the appointment as governor because of the "opportunities for accumulating wealth" and he was eager to open the territory to development and transportation, both of which depended upon the removal of the Indians.

Evans had yet another reason for wanting to settle the land question with the tribes. In June the Second Colorado Regiment, formed in Denver under Col. Jesse H. Leavenworth while the First was still in New Mexico, had been ordered to Fort Larned. The movement of troops outside the territory, at a time when the governor was attempting to have additional troops transferred

[21] "Chivington Massacre," p. 45.

[22] Unrau, "Prelude to War," p. 307n.; Undergraff to Commissioner of Indian Affairs, May 12, 1861, Letters Received, and Dole to Undergraff, May 29, 1861, Letters Sent, Upper Arkansas Agency, *OIA*, Record Group 75, National Archives.

[23] Chivington to Schofield, September 12, 1863, *WRR* series 1, vol. 22, pt. 2, pp. 527–29.

within, greatly increased his concern over a possible Indian uprising.

In this atmosphere of restlessness and uncertainty, Evans set the date of the new treaty council for September 1. The place was to be the Arikaree Fork of the Republican River, in the southwest corner of Nebraska. On June 28 the governor sent two traders, Elbridge Gerry and Antoine Janisse, to notify the northern tribes. Gerry, a grandson of the Elbridge Gerry who signed the Declaration of Independence and a twenty-five-year veteran of the plains, left his ranch on the South Platte and set out with the Frenchman Janisse, another plains veteran, to find the Northern Arapahos and Cheyennes. Agent Colley, charged with getting the message to the Southern Arapahos and Cheyennes, dispatched John Smith to notify the scattered bands. To be sure that the tribes would come, Evans had instructed the messengers to tell them he would distribute annuities at the council.[24]

In July an incident occurred that would affect Evans's plans. Little Heart, a Cheyenne warrior, was making his way from a Southern Arapaho camp to Fort Larned when he was fatally shot by a sentry who claimed the Indian was drunk and had tried to run him down. There are different versions of the Cheyennes' reactions. According to the historian George Bird Grinnell the tribe considered the killing justifiable and accepted gifts to pay for the death. John Smith said later, however, that the Cheyennes were enraged by Little Heart's death and were only kept from taking revenge on whites by the Southern Arapahos. Although Smith did not enjoy a reputation for veracity, subsequent events tend to support his version.[25]

By August word filtered back to Evans that the tribes were not disposed toward a council. Agent Colley reported that the Arkansas River bands refused to attend, ''some making one excuse and some another, their horses are worn out, there is no water in the country they would have to cross,'' or ''they are busy making lodges and the journey is long.''[26]

Nevertheless, on August 27 a determined Evans boarded the

----

[24] ''Chivington Massacre,'' p. 46.
[25] George B. Grinnell, *The Fighting Cheyennes*, p. 132; Donald J. Berthrong, *The Southern Cheyennes*, p. 167.
[26] ''Chivington Massacre,'' p. 46.

stage in Denver and headed onto the Platte Road, now called the Overland. He traveled to Julesburg, where he planned to meet Gerry and Janisse and an escort of troops before turning south toward the Republican River.

That summer Gerry had covered about six hundred miles visiting the Indian bands and trying to persuade them to attend the council. By the time he met Evans, he believed that only one village would comply, but, when the party arrived at the Arikaree Fork, only four lodges of Cheyennes, and no Arapahos, were waiting.

While Evans stayed at the fork, Gerry set out again in search of the bands. In the report he later gave Evans, he wrote that he found Black Kettle and White Antelope's villages at Beaver Creek, still a favorite camping site for the tribes. Although he did not speak with Black Kettle, who was ill in his lodge, White Antelope and other leaders made it clear they had no intention of attending another council. "The white man's hands are dripping with blood," they said, referring to Little Heart's death, "and now he calls us to make a treaty."[27] Only one chief, Bull Bear, indicated willingness to accompany Gerry to the treaty site. Bull Bear was the leader of the elite Dog Soldiers, a band of highly skilled warriors, and a brother of the Lean Bear who had served as spokesman for the Indian delegation in Washington. The other chiefs held a council, however, and forbad him.

Little Heart's death was only one of their reasons for refusing to meet Evans. The chiefs told Gerry they believed they had been swindled by the Fort Wise Treaty, and, although they had become reconciled to the hard fact that they would never recover their lands along the South Platte, they had no intention of giving up their lands on the Republican and Smoky Hill rivers, the last of their buffalo ranges. The buffalo herds there, they contended, would last a hundred years and they could continue to live as before. When Gerry replied that this was not what the governor intended, Bull Bear asked what it was the governor wanted. "Now do you say that the governor wants us to settle down and live like white men?" he inquired.

"Yes," replied Gerry. "That is just what he wants."

27 *BIA Reports*, (1863), pp. 247–48.

"You go straight back to him and tell him that we are not quite so low as that yet," Bull Bear replied.[28]

Evans waited two weeks in camp among the cottonwoods on the Arikaree Fork, and, when it became apparent the chiefs were not coming, he returned to Denver. From this time on, Evans's attitude toward the Indians hardened in anger. As the historian Grinnell put it, the governor, when his attempt to remove the Indians from the land by legal means failed, lost his head and resolved to remove them by any means possible.[29] On September 21 he wrote to Chivington, ordering him to stop all Indians from hanging around small military outposts (the Indians sometimes drew provisions and traded with the troops to supplement their food supply). "Indians near the camps," Evans stated, "are difficult for the agents to control."[30]

Despite Evans's failure to convene the council, Major Loree, under orders from the governor, successfully obtained signatures from some of the northern chiefs to a document stating that they accepted the terms of the Fort Wise Treaty. Evans had told Loree to have the chiefs sign at the distribution of annuities and Loree complied, obtaining the signatures before he handed out the food and other provisions that were desperately needed.[31]

Obtaining signatures was one thing, but removing the Indians to the reservation was something else, as Evans knew. His failure to convene the leading men of the tribes, those with enough influence to bring their people to the reservation, led the governor to believe that they meant to hold onto their lands by driving the whites away. In fact, Evans had attempted to convene a council at the worst possible time for the chiefs. An epidemic of whooping cough had swept through the Cheyenne village on Beaver Creek, for example, killing thirty-five children in the last two weeks of August and leaving many families devastated. Little rain had fallen during the hot, dry summer months, resulting in a drought so severe that even the lower Arkansas River had dried up. Not

[28] Hubert Howe Bancroft, "Interview with John Evans," Western History Division, University of Colorado Library, Boulder, Colo.

[29] Grinnell, *Fighting Cheyennes,* p. 135.

[30] Evans to Chivington, September 21, 1863, Evans Letters, CSA.

[31] *BIA Reports,* (1863), pp. 125, 131–32.

only was food more scarce than at any time in the past, but so was water. The chiefs had told Gerry that the village had assembled for the annual religious celebration, but the people would soon be scattering again into small bands in order to survive.[32]

Even Left Hand, who had always been eager to meet with whites and attempt to clear up misunderstandings, had been unable to leave his people that September and travel 250 miles to the Arikaree Fork to meet Evans. The Southern Arapaho leaders, like the Cheyennes, were weighed down by accumulating hardships brought on by drought, famine, and disease. In late September, Left Hand and Little Raven came into Fort Lyon with two thousand Arapahos, including some northerners, all of whom were starving and desperate for annuities, according to Colley. The agent also reported that the chiefs were "anxious to settle down on reservation lands," but since the reservation was not yet ready, he distributed annuities and sent the Indians on their way.[33]

This was the second time the Southern Arapahos had come to Colley and indicated their willingness, even eagerness, to move onto a reservation not yet ready for them. It could be argued that this willingness amounted to a tacit acceptance of the Fort Wise Treaty. At the very least, the Indians' realization that the gameless, arid tract was the only land left to them was a measure of the hopelessness engulfing the tribe.

That fall Colley was busy laying out an irrigation system and beginning construction on a blacksmith shop and tenant house. Although he turned the Southern Arapahos away, within a few months he would lease part of the reservation lands to white tenants who would plant the first crops.[34]

In some ways Colley was moved by the Southern Arapaho plight, however. "There is not a buffalo within 200 miles [of the reservation] and little game of any kind," he wrote Commissioner Dole. "Wild game is fast disappearing from the plains." Thousands upon thousands of buffalo had been killed during the summer and fall by whites, he said, for their "hides and tallow,

---

[32] Ibid., pp. 247–48; George Hyde, *Life of George Bent*, p. 119.
[33] *BIA Reports*, (1863), p. 253.
[34] Evans to Colley, September 12, 1864, Evans Letters, CSA.

to the Indians' injury. Most of the depradations committed by them are from starvation."[35]

With winter closing in, the situation worsened. Just how desperate the Southern Arapahos and Cheyennes became during those winter months was documented by a special agent, Dr. H. T. Ketchem, sent to the plains to vaccinate the tribes. In his first report to Evans, dated October 16 from Fort Lyon, Ketchem described the Southern Arapahos as "suffering terribly from smallpox. Many are badly pitted. All are anxious to be vaccinated."[36]

Moving down the Arkansas from Lyon, Ketchem came upon isolated bands of Southern Arapahos, "so poor and sick," he wrote Evans, "they are unable to hunt." Ketchem was horrified to learn that these starving people were subsisting on the festering carcasses of cattle that had died from disease while crossing the plains with wagon trains. Everywhere he went between Forts Lyon and Larned, the special agent found knots of Indians hungry and sick with "erysipilas, whooping cough and diarrhea." Their ponies were also dying from cold, hunger, and thirst, he reported. As 1863 wore on, Ketchem continued his work of mercy, inoculating eleven hundred persons. When he ran out of vaccine, he crossed the plains in the dead of winter to obtain more in St. Louis and returned immediately, so great was the need.

In one of his later reports, Ketchem gave Evans a frank picture of life around the forts. "Dissipation, licentiousness, and venereal diseases prevail in and around all the military posts that I have visited to an astonishing extent," he wrote. Traders were everywhere continually cheating the Indians who, he said, "do not realize one-fourth value of their robes in trade for flour, sugar, coffee, dry goods and trinkets." Hunger was commonplace and the warriors were turning more and more to whiskey, which for a time calmed both hunger and rage. They traded whatever they could for whiskey at the forts, Ketchem reported, even bringing in their women for prostitution.[37]

Ketchem also provided the only hint that Little Raven and Left

[35] *BIA Reports*, (1863), p. 253.
[36] Ibid., pp. 400–401.
[37] Ibid.

Hand were also beginning to turn to alcohol. "I saw Little Raven several times drunk," he wrote, "and was credibly informed that he and Left Hand could obtain whiskey by the bottle full anytime from the sutler's store at Fort Lyon"—the store managed by Agent Colley's wife.[38] Both chiefs recognized the problems brought about by whiskey, and Left Hand had pledged earlier in Denver to do all in his power to keep his young men away from it. That he now may have sought the escape it offered can be taken as a sign of his own depression that winter.

Despite the heavy sufferings brought on by drought, famine, and the invasion of their lands by whites, the Southern Arapahos showed their customary friendliness and expressed deep gratitude for Ketchem's help. As he told Evans, "all the Indians treated me with kindness and hospitality."[39]

It is curious that twenty years later, Evans, sere and shrunken in his seventieth year, would tell the historian Bancroft that he had distributed "a good many thousand sheep" among the Indians during this desperate period.[40] There is no evidence to corroborate his claim, nor is there evidence that the governor, who was ex-officio superintendent of Indian Affairs, did anything to relieve the immense suffering of people in his jurisdiction, although Ketchem's reports from October, 1863, to the following July kept him fully aware of the horror on the plains.

What he did do was order a military force after a group of young Arapahos who had run off cattle and horses from the J. P. Van Wormer ranch east of Denver in early November. Before Chivington could field the troops, however, the rancher and Robert North, another trader, who was married to an Arapaho and spoke the language, tracked the stock to an Arapaho camp. There the young warriors readily admitted they had stolen the cattle and slaughtered it for food. They returned one horse, also stolen, but it turned out not to belong to Van Wormer.[41]

North then rode to Denver and met with Evans, to whom he spun out a fantastic tale of Indian conspiracy. According to the

[38] Ibid.
[39] Ibid.
[40] Bancroft, "Interview with John Evans," p. 14.
[41] Evans to Dole, November 4, 1863, and Evans to Chivington, November 7, 1863, Evans Letters, CSA.

trader, he had recently been in a Southern Arapaho camp on the
Arkansas where, he said, Comanche, Kiowa, Kiowa-Apache,
Northern Arapaho, Cheyenne, and Sioux chiefs smoked the war
pipe and pledged to attack white settlements "as soon as grass
was up in the spring."[42]

It was a tale that coincided with Evans's own beliefs. To make
matters worse, Colorado troops were rapidly being pulled out of
the territory. Some were already in Kansas City awaiting further
orders, and, during November and December, the Second Colorado Regiment under Colonel Leavenworth was being moved
farther east from Fort Larned to St. Louis as part of the Union Army's District of the Frontier.

Leavenworth had even requested Chivington to send additional troops from Denver, but Chivington refused. Lieutenant
Colonel Tappan complied, however, sending companies of the
First from Fort Lyon. Tappan's compliance with the request of
one colonel brought the wrath of the other. Chivington removed
him from command of Fort Lyon, precipitating bitter feelings
between the two men.[43]

Although other companies of the First were still at Fort Lyon
and in Denver, Evans clutched at North's report as proof that the
tribes meant to stage an uprising while the territory, in his view,
was virtually defenseless. He accepted North's tale at face value,
writing Dole: "I am fully satisfied with the truthfulness of his
statements."[44]

He should not have been. No evidence exists to suggest that
any such council was held or that the tribes, battling widespread
hunger and sickness, were in any condition to make such a plan.
George Bent, William's son, who was living with the Cheyennes
at the time, later strongly disclaimed the report of "this
miserable white man who had been loafing around Arapaho
camps and living off the Indians for years," calling it "a lie from
beginning to end." Bent said that he was in the Hill band of

[42] Evans to Dole, November 10, 1863, Evans Letters, CSA: Hyde, *Life of
George Bent,* p. 121.

[43] Leavenworth to AAG, July 22, 1863, *WRR* series 1, vol. 22, pt. 2, pp.
401-402; Chivington to Schofield, September 12, 1863, ibid., pp. 527-29;
Stan Hoig, *Sand Creek Massacre,* pp. 28-29.

[44] Evans to Dole, November 10, 1863, Evans Letters, CSA.

Cheyennes on the Smoky Hill River that winter and "everything was quiet, and the First Colorado Cavalry which was guarding the Upper Platte and Upper Arkansas roads had no work to do."[45]

Although the historian Grinnell has found evidence to suggest that North was an unsavory character, illiterate and possibly insane, Evans made no effort to check North's story against more trustworthy sources.[46] Fair-minded men like Elbridge Gerry and William Bent were in close contact with the tribes during this period, yet neither reported a conspiracy. Had Evans spoken with them, they would have contradicted North's report.

Evans, however, did not want contradictory opinions. Several days after his meeting with North, the governor met Medicine Man, the Northern Arapaho chief, who assured him that the Arapahos intended to remain peaceful. As soon as Medicine Man left the governor's office, John Smith and Agent Colley, who were there, played upon his fears by suggesting that the chief was part of the conspiracy and had only been trying to throw Evans off guard.[47]

The governor agreed, and on November 9 he wrote Chivington to inform him of the Indian alliance and to point out that a "combination [of tribes] would be a forewarning to mischief."[48]

A month later he was still dwelling on the Indian conspiracy, and on December 14 he sent an urgent request to Secretary of War Edwin M. Stanton, pleading for additional troops. He said that he had evidence of an alliance of "several thousand warriors, Sioux, Cheyenne, Kiowa, Comanche, Apache, and part of the Arapahos, capable of sweeping off white settlers."[49]

The letter was hand-delivered in Washington where the governor had gone in late November in order, as he wrote later, "to personally make preparations for the probable conflict."[50]

[45] Hyde, *Life of George Bent,* p. 121.
[46] Grinnell, *Fighting Cheyennes,* p. 134n.
[47] *BIA Reports,* (1863), pp. 540–41. Medicine Man was also called Roman Nose, but he should not be confused with the Cheyenne Dog Soldier Roman Nose who would later lead an attack on Beecher's Island. See also Evans to Dole, November 9, 1863, Evans Letters, CSA.
[48] Evans to Chivington, November 9, 1863, Evans Letters, CSA.
[49] Evans to Stanton, December 14, 1863, Evans Letters, CSA.
[50] Evans to Curtis, May 28, 1864, Evans Letters, CSA.

13

The yellow-hide, the white-skin
I have now put him aside,
I have now put him aside,
I have no more sympathy for him.

Southern Arapaho song

The winter months of 1863 and 1864 were markedly quiet. For a while it appeared that Evans and Chivington, expecting an Indian uprising, were to be disappointed. For weeks heavy snowstorms and fierce winds punished the plains, forcing both white and Indian traffic to a standstill. Apart from the weather, however, the Plains Indians were in no condition to undertake an uprising.

The Southern Arapahos were scattered in small bands close to the buffalo range along the Smoky Hill River, their primary efforts bent toward obtaining food. That they were often unsuccessful can be determined from the fact that Left Hand, Little Raven, and Storm brought their bands to Fort Larned several times for army rations, even though, according to Evans's report, the Cheyennes, Kiowas, and Comanches warned them to stop dealing with whites. Although these tribes suffered from the same food shortages as the Southern Arapahos, Evans considered the warning another piece of evidence that conspiracy was abroad on the plains.[1]

At the same time Left Hand was telling every white man who would listen, including Colley, the officers at Fort Larned, and Col. Jesse Leavenworth, that the Southern Arapahos did not want war with the whites. Both Left Hand and Little Raven had been hired from time to time by Leavenworth to act as guides for the Second Colorado Regiment before it had left for St. Louis, and Leavenworth said later that Left Hand always stood for peace. He had told the colonel he would not be provoked into war with

---

[1] *BIA Reports* (1864), House Exec. Doc. 1, 38th Cong., 2d sess., pp. 236–37.

whites, not by murder, imprisonment, or any other injustice they might choose to inflict upon his people or him.[2]

While the tribes remained at peace, another Confederate threat loomed south of the Arkansas River that winter. Maj. Gen. Sterling Price and eight thousand troops began massing on the border, ready to invade Missouri. In March, Maj. Gen. Samuel R. Curtis, the former Iowa congressman who had shepherded the Union Pacific bill through Congress and who was now commanding the Department of Kansas, notified Evans that all available troops were to be pulled out of the plains to meet this latest threat.

Panic gripped Evans when he received the notification, which, he believed, would leave the territory defenseless and bring about the violence he seems to have both feared and desired. "I protested," he said later, "as Indians seeing troops going away would become more troublesome."[3] The governor's belief that all-out war would be launched in the spring had remained unshaken during the peaceful winter. On March 15 he had written Colley that "our vigilance must be preserved," and had ordered him to "get spies into Indian confidence and report promptly all you hear."[4]

In April a series of skirmishes occurred that convinced Evans that the uprising he had long predicted was upon him. Several groups of Cheyenne warriors raided white ranches, stealing stock, but no settlers were molested and no lives were lost. Yet Evans and Chivington looked upon the raids as the first skirmishes of an Indian-white war—not as the simple cases of theft that they were—and ordered armed and mounted troops to the plains against the Cheyennes.

The first raid occurred on April 5, when 175 head of cattle was lost from a herd belonging to Irwin, Jackman and Company, government contractors, in the area of the Big Sandy River, also known as Sand Creek. Herders reported that Cheyenne warriors

---

[2] U.S., Congress, Senate, "Massacre of Cheyenne Indians," *Report of the Joint Committee on the Conduct of the War*, Sen. Report 142, 38th Cong., 2d sess. (1865), pp. 1, 31 (hereafter cited as "Cheyenne Massacre").

[3] "Chivington Massacre," p. 46.

[4] Evans to Colley, March 15, 1864, Evans Letters, CSA.

had driven off the cattle, but the Indians later denied responsibility, claiming the herders had let the cattle wander.[5]

Chivington's response was to order Lt. George Eayre to take a detachment of troops and a howitzer from Camp Weld across the plains in pursuit of the cattle. Eayre moved eastward to the Republican River in west-central Kansas, where he came upon five lodges of Cheyennes under Crow Chief. Frightened by the approaching soldiers, the Indians fled, leaving behind their lodges, clothing, robes, and food. Eayre and his men marched into the deserted camp, helped themselves to whatever robes, skins, and food they wanted, and torched the rest.

Then Eayre turned north toward Beaver Creek, where he discovered another small Cheyenne camp. Again the Indians fled and the soldiers burned the camp. In that vicinity, Eayre recovered twenty head of missing cattle, which he brought to Denver. Chivington promptly notified Curtis that the troops had recovered a hundred head of cattle.[6] It would not be the only time Chivington would alter numbers to his advantage.

Whether the cattle had been stolen, as the herders claimed, or had wandered away and been found later by the Cheyennes, as they claimed, will never be known. But the incident resulted in the destruction of two small Cheyenne camps and burdened the Indians with added hardships in a time replete with hardships.

The second incident took place on April 11. W. D. Ripley, a white rancher, rode into Camp Sanborn, one of the posts Chivington had garrisoned on the South Platte, and notified Capt. George L. Sanborn that Cheyennes had run off his stock. According to another rancher (a man named Bourser, who happened to be present), Sanborn turned to Lt. Clark Dunn and ordered him to "disarm and fetch in the Indians. If they refuse . . . sweep them off the face of the earth."[7]

With Ripley along, the troops marched sixty miles before overtaking a small group of Cheyennes who were leading the stolen stock. Dunn claimed later that, although he had no interpreter, he ordered them to return the cattle and hand over their arms.

[5] *BIA Reports*, (1864), p. 383; "Chivington Massacre," p. 96.
[6] George B. Grinnell, *The Fighting Cheyennes*, p. 139.
[7] "Chivington Massacre," pp. 72–73.

When the Cheyennes refused to comply, Dunn's men attempted to wrest away their arms and the Indians opened fire, killing two soldiers and wounding two others.[8]

The Indians told another story. Spotted Horse, one of the Cheyennes with the group, told Bourser later that the warriors had taken three cattle because in Bourser's words, "there was snow on the ground and the Indians were hungry. They planned to trade some ponies for cattle if the soldiers overtook them and eat the cattle. The soldiers held no talks with the Indians, [gave them] no chance to explain but pitched into them." In Spotted Horse's version, the Indians rode up to the soldiers, dismounted, and shook hands. It was only after the soldiers tried to take their guns from them that they opened fire.[9]

On April 19 a small band of Cheyennes struck again, this time raiding a ranch on the South Platte. After driving off the white owners, they took all the household goods they could carry. Chivington sent Maj. Jacob Downing—who was his close confidant and aide and a veteran of the campaign of La Glorieta Pass—in pursuit of the guilty Indians, but Downing was unable to find them, even though he and his men swept across a wide area.

Later that month the most serious raid in the series, followed by the most serious consequences, took place. Cheyenne warriors stampeded $800 worth of horses from the Moore and Kelley Overland Stage Station near Julesburg. Downing again set off in pursuit. This time he found a Cheyenne camp with eleven lodges, which he promptly destroyed. Still searching for the raiders, Downing's men happened upon a lone Cheyenne-Sioux, whom they captured. On May 1, Downing reported to Chivington that he had spared the prisoner's life, against Chivington's apparent orders to not encumber his command with prisoners, in order to learn the location of the main Cheyenne camp. Years later Downing would brag in an interview with the *Denver News* that he got the information he wanted from his prisoner by "toasting his shins" over the fire.[10]

[8] U.S. Congress, Senate, "Sand Creek Massacre," *Report of the Secretary of War*, Sen. Exec. Doc. 26, 39th Cong., 2d sess. (1867), pp. 68–69 (hereafter cited as "Sand Creek Massacre").

[9] "Chivington Massacre," p. 73.

[10] Downing to Chivington and Sanborn to Chivington, April 20, 1864,

The hapless Indian in tow, Downing's troops pushed north of the South Platte for some sixty miles to an area called Cedar Bluffs. In the early morning of May 3 they attacked a sleeping Cheyenne camp which, Downing later estimated, contained about a hundred people. He claimed his troops killed twenty-five and wounded thirty or forty while his only loss was one dead and one wounded. The troops also captured a hundred Indian ponies which, Downing said, he "shared with the boys." [11]

Downing's account of "enemy" fatalities was not quite as glorious as he wanted Chivington to believe. Cheyenne chiefs said later that the camp was a small one composed mostly of women and children who were unaware of the horse raid at the stage station. The soldiers marched in without warning and killed four people—two women and two children. [12]

These skirmishes left no doubt that Evans and Chivington meant to win the war they believed they were in with the Indians by meeting every aggressive act with swift, harsh retaliation. On May 31, Chivington informed Major Wynkoop, who was now in command at Fort Lyon: "The Cheyennes will have to be soundly whipped before they will be quiet. If any of them are caught in your vicinity, kill them, as that is the only way. [13]

While Downing was scouring the country north of the South Platte, Chivington again ordered a command under Lieutenant Eayre to the eastern plains "to burn bridges [lodges] and kill Cheyennes whenever and wherever found." [14] Chivington issued this order although no Indian raids had taken place in the area

---

WRR series 1, vol. 34, pt. 3, pp. 242-43; Downing to Chivington, April 21, 1864, ibid., pp. 250-52; Downing to Chivington, May 2, 1864, ibid., p. 407; Downing to Chivington, May 3, 1864, ibid., pt. 1, pp. 907-908. See also Evans to Dole, June 15, 1864, Evans Letters, CSA; Grinnell, *Fighting Cheyennes,* p. 143. Later Chivington gave specific orders not to take prisoners ("Chivington Massacre," p. 74; Chivington to Wynkoop, May 31, 1864, WRR series 1, vol. 34, pt. 4, p. 151).

[11] "Chivington Massacre," p. 15.

[12] Ibid.

[13] Chivington to Wynkoop, May 31, 1864, WRR series 1, vol. 34, pt. 4, p. 151.

[14] Chivington to Eayre, May 31, 1864, ibid., p. 151; McKenney to Charlot, June 15, 1864, ibid., pp. 402-404.

apart from that on the stage station, and Downing was already attempting to even that score.

Eayre commandeered fifteen light wagons off the streets of Denver and, with eighty-four men from Camp Weld, headed southeastward toward Fort Larned. Nearing the Fort on May 16 he caught sight of a large group of Cheyennes and Sioux who were moving north. George Bent later gave an account of what happened based on information given him by Wolf Chief, who was with the Cheyennes. The Indians were frightened at the sight of the troops, Wolf Chief said, and Lean Bear, the dignified, respected leader whom the other Indians had designated their spokesman in Washington, offered to ride out to meet the soldiers and inform them that the band was friendly.

Taking one warrior named Star, Lean Bear started toward Eayre's troops, waving papers he had received in Washington as proof of his good will and proudly sporting a medal on his shirt, another souvenir of Washington. When they came within twenty or thirty feet of the soldiers, Eayre gave the order to fire. Frontline troopers lowered their rifles, took careful aim, and blasted the two Cheyennes off their horses. Then they rode forward and fired into the fallen bodies.[15]

In his eagerness to mete out punishment, Eayre had made a grave miscalculation and had placed his command in extreme danger. The two dead Cheyennes had been traveling with four hundred Indians, more than four times the number of Eayre's troops. He had opened fire with his command separated: Unguarded wagons were some distance in the rear, the artillery in the center, and the cavalry one mile in advance. The Cheyenne warriors immediately began firing on the troops, and had it not been for the efforts of Black Kettle, who ordered the warriors to cease their attack, the entire command would have been slaughtered. As Eayre's men retreated hastily to the safety of Fort Larned, a group of renegades who defied Black Kettle kept up a volley of fire, and at battle's end the bodies of seven Cheyennes, ten Sioux, and four troopers littered the area.[16]

[15] Bent to Hyde, March 6, 1905, George Bent Letters, Western History Division, Denver Public Library, Denver, Colo.

[16] Jones to Osburn, May 31, 1864, WRR series 1, vol. 34, pt. 4, pp. 149–50; George Hyde, Life of George Bent, p. 162.

Lean Bear's senseless death marked a turning point in the troubles of 1864, causing otherwise independent warriors to feel a common outrage toward the whites. Not only was Lean Bear a respected chief in his own right but he was also the brother of Bull Bear, leader of the Dog Soldiers, the crack Cheyenne fighting group.

While Black Kettle and White Antelope continued to counsel peace, many warriors would no longer listen. In the short space of two months, four Cheyenne camps had been destroyed and many innocent people had paid with their lives for the thefts perpetrated by a few. As soon as Eayre's troops were out of sight, the Cheyennes began holding war councils and voted to retaliate against the whites. Almost immediately, bands of Cheyennes attacked ranches that lay along the stage road east of Larned, killing one white and running off several others. Evans was now certain that the long-predicted war, one he had himself precipitated, had begun in earnest.[17]

In a panicky letter to Curtis of May 28, he wrote: "We are at war with a powerful combination of Indian tribes pledged to sustain each other and drive white people from the country."[18] From his spies—Robert North, John Smith, and Smith's son Jack—Evans learned that the allied tribes were camped at the headwaters of the Republican River. Sioux warriors, veterans of New Ulm, were inciting the Cheyennes who, Evans said, were "already a warlike and powerful tribe." Kiowas and Comanches filled out the war party, the governor contended, although "a band of Arapahos. . .have declined to join in."[19]

That band was Left Hand's. Evans's comment shows that at this point he accepted Left Hand's protestations of peace. But even without Left Hand's band, Evans viewed the alliance as formidable, pleading with Curtis to send forces to "chastise the combination at once." Troops on the border must not be moved further away, he wrote, "in the name of humanity."[20]

[17] Parmetar to AAG, District of Kansas, May 17, 1864, *WRR* series 1, vol. 34, pt. 3, p. 643.
[18] Evans to Curtis, May 28, 1864, Evans Letters, CSA.
[19] Ibid.
[20] Ibid.

In other letters, Evans hammered away at the same theme. On June 3 he wrote to Curtis: "I would especially ask that troops may be allowed to skin rebels into submission at once," and on June 8, to Dole: "I am satisfied that a severe chastisement of these Indians is the only mode in which we can obtain peace and security from these murderous raids and depredations on the settlements."[21]

At the time Curtis was receiving Evans's increasingly emotional communications, the general was sorely tried to keep eight thousand Confederate troops from overrunning Missouri, sweeping into Kansas, and capturing Fort Leavenworth—this, with a force of three thousand.[22] A general uprising of the Plains Indians did not strike the general as particularly imminent, or even as a serious enough possibility to warrant moving troops out of the main, hard-pressed arena. When he indicated as much to Evans, the governor replied hotly: "If you have evidence that my information of Indian hostilities and alliances for war are not well founded, I shall be most happy to be informed of it."[23]

Curtis decided to assess the situation for himself, and in June he dispatched his aide Major T. I. McKenney to Fort Larned for an objective, firsthand report from the plains. McKenney arrived shortly after Eayre's pointless attack on Lean Bear. Referring to the chief's death, he wrote Curtis on June 15:

In regard to these Indian difficulties, I think if great caution is not exercised on our part, there will be a bloody war. It should be our policy to try and conciliate [the Indians], guard our mails and trains well to prevent theft, and stop these scouting parties that are roaming over the country who do not know one tribe from another, and who will kill anything in the shape of an Indian. It will require but few murders on the part of our troops to unite all these warlike tribes of the plains, who have been at peace for years and intermarried amongst one another.[24]

---

[21] Evans to Curtis, June 3, 1864, and Evans to Dole, June 8, 1864, Evans Letters, CSA.

[22] Ruth A. Gallaher, "Samuel Ryan Curtis," *Iowa Journal of History and Politics* 25 (1927):352–53.

[23] Evans to Curtis, June, 1864, Evans Letters, CSA.

[24] McKenney to Curtis, June 15, 1864, *WRR* series 1, vol. 34, pt. 4, pp. 402–404.

In the meantime Black Kettle was frantically trying to prevent a bloody war before its own momentum hurtled the plains into the abyss. Desperate for advice, he sent a messenger to William Bent, the only white man the Indians felt they could trust, asking him to come at once to his camp on the Smoky Hill River. Bent set out immediately, riding northeastward from his ranch at Big Timbers on the Arkansas. When Bent reached Black Kettle's camp, the chief expressed alarm at the turn of events, saying he did not understand what the fighting was about. He asked Bent to convey the message to the military officials that the Cheyennes desired peace, which the old trader agreed to do. Later Bent said that at that time only about 150 warriors had become hostile; most still remained friendly. Leaving the Cheyenne camp he rode directly to Fort Lyon where he found Chivington, who happened to be on his way to Fort Larned.

Bent told Chivington bluntly that a plains war would be disastrous for whites and Indians alike, and that the Cheyennes did not want war but would fight if they had to. He also reminded the military commander that the whites did not have enough troops to protect the outlying settlements, and innocent settlers on isolated ranches or at stage stations would suffer the most in a war. Chivington, not to be turned away from the course he and Evans had embarked upon, retorted that whites would simply have to protect themselves. Still Bent persisted, pointing out that outraged warriors, goaded to war, could close the supply across the plains. Even this threat failed to dint Chivington's resolve.[25]

Evans, however, was deeply concerned by such a threat. The extent of the territory's dependence on the roads across the plains, especially the Overland Route along the South Platte which was the main freighting highway, had been forcefully brought home to him at the same time Chivington's troops were running down Cheyennes. On May 20 a wall of muddy water, swollen to ten or fifteen feet by a heavy spring runoff, had crashed down Cherry Creek and spilled through Denver's streets, tearing away buildings and sweeping cattle, sheep, and crops out onto the plains. One of the first buildings destroyed was the office of

[25] Stan Hoig, *The Sand Creek Massacre,* pp. 78–79; "Chivington Massacre," p. 93.

the *Rocky Mountain News,* perched as it was above the creek bed. Far more serious, however, was the loss of crops. Until new crops could be planted and harvested, settlers were totally dependent for food on the movement of freight from the East.

The flood had provided Evans with additional ammunition in his ongoing battle for troops to fight the Indians. On June 21 he wrote Brig. Gen. Robert B. Mitchell, commander of the District of Nebraska, requesting him to post troops along the Overland: "If this route is not properly protected," he stated, "we shall suffer the horrors of Indian war, and, as a consequence of our supplies being cut off, we shall have a famine also."[26] Another letter was dispatched to Brig. Gen. James H. Carleton, commander of the Department of New Mexico, asking for troops "to cooperate with our troops in chastising these Indians, whose alliance is extensive and extends to your department.... Our forces have been weakened here by drafts from the campaign in the States, so that we are unprepared for this emergency."[27]

At this time another view of the gathering storm on the plains was expressed in a letter written by Nathaniel Hill, a Denver settler who would later become a senator from the state of Colorado:

> The Governor is a very fine man, but very timid and he is unfortunately smitten with the belief that they are to have an Indian war. He encourages sending all the reports of Indian troubles to the states, to enable him to get armies and soldiers.[28]

Throughout the spring and early summer of 1864, the so-called Indian war consisted of conflicts between Cheyennes and whites; no Southern Arapahos were involved. Left Hand and Little Raven stayed with their villages in the vicinity of the Arkansas, away from the Cheyenne camps on the Smoky Hill, in an effort to avoid avenging soldiers and hostile raiders. It is ironic that, while the Southern Arapaho chiefs were endeavoring to keep peace between themselves and white settlers, a renegade group of

[26] *BIA Reports,* (1864), House Exec. Doc. 1, 38th Cong., 2d sess., pp. 371–72.
[27] Ibid.
[28] Nathaniel P. Hill, "Nathaniel Hill Inspects Colorado: Letters Written in 1864," *Colorado Magazine* 33 (1956):249.

four Northern Arapahos, led by John Notee, struck the blow that would prove fatal to all peaceful efforts.

On June 11 the four Indians attacked the Van Wormer ranch thirty miles southeast of Denver, killing the manager, Nathan Ward Hungate, Hungate's wife, and their two young daughters, burning the ranch house, and running off thirty horses and mules. A hired hand raced to Denver to inform Van Wormer, who happened to be in town.

The alarmed rancher set out for home where he found the scalped and mutilated bodies, which he loaded into a wagon and brought to Denver. There they were put on public display, the two children wedged between their parents in a box, and all day long a line of Denverites moved past the wagon to view the corpses. From this point forward, a strong faction of settlers stood united behind Evans and Chivington's plans not only to punish the Indians but also to drive them from the territory.

Two days later, with anxiety still at fever pitch in Denver, another rancher galloped through the streets shouting: "Indians are coming. Indians are advancing on the town to burn and massacre. Hurry our wives and children to places of safety."[29] Women grabbed their children and ran out of their homes, leaving doors flapping open and curtains moving eerily in the breeze. Those on the west side of Denver fled to the upper story of the commissary building on Ferry Street; those on the east headed toward the safety of the mint, Denver's sturdiest building. The men herded them inside, bolting windows and doors, and at the commissary two men stood guard with axes at the foot of an outside stairway, ready to chop down the stairs at the first sight of an Indian. Inside, the women and children waited out anxious hours by recounting, at length and in great detail, the horrors of the Hungate mutilations until after midnight, when scouts rode into town to report no Indians anywhere near Denver. The rancher had been mistaken.

The Hungate murders prompted an urgent telegram from Evans to Dole: "Extensive Indian murders, burning houses and

[29] Donald J. Berthrong, *The Southern Cheyennes,* p. 191; Maynard to Charlot, June 13, 1864, *WRR* series 1, vol. 34, pt. 4, pp. 353–54; Susan R. Ashley, "Reminiscences of Colorado in the Early Sixties," *Colorado Magazine* 13 (1936):219–30.

so forth on Box Elder Creek, twenty-five miles east. War reported last fall begun in earnest. Spies report large numbers in alliance." Evans pleaded with Dole to obtain permission from the War Department for him to call out the Colorado militia and raise a regiment for one hundred days to fight Indians. He also mentioned his plan to separate friendly Indians from hostiles by collecting the former at designated safety points. Under that plan, all Indians refusing to come in would be considered hostile and at the mercy of Chivington's troops. On June 16 the governor reiterated his belief that affairs with the hostiles could be settled only by force: "It is very important that Colonel Chivington operate with his command on these infernal Indians. . ."[30]

Evans's plan to cull out the friendlies while moving against the hostiles did not meet with Washington's approval, however. Charles E. Mix, acting commissioner in Dole's absence, replied on June 32:

> You will use every endeavor to keep the peace with the Indians and it is hoped that troops will soon be placed at your disposal for that purpose. It is not contemplated that the Indians should be collected and fed on the reservations, but they should be concentrated, if anywhere, about the buffalo range.[31]

The governor ignored Mix's letter and proceeded with his plan. On June 27 he issued a proclamation directing friendly Southern Arapahos and Cheyennes to report to Colley at Fort Lyon, "who will give them provisions and show them a place of safety."[32] Friendly Kiowas and Comanches were to report to Fort Larned, to be "cared for in the same way"; friendly Sioux, to Fort Laramie; and friendly Northern Arapahos and Cheyennes to Camp Collins on the Cache La Poudre.

"The object of this is to prevent friendly Indians from being killed through mistake," the proclamation read. "None but those who intend to be friendly with the whites must come to these places. The families of those who have gone to war with the

---

[30] Evans to Dole, June 14, 1864, and Evans to Curtis, June 16, 1864, Evans Letters, CSA.

[31] *BIA Reports,* (1864), p. 374.

[32] Ibid., p. 362.

whites must be kept away from among the friendly Indians.''[33] Evans sent the proclamation to Colley and ordered him to inform the tribes. Colley passed it to Bent, who rode out again to the Cheyenne camp on the Smoky Hill, stopping at Southern Arapaho camps along the way.

Following the Hungate murders and Evans's proclamation, the plains settled down to a few weeks of uneasy peace interrupted by only two minor Cheyenne attacks in late June. Several warriors robbed a stagecoach between Forts Larned and Lyon while others attacked a wagon train north of Julesburg.

It is curious that during this period—while Evans kept up a demand for additional troops and insisted that an Indian alliance had been formed which was bent on destroying the white communities—he wrote an article for the *Chicago Tribune* wherein he extolled the territory's virtues and limitless opportunities: "No country in my knowledge offers so certain a means of subsistence, and of accumulating wealth as Colorado does today."[34] Only one obstacle stood in the way, and Evans had already determined a course for its removal.

Available evidence indicates that Left Hand kept to the peaceful environs of the Arkansas River throughout that spring and early summer, occasionally bringing his band to Fort Larned to supplement their food supplies with rations. Sometime in July a band of Kiowas approached him with a plan to run off the Larned horse herd. Left Hand not only refused to take part, but he also sent a message to the commanding officer, Capt. J. W. Parmetar, warning him of the impending attack. The warning was ignored.[35]

Shortly afterward, the Kiowa chief Satanta sent a group of women to Larned to dance for the soldiers. Discipline at the fort was notoriously lax under Parmetar, an incompetent drunkard who was soon to be relieved of command by Curtis. Officers and men slouched about the parade ground, drinking and carousing, while the Kiowa women staged their traditional dances. Outside

[33] Ibid.
[34] *Chicago Tribune*, June 27, 1864.
[35] "Sand Creek Massacre," pp. 32–33; "Chivington Massacre," p. 65.

the fort, meanwhile, Kiowa warriors were running off the entire horse herd from the corral. By the time the raid was discovered, one sentinel lay dead and the dancers were gone. Hearing that the raid had been accomplished, Left Hand sent another message to Parmetar offering the services of his warriors in recovering the horses for the Larned troopers, who were now on foot. Again, he received no reply.[36]

After a few days he and his band moved up the Arkansas toward Fort Larned, situated on a gently sloping bluff that provided unobstructed views of the wide Arkansas River as it meandered along its timbered path. Leaving his people in camp along the way, he took twenty-five warriors with him. As they approached, they carried a pole with a white flag billowing overhead. About four hundred yards outside the entrance they met a sentinel, and Left Hand asked him to take a message to the commander that he and his men had come to offer their services.

The offer was not altogether altruistic. No doubt Left Hand saw the Kiowa raid as an occasion to demonstrate his people's friendliness and, at the same time, to keep his warriors busy recovering government horses instead of joining the raiding Cheyennes.

Left Hand and his men waited for the reply. Suddenly, without warning, the boom of a howitzer split the air, echoing through the valleys, as grapeshot fell wildly about them. Instantly they turned their ponies and, lying close to the animals' sides, raced down the bluff toward the Arkansas. The drunken Parmetar's reply to Left Hand's offer had been: "Fire on them."[37]

That order brought the Southern Arapahos into the Cheyenne-white conflict. Years of work in the part of Left Hand, Little Raven, and other responsible men who wished to maintain peace came unraveled. Outraged by the attempt on their chief's life, many warriors went over to the hostiles. "I was not much mad," Left Hand later told Colley, "but my boys were mad, and I could not control them."[38] Now the Southern Arapahos, like the Chey-

[36] "Chivington Massacre," p. 65.
[37] Ibid.
[38] "Cheyenne Massacre," p. 31.

ennes, had a personal score to settle with whites. As Colley put it, they began to believe now "along with the young men of the Cheyennes, that war with whites was inevitable and began making retaliations."[39]

Shortly thereafter the Overland Route came under siege. In a three-day period, July 17 to July 19, combined Cheyenne and Southern Arapaho raiding parties hit several stage stations, killing twelve white men, wounding three, and running off six hundred head of cattle.[40] Near the end of July a train was attacked near Larned and, when the gun smoke cleared, ten white men lay dead. Still other raiders swooped down in hit-and-run attacks on traffic along the Santa Fe Trail.[41]

Left Hand had no choice but to let his young warriors go, although he abhorred the raids and feared the ultimate consequences. According to Lt. Joseph Cramer, one of the officers at Fort Lyon, Left Hand remained with his village but "kept away from [the raiders], refusing to fight whites, still believing difficulty could be settled by a proclamation of the Big Chief in Denver. He made every effort to comply with Evans in good faith."[42]

But the Indian attacks accomplished what Evans's letters had failed to do. They convinced General Curtis that a war was indeed threatening to his west while his troops were held down by Confederate forces. In late July Curtis himself marched across the plains from Fort Riley to Fort Larned with four hundred men, in an attempt to find and punish the Indian raiders, but the hostiles scattered in his advance. He reached Larned and detailed a detachment farther west along the Santa Fe Trail, all without finding any Indians. While he was at Larned the general created a new military district, the District of the Upper Arkansas, under the command of Maj. Gen. James G. Blunt. Fort Lyon was removed from Chivington's jurisdiction and placed in the new district.

By the first of August, Curtis was forced to pull back to Fort Riley by the continuing drive of the Confederates under Major

[39] Ibid., p. 50.

[40] Curtis to Halleck, July 23, *WRR* series 1, vol. 41, pt. 2, p. 368; Curtis to Halleck, July 26, 1864, ibid., p. 413; Evans to Curtis, July 18, 1864, Evans Letters, CSA.

[41] Colley to Evans, July 26, 1864, Evans Letters, CSA.

[42] "Sand Creek Massacre," pp. 32-33.

General Price. But before leaving the central plains he reenforced the garrisons along the Santa Fe Trail with as many troopers as he could spare.[43]

While Curtis was marching across the plains, Left Hand brought his band to Fort Lyon and placed them under Colley, as Evans's proclamation had directed. Within a short time, however, the Southern Arapahos were forced to move away in search of game, although Evans had sent Colley $3,000 in June to feed the friendlies when they came in.[44] What Colley had done with the money is unclear, but he did not have enough provisions to allow Left Hand's people to remain in the gameless area, the only area that promised safety. The other chief who complied with Evans's circular that summer was the Northern Arapaho Friday, the English-speaking, adopted son of Agent Fitzpatrick. Friday's band came in to Camp Collins on the Cache La Poudre as directed.[45]

As the summer moved on into August, raids erupted with a vengeance. On August 7 a hundred warriors attacked two wagon trains on the Overland Route, killed many white men, and plundered food, machinery, and household goods bound for Denver. That success was followed by other attacks in quick succession along 250 miles of the road. Additional lives were lost; trains, ranches, and stations were burned and looted. Only a few wagons and mail coaches dared to move across the roads, and then only if they were heavily guarded. For the most part travel and commerce came to a halt as stage bands and freighters abandoned their posts and wagons and fled to the forts. Denver faced isolation.[46]

Evans was beside himself, his dreams of progress and development collapsing about him. A series of letters written at that time reflect his rising hysteria. A letter dated August 9 to Dole stated:

[43] Curtis to Chivington and Curtis to Evans, July 30, 1864, *WRR* series 1, vol. 41, pt. 2, pp. 483–85.

[44] *BIA Reports* (1864), p. 373.

[45] Ibid.

[46] Evans to Curtis, August 8, 1864, *WRR* series 1, vol. 41, pt. 2, p. 613; "Report of Lt. Thomas Flanagan," November, 1864, ibid., pt. 1, p. 244; Curtis to Halleck, August 10, 1864, ibid., pt. 2, p. 641; Curtis to Carney, August 10, 1864, ibid., p. 642; *Rocky Mountain News,* August 10, 1864.

"While we have patriotically furnished troops for war we are left almost defenceless at a time when the most powerful combination of Indian tribes for hostile purposes ever known on the continent is in open hostility against us." He claimed that depredations were occurring daily on the Platte, and he pleaded with Dole once more to intercede with the secretary of war for permission to raise troops for a hundred days to fight the Indians.[47] It was the same plea Dole had left unanswered in June.

The following day Evans dispatched another letter to Dole, sounding the same note: "the tribes are combined . . . [to wage] the largest Indian war the country ever had, extending from Texas to the British lines."[48] To Curtis, on August 11, he wrote that "unless troops can be stationed on the Overland Route, supplies will be cut off." Evans then demanded that the general, still tied down with the Confederate force, send five thousand additional troops to the plains and release the Colorado First and Second regiments for duty on the home front.[49] Evans also wired Secretary of War Stanton: "Pray authorize me to raise and mount a regiment of 100 day men to fight the Indians. Otherwise we are helpless."[50]

On August 11, the same day he was searching for military help, Evans issued another proclamation, rendering the June 27 proclamation null and void. He began by referring to his continuing efforts to bring about peace by having the friendlies come into designated camps. Their refusal to do so, he stated, was evidence that "most of the Indian tribes of the plains are at war and hostile to the whites." Therefore, the proclamation continued,

> all citizens of Colorado, either individually or in such parties as they may organize, are authorized to go in pursuit of all hostile Indians on the plains, scrupulously avoiding those who have responded to my call to rendezvous at the points indicated; also to kill and destroy as enemies of the country wherever they may be found, all such hostile Indians.

As reward for killing these Indians, the proclamation gave white

[47] Evans to Dole, August 9, 1864, Evans Letters, CSA.
[48] Evans to Dole, August 10, 1864, Evans Letters, CSA.
[49] Evans to Curtis, August 11, 1864, Evans Letters, CSA.
[50] Ibid.; Evans to Stanton, August 10, 1864, Evans Letters, CSA.

men permission to keep the property of their victims. "The conflict is upon us," it concluded, "and all good citizens are called upon to do their duty in the defense of their homes and families."[51]

By this incredible document the governor authorized anarchy, handing citizens a license to hunt and kill Indians, both renegades and innocents, hostile warriors and respected leaders. The admonishment to avoid pursuing friendly Indians was at best ineffective, at worst cynical. In fact, whites could kill any Indian, enrich themselves with robes, skins, ponies, and food, and claim the victim was a hostile. Who could dispute the claim?

As incredible as this document was, Evans's stand drew the full support of the *Rocky Mountain News* editor Byers, who three years earlier had cautioned moderation and reason. The day before the governor's new proclamation, Byers wrote: "A few months of active extermination against the red devils will bring quiet and nothing else will."[52]

Not long after the proclamation was tacked up on buildings and fences around Denver and published in the *Rocky Mountain News*, a hundred armed men set out to attack Friday's camp on the Cache La Poudre. On the way, learning that a small band of hostiles had been seen on the South Platte, they turned down the river after them. It was only this chance rumor, which proved to be unfounded, that saved the Northern Arapahos who had complied with Evans's June proclamation from a surprise attack. Since Evans had not bothered to inform the tribes of his latest proclamation, they had no idea that the earlier one was no longer in effect, or that they were now fair game for any white man with a gun.[53]

By August 15, Evans received his authorization to raise a regiment for one hundred days. Denver and the mining camps were in a frenzy of excitement as wheels started turning to call up, arm, and mount the Third Colorado Regiment. At this time Left Hand had already moved his band from Fort Lyon, threading a path across the plains between hostile raiding parties and army troops. His village probably camped near Little Raven's in southern Kan-

[51] *BIA Reports* (1864), pp. 374–75; "Chivington Massacre," p. 85.
[52] *Rocky Mountain News,* August 10, 1864.
[53] Grinnell, *Fighting Cheyennes,* p. 158; "Cheyenne Massacre," p. 47.

sas where, on the edge of the buffalo range, the warriors could find food and stay out of trouble.

In his report written later that month, Evans noted he had heard nothing of Left Hand, Little Raven, or Storm since Left Hand had moved away from Fort Lyon. "If, as reported, Left Hand has crossed the Platte to join Friday, he would have reached here sometime since." Yet, throughout that troubled month of August, there had been no word of him.[54]

Once again the times called for bold action. What Evans did not know was that Left Hand had left his village with Little Raven and moved northwestward toward the South Platte. Unaware of Evans's new proclamation and the extreme danger it held for all Plains Indians, he had set out across the plains alone on a difficult nine-day journey from southern Kansas to Boulder Valley.

[54] *BIA Reports* (1864), pp. 236–37.

... our women and children are scattered over the prairie, fearing the approach of your troops; they fall down and die, there is mourning throughout our whole nation.

14

One-Eye, Southern Cheyenne

Left Hand rode northwestward across the plains, avoiding the main routes along the Arkansas and South Platte which were lined with military outposts. He approached Boulder Valley, the winter campgrounds of his people before white settlers had moved in. In the distance the spectacular rock formations jutted out against the long spine of the blue white mountains. He turned his pony in the direction of Robert Hauck's ranch.[1]

Like many other settlers in the territory, Hauck had come to the plains during the frenzied days of the gold rush, but after futile months of prospecting he had turned to the steadier livelihood of ranching. Sometime during his years of ranching in the area he and Left Hand had become friends, and the chief had taken to visiting Hauck's ranch from time to time to discuss Indian-white problems.

It was early morning when Left Hand arrived, in August, 1864. Problems that the two men had mulled over in the past paled in comparison to the summer's mounting hostilities. Left Hand saw that only a policy of conciliation could prevent a great war on the plains. He described to Hauck the course he would follow, one in which "the Indians [would] make peace with the white men by arbitration," but he wanted this white man's opinion and advice, as well as his insight into the characters of the white leaders with whom the chiefs would have to deal—Evans and Chivington. He was optimistic and "certain this [arbitration] could be accomplished."[2]

---

[1] Augusta Hauck Block, "Lower Boulder and St. Vrain Valley Home Guards and Fort Junction," *Colorado Magazine* 16 (1939): 189. It is possible that Left Hand first visited Friday's camp on the Cache La Poudre, as Evans had expected, but there is no evidence of such a visit.

[2] Ibid.

The two men talked all day, going over the events of the past months and sorting out the possible means of bringing about a meeting between the Indian and white leaders. They continued talking through dinner and into the late evening until, finally satisfied his plan would work, Left Hand accepted his friend's invitation to get a good night's rest before setting out in the morning. He rose early the next day, bid Hauck farewell, and rode off; it was the last time that Left Hand would visit the beautiful and familiar Boulder Valley. Taking special care to avoid white settlements (Hauck would have warned him of Evans's latest proclamation), he headed toward Smoky Hill and the main Cheyenne camps.

During Left Hand's trip to Boulder, which consumed nearly three weeks of August, the eastern plains had erupted in vicious guerillalike attacks that ultimately had brought Evans the authority he had wanted to raise the Colorado Third. Bands of Cheyennes and Sioux, appearing from nowhere, swooped down on unsuspecting ranches and wagon trains, killed, scalped, and mutilated white families, and carried off property. In one bloody four-day period, August 6 to August 10, hostiles made far-flung strikes on points along the Platte River, west of Fort Kearny in central Nebraska; the Little Blue River in eastern Nebraska and Kansas; and the Saline River in central Kansas, leaving thirty-five white men dead.[3] William Bent's warning to Chivington that isolated settlements would bear the brunt of a plains war was fulfilled.

In the attacks along the Little Blue, which claimed fifteen lives, the Cheyennes took six prisoners. One of them was seventeen-year-old Laura Roper, who later told about the harrowing experience. On a warm, lovely Sunday, August 8, Laura said, she had walked a short distance from her home to the neighboring ranch of the Eubanks family. After a leisurely visit with her friend, twenty-four-year-old Lucinda Eubanks, she decided to start back; since it was late in the afternoon, Lucinda and her husband offered to accompany Laura part of the way home.

The little group set off down a path that meandered among the cottonwoods and bushes near the river, Lucinda carrying her in-

---

[3] Stan Hoig, *The Sand Creek Massacre*, p. 93.

fant and Eubanks leading two other children, five-year-old Isabelle and a young nephew. They had not gone far when they heard the shouts of Indians behind them. Eubanks hastened the terrified women and children into the brush, where they huddled together, scarcely breathing, as the Indians rode past. Thinking they were safe, he removed the handkerchief he had hurriedly stuffed into his daughter's mouth to stifle her cries. The moment he did so, the child let out a piercing scream and instantly the Cheyennes were upon them. They killed and scalped Eubanks "before our eyes," Laura said, "leaving his body where it fell."

The Cheyennes piled the women and children onto ponies after tying their hands behind their backs. One warrior, taking a liking to Laura's sunbonnet, snatched it from her head and pulled it over his own. Spurring on the ponies, the group rode to the next ranch where, according to Laura, a woman and two nine-year-old boys were alone. The woman was "so crazed with fright when the Indians came that she tried to fight them, scratching and biting." They killed her quickly and took the boys.[4]

The Cheyennes and their prisoners rode westward for four days and nights under the blistering August sun with little rest, food, or water until, crossing the Republican River in western Kansas, they finally reached a camp of other hostiles. Within a short time they traded Lucinda and her infant, whom she refused to allow out of her arms, to Sioux warriors camped nearby, but Laura and the other children remained in the Cheyenne camp (Lucinda Eubanks would not be released for ten months).

About a week after the Little Blue attacks, near mid-August, a small group of Southern Arapaho warriors led by Little Raven's unruly son stampeded horses and mules from the agency and moved on up the Arkansas where they stopped a wagon, killed two men, and captured another woman.[5]

The young, blond Mrs. Snyder had just arrived from the East to

4 "Chivington Massacre," pp. 90–91; Moonlight to Headquarters, North Sub-district of the Plains, May 27, 1865, *WRR* series 1, vol. 48, pt. 1, pp. 276–77; Julia S. Lambert, "Plain Tales of the Plains," *The Trail* 8 (1916): 6, 7.

5 *BIA* Reports (1864), House Exec. Doc. 1, 38th Cong., 2d sess., p. 375; Lambert, "Plain Tales of the Plains," p. 8; "Sand Creek Massacre," pp. 57, 216.

join her husband who worked in the blacksmith shop at Fort Lyon. After crossing the plains by stage, she was met in Denver by her husband and a friend, who had borrowed a wagon and four mules from the fort. The party left Denver, traveled to Boone-ville, and stopped to rest at the ranch of the former agent Boone. A black woman who had worked for the Boone family for many years took one look at Mrs. Snyder and remarked that she had ''a mighty fine head of hair'' that the Indians would find very attractive.[6] The remark, which terrified the young wife, was prophetic.

Before the Snyders had reached Bent's Old Fort, thirty-five miles west of Fort Lyon, the Indians struck. They stopped the fleeing wagon by shooting the wheel mule, and then they killed and scalped both men. Throwing Mrs. Snyder on a pony, they rode off, taking the other mules with them. Eventually the white woman was brought to the same hostile Cheyenne camp near the Republican River where Laura Roper and the four children were held.

Half-crazed with grief over her husband's murder and with fright at her own prospects, Mrs. Snyder waited for a chance to escape, and, the moment she was left alone, she stole out of camp and ran onto the plains. In no time at all, of course, the warriors tracked her down and brought her back. The next time she was left alone, she ripped the skirt of her calico dress into long strips which she braided into a strong rope and, fastening one end to a lodge pole and the other around her neck, she hanged herself.[7]

About the same time as the Snyder ambush, another band of hostiles raided a ranch on Plum Creek, thirty miles south of Denver. This time nine men were killed and a woman and boy were taken prisoner.

That the hostiles were taking women prisoners struck a particular note of terror among white settlers. The settlers knew that usually meant rape, perhaps by one warrior, if the woman prisoner were fortunate enough to have a single warrior claim her as his own, or, if not, by as many men as desired her. The thought of Indian men raping white women sent white men into murderous rage and their women into sometimes uncontrollable terror. Si-

⁶ Lambert, ''Plain Tales of the Plains,'' p. 8.
⁷ Ibid.; ''Sand Creek Massacre,'' pp. 75, 216.

meon Whitely, who succeeded Loree as agent to the Northern Arapahos and Cheyennes, reported to Evans that he had heard of three women living along the South Platte who had actually become insane from fear of being captured.[8] Chivington was incensed that the Indians were capturing women. Following the raid on the Little Blue, he immediately telegraphed the commander at Fort Kearny, "How many were killed by Indians were any women taken prisoners what their names."[9]

The attacks increased in frequency and drew closer to Denver. Evans later said that Denver citizens gave him no rest, continually filling his office with petitions and pleas for him to do something to stop the Indians. The day following the raid on Plum Creek he wired Secretary of War Stanton: "Extensive Indian depredations with murder of families occurred yesterday thirty miles south of Denver. Lines of communication cut off, crops in exposed localities cannot be gathered by scattered population. Danger of attack and starvation." Another wire went to Curtis saying, "We look to you to keep lines open."[10]

The governor's fears and the fear of the settlers fed upon one another. Ranchers and farmers abandoned their animals and crops and, in long refugee lines, headed for the safety of towns and military posts. Agent Colley complained that the crops he and tenant farmers had planted at the agency in the spring "promised a fair yield...but I am unable to get men to remain here.... Nearly everyone has left the agency and fled to some place where they will be protected." From Whitely Evans got word that everywhere the agent went along the South Platte, "panic and consternation were universal. I met scores of families en route for Denver, but a large majority of the farmers had left their ranches, and were living at improvised fortifications near the base of the mountains."[11]

In the midst of a general panic, Whitely seemed the only white man with a cool head. His report to Evans seemed to contain a

[8] *BIA* Reports (1864), p. 381.
[9] This telegram was found among the fort's records at Fort Kearny, Nebraska, but I have not discovered a copy of it anywhere else.
[10] *Rocky Mountain News,* September 12, 1865; Evans to Stanton, August 22, 1864, and Evans to Curtis, August 18, 1864, Evans Letters, CSA.
[11] *BIA* Reports (1864), pp. 232, 375-76, 381.

mild criticism of the governor's excited reactions and their effect on settlers:

> I was frequently warned of the danger of proceeding further, especially alone, and, in turn, used my utmost endeavor to convince the people that the peril, though real, was neither so immediate nor so great as the exaggerated stories in circulation had led them to believe. [12]

At about this time Elbridge Gerry rode sixty-five miles from his ranch to Denver to warn Evans that two Cheyennes had visited him with the message that warriors meant to clear whites out of the South Platte valley. The visitors admitted that "the chiefs were opposed to war," but they told him that "the young men would not be controlled; they were determined to sweep the Platte and the country as far as they could." This prompted Evans to send off another telegram to Stanton, stating he had "unlimited information" about an Indian uprising. [13] As it turned out, Gerry's was the only ranch struck in this particular "uprising"; he returned home to find the Cheyennes had run off his horse herd.

The peril was real, however, as even Whitely admitted. Bands of hostiles roved the plains, crops lay unharvested in the fields, and freight traffic no longer moved along the Overland Route. Enterprising Denver businessmen made the most of this unprecedented opportunity to buy up and hoard the town's supply of flour, which they afterwards sold at the outlandish price of $33.00 per 100 pounds. The men who turned over meager savings for a bag of flour to feed their families naturally blamed the Indians for this new and dreadful hardship. [14]

From August 15 to September 29, Denver was virtually cut off from the rest of the country. Mail from the East had to be sent by ship to Panama, trucked across the Isthmus, shipped to San Francisco, transferred to coach, and carried eastward across the Rocky Mountains. The trip took from seven to ten weeks.

[12] Ibid., p. 381.
[13] Ibid., p. 376.
[14] Jerome C. Smiley, *History of Denver,* pp. 404–405.

Although no traffic moved over the Overland during the last two weeks of August, by August 28 Curtis had succeeded in opening the road east of Julesburg by stationing troops every ten or fifteen miles along the way. A few mail wagons, stalled at Julesburg, cautiously began moving under heavy guard. Other wagons, also under heavy guard, made their way along the Santa Fe Road between that old city and Kansas City, but the road between the Arkansas and Denver remained closed during the last half of August. [15]

The Plains Indians once again controlled the plains, or so it seemed. Hostile Cheyennes, sometimes joined by Southern Arapaho warriors, attacked at will, driving whites into isolated enclaves. Starvation and death at the hands of allied warriors, which Evans had long predicted, now seemed imminent. The governor himself walked the streets of Denver with pistols slung on his hips, calling attention to his well-known belief that each man must be ready to protect himself and his family at a moment's notice. Denver citizens lived from day to day suspended in fear and unconcealed anger. Later an officer on Chivington's staff described the atmosphere in the waning days of that summer, "[Denver townspeople] wanted some Indians killed; whether friendly or not, they did not stop long to inquire."[16]

On August 23, Chivington declared martial law, closing down all businesses except pharmacies and grocery stores; these were allowed to remain open three hours each day. The drive to enlist volunteers in the Third Regiment was now in full swing and posters urging every able-bodied man to join and fight the Indians plastered the walls of Denver's buildings and littered the mining camps. Gradually, regiment companies were filled and sent to Camp Evans, near Denver, where they were outfitted with makeshift uniforms and issued arms—mostly outdated Austrian muzzle-loading muskets of large bore. Horses were gathered from local ranches. After receiving the minimum amount of what

[15] *BIA* Reports (1864), p. 375.
[16] Nathaniel P. Hill, "Nathaniel P. Hill Inspects Colorado: Letters Written in 1864," *Colorado Magazine* 34 (1957): 25; "Chivington Massacre," p. 14.

might pass for military training, recruits were sent to stations along the South Platte.[17]

In Boulder Valley, David Nichols, a veteran of the Mexican War who had found his way to the Colorado gold mines in 1859, received a captain's commission from Chivington that enabled him to recruit Company D from among Boulder settlers. Although other companies purchased horses from ranchers, the Boulder volunteers went from ranch to ranch, confiscating the best animals. Bob Hauck was forced to furnish six horses, but he refused to join the regiment.[18]

Denver's residents were also embroiled in political struggles over the question of statehood that August of 1864. Congress had earlier passed an ennabling act that allowed Colorado, Nebraska, and Nevada to hold elections on the question of joining the Union. In July a constitutional convention had met in Denver and drawn up a proposed state constitution. So certain was the prostatehood faction that their views would carry that they had already nominated a slate of state officers. The whole package—statehood question, constitution, and slate—was to be submitted to the voters on the second Tuesday in September.

Despite the unrest in the territory, both Evans and Chivington, leaders of the prostatehood faction, were deeply engrossed in these political activities, their eyes fixed on federal offices. The colonel had been nominated for Congress and the governor was slated to be elected to the Senate as soon as the new state legislature convened, provided the statehood question carried. Chivington had spent so much time ensuring his nomination, in fact, that Curtis had felt compelled to upbraid him earlier in the summer for neglecting his military duties in favor of politics, a charge vehemently denied by the colonel.[19]

Another event was unfolding that summer which throws a glaring light on the ambitious colonel's frame of mind. A gang of desperadoes led by Jim Reynolds had been raiding mountain

[17] *Rocky Mountain News,* August 23, 1864; Irving Howbert, *Memories of a Lifetime in the Pike's Peak Region,* p. 119.

[18] Block, "Lower Boulder and St. Vrain," p. 189.

[19] Wynkoop manuscript, p. 37; Chivington to Curtis, August 8, 1864, *WRR* series 1, vol. 41, pt. 2, pp. 613–14; Curtis to Chivington, July 30, 1864, ibid., pp. 483–84.

roads and stealing gold dust from mine wagons. Finally chased down by a posse of seventy-five men out of Fairplay and companies of the First Colorado under Lt. George Shoup, five of the gang were captured and brought to Denver, where Chivington demanded they be turned over to the military for trial. On August 23 he wired Curtis: "Have five notorious guerillas. Will try by military commission. If convicted can I approve, and shoot them?"[20]

Curtis was absent from headquarters, but his adjutant (who was also named Curtis) replied that "The authority to confirm sentence of death is vested in the department commander. I do not think it can be delegated."[21] Despite this reply, or perhaps because of it, Chivington turned the prisoners over to Capt. T. G. Cree of the Third, supposedly for the purpose of escorting them to Fort Lyon for trial. When Cree and a detachment of troops left Denver on the nine-day trip, however, they carried no food rations for the prisoners. Nearing Russellville, the captain ordered the five men shot. Later Cree said that he had orders from Chivington to "leave them on the prairie."[22]

Outraged by this blatant abuse of power, U.S. Attorney Browne, the same man who had tried to settle the land question in favor of the Indians, wrote Curtis:

> . . . the whole five were butchered, and the bodies, with shackles on their legs, were left unburied on the plains and yet remain there unless devoured by the beasts of prey that don't wear shoulder straps. . . . When the news was first brought to Chivington of the death of these persons, and of the manner of their death, he sneeringly remarked to the bystanders: "I told the guard when they left that if they did not kill those fellows, I would play thunder with them." There is no doubt in the minds of our people that a most foul murder has been committed, and that, too, by the express order of old Chivington."[23]

[20] Chivington to Curtis, August 23, 1864, *WRR* series 1, vol. 41, pt. 2, p. 828.

[21] Maj. S. S. Curtis to Chivington, August 24, 1864, ibid., p. 843.

[22] "Sand Creek Massacre," pp. 51, 191.

[23] Brown to Curtis, October 3, 1864, *WRR* series 1, vol. 41, pt. 3, pp. 596–97.

Curtis took no official action against Chivington. Even if he had wished to issue a reprimand or order a court martial, it would have been difficult during the weeks when communication between Denver and the military headquarters at Fort Riley had been cut off by the hostiles. By the time roads and lines were reopened, the matter was old and Curtis was weighed down with more pressing concerns.

The lack of official censure, however, confirmed Chivington in his growing belief that he was answerable to no one and that harsh, extralegal measures were justifiable against persons who, in his righteous view, were unfit. He had reached his zenith: the Third stood ready for duty, awaiting his command; the First, stationed throughout the territory, took orders from him. He was riding the crest of the statehood movement in full confidence that he would soon sit in Congress, and his steadily growing power was sweet to savor.

While Evans and Chivington geared for war that August, the Southern Arapaho and Cheyenne chiefs continued their long, desperate pursuit of peace. Shortly before the month closed, Left Hand reached Black Kettle's camp on the Smoky Hill near Hackberry Creek hoping to form an alliance with the Cheyenne chief who opposed war as strongly as he did. In July Black Kettle had asked Bent to carry a peace message to the military officials, and, although the trader had tried to reason with Chivington and lay the groundwork for a negotiated peace, the effort had come to nothing. Bent had not been Black Kettle's only messenger: the chief said later that throughout the summer he sent peace messages to Fort Lyon "many times," only to have his messengers fired upon.[24]

Now the Southern Arapaho and Cheyenne chiefs joined forces to bring about a meeting with white officials and stop the conflict. First they sent runners to the various scattered bands of their tribes asking the chiefs to come to the Smoky Hill for a council. That Left Hand had just returned from Boulder gave even the most hostile leaders a strong incentive to come.

According to George Bent the hostiles were living in camps on

[24] Bent-Hyde Papers, Western History Division, University of Colorado Library, Boulder, Colo.

the Solomon River in central Kansas, and, ranging from there across the plains, they were making raids along the Overland and Santa Fe roads and on the Little Blue settlements. War parties had been setting out and returning daily, said Bent, who had been in the camps that summer:

> I saw fine silks heaped up on the ground in the lodges, and cloaks, groceries of all kinds, ladies' fine bonnets, canned goods, bolts of fine cloth, sides of bacon, bags of coffee and sugar, boxes of crackers, boots and shoes. . . young warriors were wearing fine silk shirts of bright colors and stripes which the women had made out of captured bolts of silk.[25]

The Southern Arapahos under Little Raven and Neva were the first to arrive in answer to Left Hand and Black Kettle's summons. Later, even those hostile Cheyenne and Sioux bands who were benefiting the most from the raids came in. A council was convened and the two leaders argued the necessity of working out peace with the whites. Ranged against them were the hostile warriors who were determined to fight a war they knew they could not win; they expected to die fighting. Fortunately, Left Hand was not limited to the sign language for this crucial council. He could argue with the warriors, reason, cajole, even threaten them, in Cheyenne or Sioux, their own languages, and on their own terms. There would be no misunderstanding of the issues at stake.

In the end, his views prevailed. The other chiefs reached a decision based on what they believed best for their people—especially those who could not protect themselves—and not on the desires of the warriors. They would send another message to the whites, asking for a meeting.

Still there was the main problem of getting the whites to agree to meet with them. Black Kettle's previous peace overtures had been repulsed. The new plan was probably suggested by Left Hand, since it had not been tried before his arrival. The chiefs would offer to return the prisoners at the meeting; the whites, they thought, could not refuse those terms.

According to Bent, who was there, the chiefs agreed to write a

[25] George Hyde, *Life of George Bent*, p. 140.

letter and send a copy both to Colley and to Major Wynkoop at
Fort Lyon. He and Edmond Guerrier, also in the camp, were
asked to write the letter that the chiefs dictated. Dated August
29, 1864, Cheyenne Village, it began by referring to Evans's
proclamation, which William Bent had brought in July:

> Sir: We received a letter from Bent, wishing us to make peace. We
> held council in regard to it. All come to the conclusion to make
> peace with you providing you make peace with the Kiowas, Com-
> anches, Arapahos, Apache and Sioux.
>
> We are going to send a messenger to the Kiowas and to the
> other nations about our going to make peace with you.
>
> We heard that you have some [prisoners] in Denver. We have
> seven prisoners of yours which we are willing to give up, providing
> you give up yours.
>
> There are three war parties out yet, and two of Arapahos. They
> have been out some time, and expected in soon. When we held
> this council, there were few Arapahos and Sioux present. We want
> true news from you in return—this is, a letter. Black Kettle and
> other chiefs.[26]

The danger of delivering the copies of this letter was not lost on
warriors who had been fired upon trying to deliver other peace
messages. Since it was not an errand the chiefs would assign, they
asked for volunteers.

An elderly warrior, who had earned the name One-Eye years
before—he had lost an eye defending William Bent against a
group of Kiowas—stood up. "Give me true news," he said,
"such as is written to carry to the chiefs at the fort and I will go."
Later he explained to Major Wynkoop that he had been moved by
the Great Spirit to try and save his people. "I am young no
longer," he said, "I have been a warrior, I have not been afraid to
die when I was young, why should I be when I am old?"[27]

Minimic, a young Cheyenne warrior, also stood and said he
would not let One-Eye go alone. He was willing to die with him,

---

[26] Ibid., p. 142; *BIA* Reports (1864), p. 377.

[27] Wynkoop manuscript, p. 28; George Bent states that Eagle Head
agreed to take one letter, but the fact remains that it was Neva who attempted
the delivery of it (Hyde, *Life of George Bent*, p. 142).

he said, to make his people happy once more. One-Eye also decided to take along his wife, who probably had no choice about joining the brave expedition.

Neva agreed to deliver the other copy to Agent Colley. Taking fourteen Southern Arapahos, he rode southwestward toward the agency. Near Fort Lyon the party met a soldier who raced into the fort to report hostile Indians in the vicinity. Wynkoop had notified headquarters earlier that month that he intended to kill all Indians he came across until ordered otherwise. He immediately dispatched thirty mounted troops after Neva's party. The troops split into two squads and headed in different directions. One squad, under Lt. Joseph Cramer, caught sight of the Indians and gave chase for fifteen to twenty miles before engaging them in a four-mile running battle in which four of the warriors were wounded.

At one point the warriors cut Cramer and six troopers from the rest of the squad, whose tired horses had lagged behind. Later Cramer said that the warriors "wanted to kill us and Neva knew they could but would not let them because they were sent on a peace mission."[28] Unsuccessful in his attempt to reach Colley, Neva returned to camp with his wounded men and waited anxiously with the chiefs for word from One-Eye.

There was a great feeling of unease at Fort Lyon at this time. During the last days of August hostiles had struck several wagon trains along the Santa Fe Road and near the Cimarron River. The pattern of destruction was always the same: white men were killed and scalped and their animals captured. To help Lyon troops protect the roads, a detachment had been sent from the Department of New Mexico, probably in answer to Evans's earlier request. Nevertheless, Major Wynkoop meant to take no chances with hostiles. "My garrison was small," he wrote later, "and I was surrounded by five of the hostile tribes. I had issued the most stringent orders to kill all Indians that could be reached."[29]

[28] Cramer to Wynkoop, August 12, 1864, *WRR* series 1, vol. 41, pt. 1, p. 238; "Sand Creek Massacre," pp. 17, 32, 33; "Chivington Massacre," p. 31. The "Sand Creek Massacre" citation gives the date of delivery as August 11, but the letter was not written until August 29. The date was probably an error meant to be written as August 31.

[29] Wynkoop manuscript, p. 27.

Wynkoop was no longer the light-hearted adventurer who had crossed the plains in 1858 as sheriff of the illegal Arapaho County. He had placer-mined for a short time on Clear Creek, but, like most other goldseekers, had failed to find a fortune. In 1860 he had married Louisa Matilda Brown, and the following year the first of their eight children was born. By 1862, Wynkoop was ready to turn in his pick and shovel for regular pay as captain of Company A, First Colorado Regiment. Instead of finding a life of wealth and ease on the plains, he had found high adventure. He had marched over mountainous Colorado country to New Mexico and taken part in the Civil War battles at La Glorieta Pass. Now he was in command of an isolated fort surrounded by hostile Indians.[30]

Wynkoop's attitude toward Indians was not unlike that of Evans, Chivington, and other leading men in the territory at that time. Later he wrote that he had believed, without question, that the Indian could never be

> assimilated with the spirit of progress, that he was degraded, treacherous and cruel, that he must make way for civilization or be trampled on, that he had no rights that we were bound to respect, in fact that he had nothing but the instincts of a wild beast, and should be treated accordingly.[31]

That attitude was soon to undergo a change.

On September 3, Wynkoop was at work in his quarters at Fort Lyon when a sergeant interrupted him to say he had captured three Indians, two men and a woman. Wynkoop reprimanded him for ignoring orders to shoot Indians on sight, but the sergeant explained he had been about to shoot them when he saw that one was waving a letter. He decided to bring the party in to the fort.

Wynkoop read the letter before sending for the Indians, as well

---

[30] Edward E. Wynkoop, "Edward Wanshier Wynkoop," *Kansas Historical Collections 13* (1913–14): 71–79; Hal Sayre claimed that Wynkoop married the region's celebrated entertainer Mlle Haidie, but this is erroneous (Hal Sayre, "Early Central City Theatricals," *Colorado Magazine* 6 [1929]: 48–49); Wynkoop manuscript, pp. 27–28.

[31] Wynkoop manuscript, p. 27.

as for John Smith, the interpreter. When One-Eye was brought in, the major asked: "Did you not know that an Indian coming within range of this post was certain to be killed?"[32]

"I knew it," One-Eye replied.

The answer astounded Wynkoop, who studied the man before him. One-Eye stood proudly erect, holding his blanket around him, and began to speak of the hardships of his people. At one time, he said, the young men could go off and hunt, knowing their wives and children were safe. Now, he went on, the whites had made war, had struck the Indians, and they had struck in return. "They are many and we are few, they have guns and ammunition and cannons, while we have but bows, arrows and spears."

One-Eye said that the Indian men were obligated to find food for their families while at the same time fighting whites. When the warriors were away hunting, soldiers would strike the villages. The people lived in constant fear, "at all hours of the day or night, in bitter cold weather, and in the storm, our women and children are scattered over the prairie, fearing the approach of your troops; they fall down and die, there is mourning throughout our whole nation."

The Indians desired peace, One-Eye continued, and believed that if the Great Father in Washington had any idea of how much his red children were suffering, "he would stretch forth his hand and say to his soldiers, stop."

Still astonished, Wynkoop persisted: "Did you not fear you would be killed when you endeavored to get into the fort?"

One-Eye replied: "I thought I would be killed, but I knew that paper would be found upon my dead body, that you would see it, and it might give peace to my people once more."

The major ended the interview with the feeling, he said, that he had been "in the presence of superior beings," and ordered the Indians taken to the guardhouse where they could eat and rest while he discussed the letter with other officers.[33]

The officers unanimously opposed sending a detachment 140

[32] Ibid., pp. 27–28.
[33] Ibid.; George Bent claimed later that the three were treated harshly (Hyde, *Life of George Bent*, p. 142).

miles into the heart of hostile territory, and Wynkoop himself was beginning to have doubts. The letter might be a trick to pull troops away from the fort and onto the plains where they could be ambushed. Even with the New Mexico detachment, Lyon would be undermanned and vulnerable to attack while the detachment was away. Guns, ammunition, and supplies could all fall into the hands of hostiles.

Despite the serious consequences that would ensue if the letter were a trick, Wynkoop decided that for the sake of the prisoners, he had no choice but to go to the Smoky Hill camps. Because his officers maintained the trip would be a "rash enterprise, foolhardy and perilous in the extreme," he did not issue orders for men to accompany him. Instead, like the Indian chiefs, he asked for volunteers.[34]

[34] Ibid., p. 29.

...it was like coming through the fire.

Black Kettle, Southern Cheyenne

15

On the morning of September 6, 1864, Major Wynkoop, John Smith, and 130 volunteer troops rode out of Fort Lyon onto the bleak, hot plains following One-Eye, his wife, and Minimic, who had agreed to lead them to the Smoky Hill camp. The two twelve-pound howitzers that Wynkoop had brought along in case of trouble clanked awkwardly over the dusty earth.

The troops marched for four days, covering about thirty miles a day and making camp at night. Each day took them deeper into the hostile country where war parties, according to the chiefs' letter, were still ranging about. One-Eye, worried about the possibility of an ambush, had advised Wynkoop to take enough men for adequate protection.[1]

The troops pressed on through the desolate country. They saw no sign of life on the parched bluffs. Warily scanning the horizon for unusual movements, they feared that hostiles were tracking their progress and waiting for the opportune moment to fall upon them.

On the fourth day Wynkoop's men reached the Smoky Hill in the vicinity of Hackberry Creek. Ahead were six hundred to eight hundred painted warriors formed into battle lines, with those in front shouting to the others to fall in behind. Wynkoop quickly ordered his men into battle formation also, and they continued moving slowly forward.[2]

Beckoning to One-Eye, Wynkoop ordered him to take a message to the warriors that he wanted to meet with the chiefs in order "to come to an understanding which might result in mutual benefit," and to let them know that he "had not come desiring strife; but was prepared for it, if necessary, and advised them to listen to what [he] had to say previous to making any more

---

[1] *BIA Reports* (1864), House Exec. Doc. 1, 38th Cong., 2d sess., p. 378; Wynkoop manuscript, p. 29.

[2] *BIA Reports* (1864), p. 378; Wynkoop manuscript, p. 29; "Sand Creek Massacre," p. 16; Bent-Hyde Papers, Western History Division, University of Colorado Library, Boulder, Colo.

warlike demonstrations.'' He also warned One-Eye not to attempt any tricks, since his wife and Minimic were still in custody.[3]

The troops halted and waited for the Cheyenne to deliver the message. Ahead, the warriors shouted and gestured toward the soldiers, their restless ponies jumping from side to side. After a few intense moments One-Eye was at last seen riding out from the Indian ranks. The message he brought was that Black Kettle, Left Hand, and the other chiefs would meet Wynkoop in council the following day. Satisfied, Wynkoop ordered his men to fall back eight miles before making camp, putting what he hoped was a safe distance between them and the menacing force of warriors.

At nine o'clock on the morning of September 10 an Indian delegation arrived at Wynkoop's camp. Left Hand, Neva, Little Raven, and Big Mouth represented the Southern Arapahos; the Cheyenne chiefs included Black Kettle, White Antelope, Bull Bear, Sitting Bear, and Big or White Wolf. ''They did not immediately greet me cordially,'' Wynkoop wrote later, ''but in a business like manner.''[4]

Wynkoop, John Smith, and the chiefs sat in a large circle while the soldiers and other Indians crowded around, straining to hear. The council got under way when Black Kettle asked the major what he had to say. Wynkoop stood and, glancing at the faces before him, began to read Black Kettle's letter aloud. When he had finished, he asked if the letter had been sent on their authority. The chiefs replied that it had.[5]

Wynkoop then told them he did not want to deceive them; he was not a big enough chief to negotiate peace. If they sincerely wanted peace, as the letter stated, he proposed that they turn over the white prisoners as a sign of their good faith. In return, he said, he would take those chiefs they selected to Denver to confer with Evans and Chivington, the men who had the power to negotiate with them. ''I also told them,'' Wynkoop wrote later, ''that I would use my utmost endeavors to re-establish pacific relations.''

[3] *BIA Reports* (1864), p. 378.
[4] ''Sand Creek Massacre,'' p. 29, 84; Wynkoop manuscript, p. 29.
[5] Wynkoop manuscript, p. 29.

From the chiefs' expressions Wynkoop could detect a sharp division among them. The truth was that Left Hand and Black Kettle had already purchased some of the white prisoners from the hostiles with their own ponies and robes and had intended to turn them over to Wynkoop, as their letter had indicated. Some of the other chiefs saw no reason to give up their only bargaining power without a guarantee of peace from white officials.

Bull Bear, whom Wynkoop called a "gigantic chief," sprang to his feet, strode over to the major who had sat down by now, and motioned him to rise. Wynkoop again pulled himself upright as Bull Bear harangued him. "This man," the chief of the Dog Soldiers shouted, "thinks we are children, but I tell him we are neither papooses nor squaws, that we are men." Bull Bear reminded the others forcefully that they had given many ponies and buffalo robes to the hostiles for the prisoners; "we now say we will trade them for peace, and this white soldier chief says 'give me the white prisoners, and I will give you nothing in return.' Does he think we are fools that he comes to laugh at us?"[6]

Bull Bear then said that his brother Lean Bear had been a friend of whites but nonetheless had been killed by them. No peace can be brought about with white men, he shouted. The Indians must fight. Little Raven jumped up in agreement. His experiences had taught him, he said, that peace with whites was impossible, no matter how much the Indians might desire it. Others shouted in agreement.

At this point One-Eye, who had been standing outside the circle, pushed his way into the center, brandishing a tomahawk— his voice "hoarse with passion," according to Wynkoop—and demanded the right to speak. He had pledged his faith that the soldiers could come to the council and return unharmed, he shouted, and such would be the case. If anyone moved against them, he would defend them against his own people.

Then One-Eye turned to Bull Bear saying he was ashamed to hear a Cheyenne chief go on so about a few ponies. If he was so worried about his ponies, he was welcome to go out to the herd and take his pick of One-Eye's animals, an offer Bull Bear later accepted.

[6] Ibid., p. 29-30.

Throughout One-Eye's impassioned speech, Wynkoop said, Black Kettle sat "immovable as a statue, with a slight smile upon his face. He saw my bewilderment, I might say trepidation, and as his eye caught mine, he gave me a look of encouragement which assured me more than if I had the knowledge of a thousand bayonettes within call."[7]

Black Kettle quietly motioned One-Eye to return to his place as Left Hand rose to speak. He probably spoke in Arapaho for the benefit of the chiefs and others from his tribe. Then he may have turned to Wynkoop and spoken in English because the major said later that Left Hand spoke English well. Since Smith could not speak Arapaho, Left Hand was the only man at the council with command of the three languages in use, Arapaho, Cheyenne, and English.[8]

Left Hand began by saying he had been friendly with the whites until the present season. He told of how he had gone to Fort Larned in July to help the soldiers recover horses stolen by the Kiowas and had nearly been killed for his efforts. After that, he said, many of his young men went over to the Dog Soldiers and the hostile Kiowas, believing that it was the intention of the whites to make war upon them.[9]

These young men had taken part in raids against his orders, Left Hand continued, emphasizing that he and the other Arapaho chiefs opposed hostilities and only wanted peace. He had tried to get peace messages to Colley, he said, but his men had been fired upon.[10]

Now it was Black Kettle's turn. The Cheyenne chief rose to his medium height and pulled a blanket around his muscular body. At this time, according to George Bent (who later married the chief's niece), Black Kettle was about fifty-seven years old, a man of strong character, serene and dignified. He was a member of the Sutaio, an elite band of progressive Cheyennes who had given the tribe the Sun Dance and other religious ceremonies. For twenty years he had lived with one wife, Woman to be Hereafter, whom

[7] "Sand Creek Massacre," pp. 29–31; Wynkoop manuscript, p. 30.
[8] "Chivington Massacre," pp. 76, 41.
[9] Testimony of John Smith, January 15, 1865, WRR series 1, vol. 41, pt. 1, p. 966; "Sand Creek Massacre," p. 30.
[10] "Sand Creek Massacre," p. 30.

he had married after his first wife was captured by the Utes in the 1840s. He had no living children. In 1850, after earning a reputation as a brave warrior and a man of outstanding ability, Black Kettle had been elected chief.[11]

Now the chief reminded Wynkoop that both Cheyennes and Arapahos had treated whites with kindness when they had come to the plains. "Some years previously," he said, "when the white emigration first commenced coming to . . . the country which was in possession of the Cheyenne and Arapaho nations, they could have successfully made war against [the whites]. They did not desire to do so."[12]

The chief then recounted recent events which had led to the Indian raids. A Cheyenne hunting party near the South Platte had found loose stock last spring, he said, and was trying to return it to a ranch when soldiers, led by Lieutenant Dunn, approached and tried to disarm them. The scuffle resulted in the deaths of both Indians and whites, for no reason. Wynkoop accepted Black Kettle's version of this incident, saying later that he personally knew of many instances where the Indians returned lost stock for rewards of sugar and coffee.

Next, Black Kettle gave the Cheyenne version of the senseless attack near Cedar Canyon, north of the South Platte. Captain Downing's troops had marched in on a small camp of women and children, destroyed the lodges, and killed some of the occupants before driving off the stock.[13]

But the most outrageous act had been the killing of Lean Bear. Black Kettle described how the chief had approached a column of troops, "not dreaming there was any hostility between his nation and the whites. He was immediately shot down."[14]

These and other incidents, he concluded, had convinced the young warriors that war was inevitable, and they began raiding white trains and settlements, although he and the other chiefs

[11] George Hyde, *Life of George Bent,* pp. 322-33; Bent to Tappan, February 23, 1889, George Bent Letters, Colorado State Historical Society, Denver, Colo.

[12] Testimony of John Smith, January 15, 1865, *WRR* series 1, vol. 41, pt. 1, p. 966-67; Wynkoop manuscript, p. 31.

[13] "Sand Creek Massacre," pp. 31-32; Wynkoop manuscript, p. 26.

[14] "Sand Creek Massacre," pp. 31-32.

opposed war and were doing everything in their power to restore peace. Many times, he said, he had sent his men to the military posts with messages that he wished to hold a peace council. Each time the warriors had been fired upon. The whites had forced the tribes into the present difficult situation, and it was only because the chiefs were anxious about the welfare of their villages that they had agreed to make this last effort to communicate with white officials. With this, Black Kettle walked over to Wynkoop, shook his hand and embraced him twice, saying he was glad the effort had been successful.

The chief led the major to the center of the circle to answer Bull Bear's charges. "This man," he thundered to the others, "has not come here to laugh at us, nor does he regard us as children. He has followed on the trail of him whom we had sent as our messenger. It was like coming through the fire. . . . He has not come with a forked tongue or with two hearts, but his words are straight and his heart single."

Black Kettle said that if Wynkoop had promised a peace he could not deliver, he himself would have despised him. "But, he has come with words of truth; and confidence in the pledges of his red brothers, and whatever be the result of these deliberations, he shall return unharmed to his lodge from whence he came." Fixing the eye of Bull Bear, he said, "It is I, Moka-ta-va-tah, that says it."[15]

Wynkoop's uneasiness about his isolated position was somewhat allayed by Black Kettle's show of support. From that moment, he said later, the expressions of the other chiefs assumed a friendlier aspect. Black Kettle then told Wynkoop to take his men to a campsite about twelve miles downstream while he and the other chiefs discussed Wynkoop's proposal. He promised to let him have their decision within two days.

Before Wynkoop's men could pull away, however, new excitement erupted. Some of the Indians, fascinated by the two howitzers, had slipped over to the guns, and one of them was trying to poke grapeshot down the vent. The guards drew their pistols, ordering the Indians back, whereupon the Indians fixed their arrows.[16]

[15] Ibid; Wynkoop manuscript, p. 31.
[16] Wynkoop manuscript, p. 31; "Sand Creek Massacre," pp. 31–32.

Lt. Joseph Cramer rightly judged that the situation called only for calmness. He dismissed the guards and forbad any further aggressive reaction. At the same time he cautioned them to stand in groups on the alert. Word of the dispute was also brought to Black Kettle, who called the offending Indians to the circle and spoke sternly to them. Immediately afterward, they mounted their ponies and rode off.

Wynkoop and his troops broke camp and marched twelve miles along the dry creek before setting up another camp. Although he claimed later that his trust in Black Kettle never wavered, he nonetheless had ordered his men to take up "a strong position to act on the defensive should any treachery be intended."

Whatever confidence Wynkoop may have had, it was not shared by the other officers and men, some of whom demanded that the detachment return immediately to Fort Lyon. As the evening wore on, their demands grew so insistent that Wynkoop feared mutiny. But he stood his ground and ordered the men to stay in place until Black Kettle's message arrived. "With mutiny in camp, and surrounded by thousands of fierce barbarians, whether hostile or not an open question, my feelings that long and sleepless night were not to be envied," he wrote later.[17]

The night passed quietly enough, but the anxiety of the troops rose as steadily as the sun throughout the long morning. About noon, Left Hand and several warriors were seen approaching the camp, and riding with the chief was seventeen-year-old Laura Roper. When the party pulled in, Left Hand dismounted, helped the girl down, and handed her over to Wynkoop, saying he was glad to see her go back to her friends.[18]

The return of the first prisoner meant that the peace faction, led by Left Hand and Black Kettle, had prevailed once again, and Wynkoop's proposal had been accepted. Left Hand told the major that Black Kettle had gone to the hostile camps to purchase other prisoners and would return with them the following day. To prove their continuing good faith, he and his warriors then of-

[17] Wynkoop manuscript, pp. 33–34; "Sand Creek Massacre," p. 44.
[18] "Sand Creek Massacre," pp. 27, 44, 99; Julia S. Lambert, "Plain Tales of the Plains," *The Trail* 8 (1916):7.

fered to remain in Wynkoop's camp as hostages until Black Kettle's arrival.[19]

With Laura's return, the troops became more confident of their undertaking, but their situation was still full of uncertainties. The same was true for the Indians. In the past, when Left Hand had visited camps of white friends, evenings had passed in friendly conversation around the campfire. But Wynkoop's memoirs mention no friendly conversations that evening, suggesting that Left Hand and his men stayed to themselves.

Wynkoop questioned Laura closely about her captivity, however. She told him that generally she had been treated well, although she complained about riding under the blistering sun for days on end. Left Hand had purchased her freedom, she said, and had treated her kindly, promising even before the soldiers had come to the Smoky Hill that he would see she was returned safely because "she belonged with her people." According to Lieutenant Cramer, who probably also talked to Laura, Left Hand had given the promise "if the whites would make a treaty." But Laura's words indicate her belief that the man who had traded his ponies for her freedom meant to see that she got it, without condition.[20]

Much later, Laura gave a different version of her captivity to Julia Lambert. According to Lambert, Laura maintained she had been held captive for four months, although in fact she had been captured on August 8 and was returned by Left Hand on September 11.[21] That exaggeration was of less importance than the charges she made against Black Kettle, however. "I was the property of Black Kettle," Mrs. Lambert quoted Laura as saying, "to do with as he saw fit, submit or be killed."[22] Laura claimed that, when the soldiers arrived at Smoky Hill, the chief had handed his wife a knife and instructed her to cut Laura's throat should the soldiers attack.

This later version is not consistent with the evidence or with Black Kettle's character. Laura had been kidnapped by hostile

[19] Wynkoop manuscript, p. 33–34.

[20] "Sand Creek Massacre," p. 27, 44, 99; Lambert, "Plain Tales of the Plains," p. 7.

[21] "Sand Creek Massacre," 27, 44; Lambert, "Plain Tales of the Plains," pp. 6–7.

[22] Lambert, "Plain Tales of the Plains," p. 7.

Cheyennes, who took her to their camp near the Republican River, and she had not been brought to the Smoky Hill camps until the hostiles came for the council at the end of August. Shortly afterward she was ransomed by Left Hand and turned over to Wynkoop. It is doubtful she was ever in Black Kettle's control.

Even if she had been, however, she would have been as well treated by him as she was by Left Hand. Both chiefs were men of moderation, responsible for the welfare of many people. Their overriding concern that summer and fall was to prevent a war between their men and the whites. Certainly Black Kettle would not have mistreated a young white prisoner, an act that could only stir feelings of anger and vengeance among whites, at the very moment he was trying to arrange a peace council.

It is true that Laura had probably been raped by the hostiles who captured her, as were the other white women who had fallen into their hands. It is unfortunate that, in recounting the girl's story, Mrs. Lambert erroneously identified the hostile leader as the Cheyenne chief Black Kettle.

It is also true that women of both races paid a heavy toll in personal suffering during this period on the plains. As harrowing as Indian captivity was for white women, it did not differ markedly from the abuse suffered by Indian women at the hands of white men. Left Hand's wife, possibly his ten-year-old daughter, and other women in his band had been raped in Denver by Phil Gardner's gang of outlaws in the spring of 1860, and this had not been an isolated incident.[23] Such assaults, vicious and frequent, had forced Left Hand to move his village away from Denver in the autumn of 1861. Indian women were continually abused by white soldiers at the forts, sometimes with the connivance of their own husbands. Nevertheless, such abuse frequently resulted in the births into the tribes of fair-haired, blue-eyed children, children the Indian men accepted and provided for as their own.

Whites tended to overlook the ongoing abuse of Indian women as of no consequence, although they were outraged by the thought of warriors raping white women. For an Indian to ride

[23] Assaults by whites on Indians in Denver were frequent occurrences. See Frank Hall, *History of the State of Colorado*, 1:59–60.

into a white camp with a white teen-age girl on his pony and give himself over as a hostage, as Left Hand did, was an act of stunning courage. (Nine months later two warriors, a Sioux named Black Foot and a Cheyenne, Big Crow, ransomed Lucinda Eubanks and her infant and brought them to Fort Laramie. The commander, Col. Thomas Moonlight, ordered the men hanged in chains until they were dead.)[24]

The day after Laura's return, a warrior brought a message that Black Kettle was on his way with three other prisoners, and Wynkoop immediately rode out to meet the party. When he sighted the soldiers, a young boy of the group spurred his pony out ahead, reaching Wynkoop first. "Well, my boy, who are you?" asked the major. "My name is Dan," he replied, "I've been a prisoner." Then he added quickly, before the others drew close, "Can I keep the pony?" "No," Wynkoop answered, "You should have a better one." The boy was eight-year-old Daniel Marble, who had been captured on the South Platte. At that moment a second boy, eight-year-old Ambrose Archer, rode up. Later Lieutenant Cramer said that Ambrose confided that he would "just as lief stay with the Indians as not."[25]

The two boys were the right age and sex to make Indian captivity a memorable adventure. Both had been given ponies and allowed what was, to them, an unaccustomed degree of freedom to ride over the plains, play games, and romp with the Indian boys. There were few chores assigned, little responsibility, and no studies.

As Black Kettle's party drew alongside Wynkoop, the major spotted a head of golden ringlets bobbing out of a squaw's blanket. He took the child, five-year-old Isabelle Eubanks, who began crying for her mother. "I galloped with my prize some distance ahead," Wynkoop recalled later, "to gain time to control feelings I did not wish the Indians to see."[26]

[24] Hyde, *Life of George Bent,* p. 208; Moonlight to Headquarters, North Sub-district of the Plains, May 27, 1865, *WRR* series 1, vol. 48, pt. 1, pp. 276–77 (Moonlight says that Chiefs Two Face and Black Foot were both Sioux); Bent to Hyde, May 3, 1906, "George Bent Letters to George Hyde," Western History Division, Denver Public Library, Denver, Colo.
[25] "Sand Creek Massacre," p. 44; Wynkoop manuscript, pp. 31–32.
[26] Wynkoop manuscript, p. 32.

Wynkoop brought the children into a camp wild with joy. The men gathered around them, hugging and swinging them in the air, shouting and cheering at the success of their mission. According to the major, one of the men who had led the mutiny now hugged Isabelle, ''tears streaming down his craggy face.''[27]

When Wynkoop received the children they were in good health and showed no signs of abuse or ill treatment. Unfortunately, Isabelle and her cousin, who was returned later, would die in Denver in the early part of 1865. Although Lucinda said later that she was told they died from injuries suffered while in captivity,[28] it is more likely that they died from some disease to which they had been exposed in the Indian camps.

Black Kettle's party followed Wynkoop into the camp where the chief explained that he had been unable to find the other three white prisoners—Lucinda Eubanks, her infant, and a Mrs. Morton, who had been captured on Plum Creek. They had been traded to the Sioux who had taken them north, he said, but he promised to continue his efforts to free them. He also informed Wynkoop that a delegation had been selected to accompany him to Denver for a council with Evans.[29]

When Wynkoop and his troops headed back to Fort Lyon, the three white prisoners riding alongside and Isabelle riding with one of the officers, some of the head men of the Southern Arapahos and Cheyennes went with them. Neva, Bosse, Heap of Buffalo, and No-Ta-Nee, all relatives of Left Hand, had been selected to represent the Southern Arapahos.[30] The Cheyenne delegation included Black Kettle, White Antelope, and Bull Bear.

Shortly after their arrival at the fort, another Indian party numbering twenty to thirty families, including the families of the delegation members, moved to the Arkansas River area where

[27] Ibid.

[28] Jacob P. Dunn, *Massacres of the Mountains,* p. 265. Lucinda's testimony was given on June 22, 1865, in Julesburg. See ''Chivington Massacre,'' pp. 90–91.

[29] *BIA Reports* (1864), p. 378.

[30] Heap of Buffalo and No-Ta-Nee are described as half-brothers to Left Hand in ''Sand Creek Massacre'', p. 39.

they would remain while the leaders traveled to Denver.[31]

As before, Little Raven refused to take part in another talk with whites. His attitude had hardened now into a middle-of-the-road position, neither seeking war nor actively working for peace. Deeply distrusting whites, the Southern Arapaho chief's main concern was to keep his own band out of the conflict which, in his view, was inevitable.

Left Hand also stayed behind, but for different reasons. Allied with Black Kettle as a leader of the peace faction, Left Hand remained with the villages on the Smoky Hill in order to keep the young warriors from further acts of aggression that could destroy his efforts. Neva would speak for him in Denver.[32]

[31] "Sand Creek Massacre," p. 60-61.
[32] "Chivington Massacre," p. 90.

Seventeen-year-old Laura Roper, who was ransomed and returned to safety by Left Hand, is shown here with fellow captives, Daniel Marble and Isabelle Eubanks. This photograph was taken in Denver shortly after their release. *Courtesy of Ruth Dunn.*

A cavalcade of carriages formed at Denver's Sixteenth and Lawrence streets in September, 1864, awaiting the arrival of the Indian leaders who were coming to meet with Governor Evans and sue for peace. *Courtesy of the Colorado State Historical Society.*

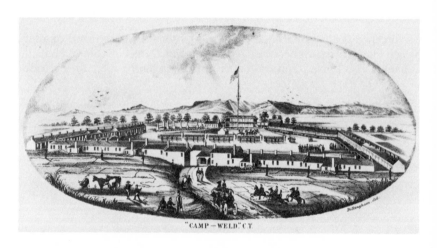

"CAMP—WELD" C.T.

Camp Weld, February, 1862, from a sketch by J. E. Dillingham. *Courtesy of the Colorado State Historical Society.*

Wagons carrying the Indian delegation, including Chiefs Black Kettle and White Antelope, as well as Neva, roll along Fourteenth Street between Lawrence and Larimer. Governor Evans's brick home is on the left. At the top is the imposing Lawrence Street Methodist Church. *Courtesy of the Colorado State Historical Society.*

Following the Camp Weld Council, September 28, 1864, most of the participants posed for this famous photograph. Edward W. Wynkoop is front left, and Silas Soule, front right. Seated, left to right, are Cheyenne leaders White Antelope, Bull Bear, and Black Kettle (center) and the Southern Arapaho leaders Neva and No-Ta-Nee. Standing, left to right, are an unidentified trooper, Agent Samuel Colley's son Dexter, John Smith, Heap of Buffalo, Bosse, Secretary of Colorado Territory Samuel H. Elbert (Governor Evans's son-in-law), and another unidentified trooper. *Courtesy of the Colorado State Historical Society.*

The Indian delegation posed alone for a second Camp Weld photograph. Seated, left to right, are Neva, the ranking Southern Arapaho present, Cheyenne chiefs Black Kettle (leader of the delegation), Bull Bear, and White Antelope. Standing, left to right, are the less prominent Southern Arapahos Bosse, No-Ta-Nee, and Heap of Buffalo. *Courtesy of the Western History Collection, University of Colorado Libraries, Boulder.*

Little Raven, holding his daughter, is shown at Fort Dodge with William Bent and two of Little Raven's sons. On the right is the man who had earlier joined the hostiles. *Courtesy of the Western History Collections, University of Oklahoma Library, Norman.*

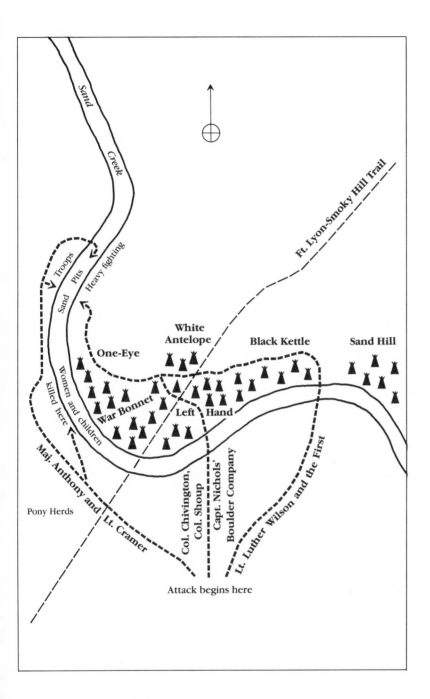

Map of the Sand Creek battle showing the deployment of Chivington's troops.

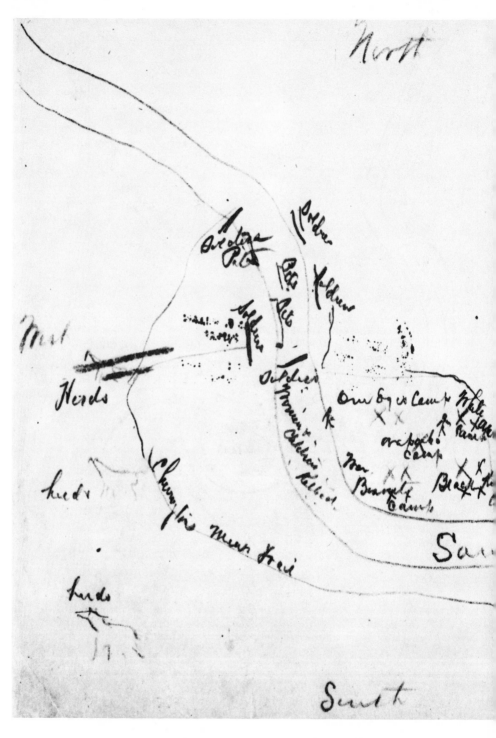

The original map of the Sand Creek battle drawn by George Bent. *Courtesy of the Western History Collection, University of Colorado Libraries.*

This famous photograph of the second Chief Left Hand was taken in Washington, D.C., by Alex Gardner in 1872, eight years after the first Chief Left Hand's death. *Courtesy of the Colorado State Historical Society.*

All we ask is that we may have peace
...We want to hold you by the hand.

Black Kettle, Southern Cheyenne

16

The Third Colorado Regiment, the hope of the territory, was fully organized and ready for action by September, 1864. On Chivington's recommendation Evans appointed Lt. George Shoup— the man responsible for rounding up the unfortunate Reynolds Gang—to the coveted position of regiment colonel.[1] The only remaining problem was that of obtaining an adequate supply of arms and ammunition.

On September 19, Evans sent an urgent wire to Secretary of War Stanton asking for the authority and appropriations to arm the one-hundred-days men. Chivington even sought permission from Stanton and Major General Halleck to divert a supply train bound for the Department of New Mexico on the excuse that the Third needed it against "Indian warriors congregated eighty miles from Fort Lyon, 3,000 strong." Major General Halleck was not taken in by this, however, and he curtly told Chivington to order supplies through regular channels.[2]

Communications from the governor to regional military headquarters and to Washington concerning the Indian threat seemed hardly to abate that autumn, even though the hostiles at times controlled the roads and cut the wires. Evans telegraphed when he could—there was a greater sense of urgency to a telegram—and, when he could not, he dispatched letters which eventually got through. Early on September 4, 1864, he wrote Stanton "praying that the Second Colorado Regiment [could] come out" to join the Third against the Indians. Explaining why the general uprising he had been predicting had not yet occurred, despite the extensive troubles, he added that the plans of a thou-

---

[1] "Sand Creek Massacre," p. 175.
[2] Evans to Stanton, September 19, 1864, Evans Letters, CSA; Chivington to Stanton, (telegram), September 19, 1864, WRR series 1, vol. 41, pt. 3, pp. 260-61; "Cheyenne Massacre," p. 68.

sand warriors to strike the Platte had been "frustrated but not set aside."[3]

In fact, the uprising had not taken place because the chiefs had bent their efforts toward bringing about peace and, although Evans refused to recognize it, peace was at hand. Left Hand and Black Kettle had gathered enough support among the other leaders and their people to force the hostiles to remain quiet while peace was negotiated. As Colley put it later, the chiefs "were unanimously opposed to war with the whites, and desired peace at almost any terms that the whites might dictate."[4] The Smoky Hill Council was held on September 10. By September 23 Indian raiding had stopped and even Chivington admitted that travelers could safely cross the plains.[5]

Peace in winter, after the many raids of the spring and summer, did not suit Evans's plans. Both Colley and Wynkoop had kept the governor informed of the chiefs' peace overtures, but he stubbornly dismissed them. On September 4, Colley had written him of One-Eye's arrival at Fort Lyon, enclosing Black Kettle's letter. He also mentioned that Southern Arapahos, Cheyennes, and two large bands of Oglala and Brulé Sioux were camped near the Bunch of Timbers, eighty to a hundred miles northeast of the fort. Evans focused on the last piece of information, the location of the Indian camps, and on September 14 he forwarded Colley's letter to Chivington with a note calling the colonel's attention to the location.[6]

It was this note from Evans that had prompted Chivington's attempt to divert the New Mexico supply train for the purpose of quickly arming the Third and taking to the field against the Indians while he still knew of their position. The note also marked the first of a series of communications that autumn by which the

[3] Evans to Stanton, September 4, 1864, Evans Letters, CSA.

[4] Testimony of Samuel Colley, January 27, 1865, WRR series 1, vol. 41, pt. 1, p. 969.

[5] Report of Major Wynkoop, January 15, 1865, WRR series 1, vol. 41, pt. 1, p. 961; Chivington to Curtis, September 13, 1864, ibid., pt. 3, p. 181; Holliday to Curtis, September 23, 1864, ibid., p. 334; Chivington to Curtis, September 23, 1864, ibid., p. 335.

[6] BIA Reports (1864), House Exec. Doc. 1, 38th Cong., 2d sess., p. 377; Evans to Chivington, September 14, 1864, Evans Letters, CSA.

governor informed the colonel of the whereabouts of the Southern Arapahos and Cheyennes.

On September 18, Wynkoop sent Evans a detailed report of the Smoky Hill Council and notified the governor that he was bringing the chiefs to Denver for a meeting which, he was certain, "would result in what it was their desire to accomplish—peace with their white brothers." Wynkoop concluded with the terse announcement, "We are starting immediately for Denver."[7]

Evans was most unhappy with this turn of events. He had no desire to meet with the chiefs and no plans to negotiate peace. In his view, Wynkoop failed to grasp the central issue of the Indian-white conflict, which was nothing less than who would occupy and control the land. By his meddling the major had placed the governor in an awkward position. There was nothing he could do, however, but await Wynkoop's arrival.

The peace delegation pulled out of Fort Lyon for the nine-day trip to Denver on September 18, shortly after Wynkoop had dispatched the letter. Accompanying the seven leaders were John Smith, his son Jack, and Dexter Colley, son of the agent and Smith's partner. An escort of eighty troops under Wynkoop and two other officers, Lieutenants Cramer and Soule, rode with them.[8]

The party reached Booneville and made camp while Wynkoop and Colley continued on to Denver to make arrangements for the council. The major wrote later that he found Denver residents "in a state of considerable excitement" over Indian affairs and sharply divided into two factions.[9] The first comprised most of the responsible persons in town, who opposed war and applauded his humane rescue of the white prisoners and his actions on behalf of peace.

The second faction, led by Evans and Chivington, and including volunteers of the Third Colorado Regiment, which was camped outside town impatient to get on with fighting Indians, condemned his actions, giving him reason to fear for his own

[7] *BIA Reports* (1864), p. 378.
[8] Wynkoop manuscript, p. 34. Other sources place the number of troops with Wynkoop at forty (see "Sand Creek Massacre," pp. 86, 213).
[9] Wynkoop manuscript, p. 34.

safety in Denver, as well as for the safety of the chiefs. It was fortunate, he said later, that his escort of troops were men who had
gone to the Smoky Hill with him and "felt equally with myself
the sacredness of the pledge I had given to the Indians and were
ready and willing to protect them and myself against all
comers."[10]

Not only were Evans and Chivington in the vanguard of the
war faction, they were, according to Wynkoop, also among those
Denver businessmen who held contracts to supply the Third.[11]
No evidence exists to support the major's accusation, but neither
is there evidence to disprove it. Certainly civilians were in a position to profit by supplying the Third, and it is very unlikely that
Evans, who had called up the regiment, saw any reason why he
should not share in those profits. He was, after all, a brilliant
businessman, who had built a fortune by searching out and taking advantage of profitable ventures. In Illinois, for example, he
had established a supply center on the Missouri River to outfit the
hordes of goldseekers decamping for the plains.[12] Although not
as successful as his ventures into land and railroad development,
it demonstrated Evans's readiness to make bold investments.

Wynkoop's inference (that the governor opposed peace in
order to profit from outfitting the Third) accuses Evans of a short-
sightedness of which he was never guilty, however. Any profit ac-
cruing to Evans from the regiment was insignificant in comparison to the fortune Evans knew could be amassed from land
development and railroad construction if the Indians were
removed from the plains—by war if necessary. Yet, while focus-
ing on the future, the governor was not adverse to dabbling in
smaller business ventures as they presented themselves, including supplying the Third.

If Evans held supply contracts, probably Chivington did too. It
would not have been unlike the businessman-governor to steer
the colonel toward a profitable investment. The official duties of
the two territorial leaders kept them in close contact, if not in
daily communication, during this period. In addition, they were
both active members of the Methodist-Episcopal church and

[10] Ibid.
[11] Ibid.
[12] Edgar McMechen, *The Life of Governor Evans*, p. 84.

served on the board of trustees for Colorado Seminary, predeces-
sor of the University of Denver, which they both had helped
found in July of 1863.[13] But despite their many-faceted association, Evans and Chivington were probably not personal friends.
The fifty-year-old governor had eclipsed the frontier–farming
culture that both men shared. Chivington had not.[14]

Evans had been a physician, railroad builder, land developer
and university founder before he came to Colorado. He was a
man of wealth and national prominence—an acquaintance of the
nation's leaders, including Lincoln. Although he remained an
ambitious man, he had already achieved much that Chivington
still coveted from the world.[15]

The colonel, seven years younger, was semi-literate, having
had, at most, one or two years of formal education. He had
worked his way through a home study course to become an itinerant Methodist preacher, a career that had taken him to rough outposts along the Missouri River and, finally, to Colorado Territory.
He had reached his lofty position in the territory only because the
Civil War had called all trained officers into the Union Army,
leaving a gap on the frontier. Chivington, a man with no military
training, could not have otherwise risen to the post of commander of the District of Colorado.

Once there, however, he found himself sharing the political
power in the territory with the governor, a man he admired and
sought to emulate. Through association with Evans, Chivington's stature increased, both in the eyes of other townspeople and
in his own. The more the governor relied upon the colonel's
military force in his struggle against the Indians, the more prestige accrued to the ambitious Chivington. He failed to see, however, that the governor, a far-sighted man, was manipulating

[13] Ibid., p. 105; Evans is frequently credited with founding the University
of Denver. That Chivington was also an original founder has been relegated to
historical obscurity.

[14] In an interview with Hubert Howe Bancroft in 1884, Mrs. John Evans
strongly disassociated her husband from Chivington (Bancroft, ''Colorado
Notes,'' Western History Division, University of Colorado Library, Boulder,
Colo.).

[15] See McMechen, *Life of Governor Evans*, and Reginald S. Craig, *The
Fighting Parson*.

him for his own purposes. Those purposes were not to be thwarted by Major Wynkoop. When Wynkoop reached Governor Evans's brick home on Fourteenth Street, between Lawrence and Larimer, he was told that the governor was sick in bed and could not possibly see him or the chiefs.

The major was not to be deterred, however. He and Colley put up at a hotel, and the following day he sent Colley back to the governor's house with a message that went something to the effect that both he and the chiefs would stay in Denver until the governor met with them. Colley promptly returned to the hotel with Evans.

The governor told Wynkoop bluntly that he was sorry he had brought the chiefs, that they were in the hands of the military and he wanted nothing to do with them, and that it was not his policy to make peace until they had been properly punished. For the government to make peace at this juncture, he stated, would be to "acknowledge ourselves whipped."[16] Wynkoop countered that it would be a strange state of affairs if the United States were to consider itself whipped by a few Indians.

A heated argument ensued in which Wynkoop told Evans that he had given his word, as a United States officer, to bring the chiefs to Denver for an interview with the governor, that on the strength of that word, these chiefs had traveled four hundred miles from their villages, and that he meant to see that it was honored. He also forcefully reminded Evans of his responsibilities as ex-officio superintendent of Indian affairs in the territory.[17]

According to Wynkoop, Evans replied that the Third had been raised and was in camp ready for action. Wynkoop later recounted Evans's comments:

He further said, that the regiment was ordered to be raised upon his representation to Washington that they were necessary for the protection of the Territory, and to fight hostile Indians; and now, if he made peace with the Indians, it would be supposed at Washington that he had misrepresented matters in regard to the Indian difficulties in Colorado and had put the government to a useless expense.

[16] "Chivington Massacre," p. 77; "Sand Creek Massacre," p. 90.
[17] "Chivington Massacre," p. 77.

Several times, according to Wynkoop, Evans repeated, "What shall I do with the Third Regiment, if I make peace?"[18]

Wynkoop stubbornly insisted that Evans meet with the chiefs, however, and finally the governor backed down, instructing him to bring the chiefs to Camp Weld the following day, Wednesday, September 28.

Hearing that Indian chiefs were approaching town, Denver's citizens turned out in a cavalcade of carriages at Sixteenth and Lawrence streets, hoping to catch sight of them. When the two wagons that carried the chiefs, cramped and crowded on the hard seats, rolled down Lawrence Street, these carriages pulled in behind them, forming an impressive parade through Denver. Later Black Kettle said that he had "great apprehensions" about their safety at this moment, but that he had relied on Wynkoop's good faith to see them through and conduct them back to their people.[19]

The council opened at Camp Weld, the clump of low buildings that Governor Gilpin had ordered constructed on the southwest edge of town. In addition to Chivington, Evans had brought along Colonel Shoup, the Third's commander, and Simeon Whitely, who was asked to keep a record of the meeting because, the governor said, "upon the results of this council very likely depended a continuance of the Indian war on the plains."[20]

Evans began by asking the chiefs what they wanted to say. Black Kettle answered that they had come in response to the governor's cicular of June 27. He had accepted the proclamation, he said, as soon as William Bent had brought it, but it had taken some time to get his people together for a council and to get a message to Major Wynkoop. When Wynkoop responded by coming to the Smoky Hill, the chiefs had returned four white prisoners, and they intended to return others as soon as they could locate them.[21]

Having provided the governor with the background that he felt was necessary, Black Kettle launched into the real purpose of the council, the Indians' desire for peace. "We have come with

[18] Ibid.; "Sand Creek Massacre," p. 90.
[19] "Sand Creek Massacre," p. 40.
[20] Ibid., p. 213.
[21] Ibid., p. 114.

eyes shut," he said, "following his [Wynkoop's] handful of men, like coming through the fire. All we ask is that we may have peace with the whites. We want to hold you by the hand. You are our father." [22]

Motioning toward Chivington and Shoup, the chief continued: "I want you to give all these chiefs of the soldiers here to understand that we are for peace, and that we have made peace, that we may not be mistaken by them for enemies." Then, he added, "I have come to talk plain with you. We must live near the buffalo or starve."

In Black Kettle's view, the act of coming to Denver and informing Evans that the tribes desired peace—that they needed peace in order to provide for their people—was enough to bring it about. It seemed a simple thing, a matter of agreement among reasonable men. "When I go home," he continued, "and tell my people that I have taken your hand, and the hands of all the chiefs here in Denver, they will feel well, and so will all the different tribes of Indians on the plains, after we have eaten and drunk with them."

The Cheyenne chief had not reckoned on the subtle twists of the white man's logic, however. Evans replied that he was sorry Black Kettle had not responded immediately to his circular. Then he went on the attack: "You have gone into an alliance with the Sioux, who are at war with us. You have done a great deal of damage, have stolen stock, and now have possession of it." However much a few might want peace, Evans stated, "as a nation you have gone to war."

The governor spoke petulantly about his efforts to make the Arkansas River reservation habitable, saying that while the government had spent "thousands of dollars in making farms for [them], and making preparations to feed, protect and make [them] comfortable," the Indians had been attacking whites. The governor also mentioned his trip to the fork of the Arikaree the previous fall. "I wanted to make you a feast," he told Black

---

[22] Ibid., p. 213. The following account is based on Whitely's record of the Camp Weld Council in "Sand Creek Massacre," pp. 213–17, and "Chivington Massacre," pp. 87–90.

Kettle, "but you sent word to me that you did not want to have anything to do with me."

Black Kettle acknowledged this was true. According to Lieutenant Soule, the chief tried to describe the outrages whites committed against the Indians, and to explain the extreme circumstances of his people that fall—an explanation that was unnecessary since Evans knew of the tribes' severe hardships—but the governor interrupted, saying, "I was under the necessity after all my trouble, all the expense I was at, of returning home without seeing [the chiefs]."[23] Meanwhile, he continued, "your people went away and smoked the war pipe with our enemies." Black Kettle answered, "I don't know who could have told you this."

The source, of course, was Robert North. Had Evans named his informant, the chiefs would have known how to defend the accusation. North had not been in their camps at the time he claimed to be and therefore could not have witnessed a tribal war council. Such a disclaimer would not have swayed the governor, however. "No matter who said this," he persisted, "your conduct has proved to my satisfaction that was the case."

All the chiefs spoke at once. "This is a mistake," they said, "we have made no alliance with the Sioux or anyone else." Evans countered by saying that their conduct had seemed to show an understanding with other tribes. The chiefs acknowledged that the Indians' actions could have given the governor reason to believe this.

That acknowledgement, in Evans's view, constituted proof that the alliance existed. He told the chiefs he was in no position to make a peace treaty because, he said,

War is begun, and the power to make a treaty of peace has passed from me to the great War Chief. The time when you can make war best is in the summer time. When I can make war best, is in the winter. You, so far, have had the advantage; my time is just coming.

The governor concluded by saying, "My proposition to the friendly Indians has gone out; I shall be glad to have them all

[23] "Sand Creek Massacre," p. 27.

come in under it. I have no new propositions to make." He could not offer peace, Evans said, only advice: the chiefs "should turn to the side of the government." When one of the chiefs asked what that meant, the governor explained that they should make some arrangement with the soldiers to help them fight the Indians who were still hostile.

Black Kettle saw in this suggestion the means of keeping his warriors busy, just as Left Hand had hoped to do by recovering the Fort Larned stock. The Cheyenne chief told Evans that he would take this message to his young men and that he believed they would agree to it. Once again Evans advised the chiefs to place themselves under the military. "If the Indians [do] not keep with the soldiers, or have an arrangement with them, they [will] be all treated as enemies."

Although his words were taken down by Whitely, Evans later claimed he had never made this suggestion, maintaining that he had only ascertained the chiefs' views at the council and "had not offered them anything whatever."[24] White Antelope, who had been sitting quietly through the council, finally took the floor. "What do you mean by us fighting your enemies," he asked Evans. "Who are they?"

"All Indians who are fighting us," replied the governor.

"How can we be protected from the soldiers on the plains?" the chief persisted, referring to Curtis, who had made a two-week sweep of the plains beginning September 3. Although the general's troops had had two minor skirmishes with warriors and had ranged close to the Cheyenne camps on the Smoky Hill, no major battles had been fought.[25] Evans's response to White Antelope was clear. "You must make that arrangement with the military chief."

"I fear that these new soldiers who have gone out, may kill some of my people while I am here," White Antelope persisted. To that, Evans replied: "There is great danger of it."

Later, Lieutenant Soule said that time and again the chiefs tried to tell of the outrages committed by whites against their

[24] Evans to Colley, September 29, 1864, Evans Letters, CSA.
[25] Curtis to Chivington, September 2, 1864, *WRR* series 1, vol. 41, pt. 3, p. 37.

people, but they were led away from the subject by the governor's questions.[26]

At this point Evans began interrogating the chiefs on the nature of the Indian alliance that he was convinced existed. White Antelope's statement that thirteen bands of Sioux had crossed the Platte into Arapaho and Cheyenne country and were in alliance with the Kiowas, Comanches, and Apaches against whites confirmed the governor's fears. In rapid-fire succession, he asked who had committed depredations, who had stolen cattle, horses, and mules, and who had raided ranches. The chiefs answered truthfully when they could, naming Whirlwind, Powder Face, and Little Raven's son as the Southern Arapaho raiders.

The chiefs did not know who had killed the Hungate family, however. After some discussion Neva suggested that Medicine Man, chief of the Northern Arapahos, may have been guilty, but Whitely, who knew that Medicine Man had been elsewhere at the time, said that this could not be true. In fact, the murders had been committed by an outlaw band of Northern Arapahos led by John Notee.

When Evans asked who had taken stock from Frémont's Orchard, near the South Platte, White Antelope halted the barrage of questions. "Before I answer," he said, "I would like for you to know that this was the beginning of war, and I should like to know what it was for, a soldier fired first."

He then gave the same version of this incident that Black Kettle had earlier given Wynkoop. The Cheyennes were trying to return lost stock to Gerry's ranch when soldiers approached and opened fire. One of the warriors was so gravely wounded that he would never recover, White Antelope said.

At this point, Neva broke in to say he saw no reason to call up past hostilities. "I came here to seek peace and nothing else," he said, adding that "Comanches, Kiowas, and Sioux have done much more than we have." Neva also mentioned the growing dependence of his people upon the whites. "I know the value of the presents which we receive from Washington. We cannot live

[26] "Sand Creek Massacre," p. 27.

without them," he said, reiterating the Southern Arapahos desire for peace.

Despite Neva's attempt to put the council back on the main issue, Evans returned to the subject of war. "What are the Sioux going to do next?" he asked.

Bull Bear replied honestly that they wanted to clear out "all this country. They are angry and will do all the damage to whites they can." Also seeing the possibility of keeping his men occupied, the Dog Soldiers' leader offered to help troops fight the Indians "who have no ears to listen to what you say."

Evans ignored the offer and went after the information he considered critical—the location of hostile camps. "Where are the Sioux?" he wanted to know. Bull Bear replied, "Down the Republican, where it opens out." Satisfied, Evans turned to Chivington and asked if he had anything to say.

The colonel pulled himself up to his full six feet, four and a half inches and, looking down upon the chiefs sitting on the floor, began, "I am not a big war chief" (a statement which must have taken them by surprise), "but all the soldiers in this country are at my command. My rule of fighting white men or Indians is to fight them until they lay down their arms and submit to military authority. They are nearer major Wynkoop than any one else, and they can go to him when they get ready to do that."

The statement could not have been clearer. If the Indians were to lay down their arms and go to Major Wynkoop at Fort Lyon, Chivington would no longer fight them.

At no point in the council was the punishment of hostiles mentioned, yet Evans, Chivington, and Curtis stood united in the determination that warriors should pay for outlaw activities before peace could be concluded. It was not enough for them to lay down their arms and come into the forts, as the governor and colonel deliberately led the chiefs to believe.

Evans made clear his determination to punish the Indians in a report to Commissioner Dole, dated October 15: "Troops are necessary," he wrote, "to pursue [the Indians] to their hiding places and to punish and intimidate them, for this is the only means of procuring safety from their depredations, inaugurating

²⁷ *BIA Reports* (1864), pp. 365-66.

a permanent peace, commanding their regard for authority. . . . Such punishment," Evans concluded in a curious twist of logic, was the only way of "securing their enduring friendship."[27]

In the same report, Evans wrote that "hostilities must be punished to prevent their recurrence, and such an alliance as now exists, extending from Texas to the British line, must be broken up by punishment to secure a peace which would be worth the name."

Curtis was of the same opinion. On the day of the Camp Weld Council, in fact, he had wired Chivington: "I shall require the bad Indians delivered up; restoration of equal numbers of stock; also hostages to secure. I want no peace until the Indians suffer more."

In a letter to the colonel that followed this wire, he wrote: "I fear the agent of the Interior Department [Colley] will be ready to make presents too soon. It is better to chastise before giving anything but a little tobacco to talk over. No peace must be made without my directions."[28] At the time Curtis issued this directive, neither Evans nor Chivington had fully informed him of the chiefs' peace efforts. Had Curtis known that the Camp Weld Council was taking place, the directive might have been different.

As it was, Evans and Chivington could later claim they had followed the general's directive since no peace was concluded at Camp Weld. The council ended in genial, deliberate misrepresentation. Evans, conceding later that the chiefs had been "earnest in their desire for peace," told them to "make immediate application to the military authorities for, and to accept, the terms of peace they might be able to obtain." With this, he "left them in the hands of Major Wynkoop." The chiefs, believing they had been directed to bring their people into Fort Lyon, shook hands with the white officials, "perfectly contented, deeming that the matter was settled." Black Kettle even embraced the governor, saying his heart was glad he had come to Denver.[29]

[28] Ibid., p. 365.
[29] Ibid., p. 364; "Sand Creek Massacre," pp. 116–17; Testimony of John Smith, January 15, 1865, WRR series 1, vol. 41, pt. 1, p. 967.

The chiefs then piled into the wagons for the long, jolting journey to Fort Lyon, but Wynkoop remained in Denver several days to assure citizens that the Indians had ceased raiding and that farmers and ranchers could safely return to their homes and harvest their crops.[30]

Evans and Chivington, having led the Indian peace delegation to believe peace was within reach, turned their efforts toward a winter campaign. In a report to Dole, written two weeks after the council, the governor spelled out his plans:

> This winter, when the Indians are unable to subsist except in the buffalo range, is the most favorable time for their chastisement, and it is hoped that a presentation of the urgent necessity of the case to the War Department will secure the immediate organization of such military expeditions against them as to bring them to terms.[31]

Unaware of the governor's plans, Wynkoop said later that before leaving Denver he had informed both Evans and Chivington that he would have the chiefs bring their people to Fort Lyon "until such time as some action was taken by the proper authorities in relation to their proposition for peace."[32]

Thus it happened that Major Wynkoop, while trying to help the Southern Arapahos and Cheyennes obtain the peace they longed for, had pinpointed the winter location of their villages for the military leaders, and unwittingly had cast the net in which the Indians would be caught.

[30] Wynkoop manuscript, p. 36.
[31] *BIA Reports* (1864), p. 366.
[32] "Sand Creek Massacre," p. 96.

The place where crying begins,
The Thi aya
The Thi aya
When I see the Thi aya
I begin to lament.

17

Southern Arapaho song

While the Southern Arapahos and Cheyennes awaited the result of the Camp Weld Council, all was quiet on the plains. Even hostile Dog Soldiers and Sioux warriors remained in their camps on the Solomon River, giving white settlements and wagon trains a respite from fear.

Sometime before the chiefs returned from Denver, some Southern Arapaho and Cheyenne villages on the Smoky Hill began moving southward toward Fort Lyon. A scout brought word that Pawnees were hunting buffalo nearby, and a large party of warriors left the villages and moved down Hackberry Creek in pursuit of the enemy tribe. According to George Bent, one of the warriors, the group included Southern Arapahos from the bands led by Little Raven, Storm, and Spotted Wolf and Cheyennes under Black Kettle, White Antelope, and War Bonnet.[1]

As the warriors searched for Pawnees, cavalry troops from Fort Larned, under Maj. Gen. James G. Blunt, happened into the area. Blunt had taken to the field under orders from Curtis to continue his search for hostile Indians. "Before any peace can be granted the villains who have committed the crimes must be given up, and full indemnity in horses, ponies, and property must be granted as the Indians can indemnify," Curtis wrote. "Something really damaging to them must be felt by them."[2]

On the morning of September 25, a cavalry detachment under Maj. Scott Anthony, another veteran of La Glorieta Pass, overtook and opened fire on a scouting party of warriors who were

[1] George Hyde, *The Life of George Bent,* p. 143.
[2] Curtis to Blunt, September 22, 1864, *WRR* series 1, vol. 41, pt. 3, pp. 314–15.

looking for Pawnees. The Indians retreated to their camp with Anthony in hot pursuit, unaware that he was riding into a large enemy force. It was not until the bluffs swarmed with warriors encircling his detachment that the major grasped his mistake.

Fortunately, Blunt's larger force appeared in the distance at that moment and began firing, giving Anthony's beleaguered men the chance to break out of the entrapment. A fierce running battle ensued, with the outnumbered warriors attempting to outrun Blunt's troops. In time the soldiers' horses tired and Blunt was forced to give up pursuit, but not before nine warriors and two soldiers had been killed and seven soldiers had been wounded.[3]

When the warriors returned to the main villages, ten miles north of the battle area, chaos broke out. Women began hastily breaking down the lodges to move back to the Smoky Hill out of the way of the soldiers. So great was the confusion, George Bent said later, "they hardly knew which way to turn next."

Bent does not name Left Hand's band as being with the villages at this time. Left Hand probably had left the Smoky Hill earlier and headed for Fort Lyon, eager to be on hand when the peace delegation returned from Denver, and therefore had missed the skirmish with Blunt's troops. On September 28, Agent Colley wrote Evans that Southern Arapahos and Cheyennes were straggling into the post daily; Left Hand was probably among them.[4] Evans received Colley's letter on October 8. Conceiving of it as the latest news on the whereabouts of the Indians, he immediately forwarded it to Chivington.[5]

Evans then issued a directive to Colley, ordering him to withhold annuities and rations from the tribes, even though the June

---

[3] Sources differ on the number of fatalities. George Bent gave the number presented here, which is probably correct (Bent to Hyde, January 29, 1913, William Robertson Coe Collection, Yale University Library, New Haven, Conn.). See Hyde, *Life of George Bent,* pp. 144–45 (claims one dead warrior), and Blunt to Charlot, September 29, 1864, *WRR* series 1, vol. 41, pt. 1, p. 818 (Blunt claims there were a great many killed, but that the Indians carried off their dead).

[4] Hyde, *Life of George Bent,* p. 146; Colley to Evans, September 28, 1864, Evans Letters, CSA.

[5] Evans to Chivington, October 8, 1864, Evans Letters, CSA.

27 proclamation had promised that all peaceful Indians coming into the fort would receive provisions. Evans placed the burden on Colley for clearing up any misunderstandings from the Camp Weld Council.

Chiefs have been here and I have declined to make any treaty with them, lest it might embarrass the military operations against the hostile Indians of the plains. Arapahos and Cheyennes being now at war with the United States government must make peace with the military authorities. This arrangement relieves the Indian bureau of their care until peace is declared. . . . You will be particular to impress upon these chiefs the fact that my talk with them was for the purpose of ascertaining their views, and not to offer them anything whatever. They must deal with the military authorities until peace, in which case alone will they be in proper position to treat with the government in relations to the future.[6]

As far as Evans was concerned, the main result of the Camp Weld Council had been the intelligence he had gathered about the various tribes. Immediately following the council, he wired Secretary of War Stanton that he had definite information that the Sioux planned to strike the Platte. "We must have a strong force," he reiterated. No mention was made of the chiefs' anxious pleas for peace.[7]

At the same time, Evans notified Commissioner of Indian Affairs Dole of the stand he had taken at Camp Weld and of his decision to withhold annuities. Dole replied with blunt criticism of the governor's actions:

It is your duty to hold yourself in readiness to encourage and receive the first intimations of a desire on the part of the Indians for a permanent peace and amity. . . . I cannot help believing that very much of the difficulty on the plains might have been avoided, if a spirit of conciliation had been exercised by the military and others.[8]

[6] Evans to Colley, September 29, 1864, Evans Letters, CSA.
[7] Evans to Stanton, September 28, 1864, Evans Letters, CSA.
[8] Dole to Evans, October 15, 1864, in *BIA Reports* (1864), House Exec. Doc. 1, 38th Cong., 2d sess., p. 256.

Wynkoop, in the meantime, was acting on the advice that he believed had been given at Camp Weld in that very spirit of conciliation. As soon as he returned to Fort Lyon he sent John Smith to tell the chiefs, who were waiting nearby, to bring their families to the vicinity of the post, ''that he prefered to have them under his eye and away from other quarters, where they were likely to get into difficulties with the whites,'' Smith said later.[9]

According to Colley, Wynkoop also told the chiefs that he would dispatch a messenger to Curtis, informing the general of their desire for peace. He promised to let them know Curtis's reply and said that ''until that time, if they placed themselves under. . .protection, they should not be molested.''[10]

Officers at the fort later confirmed Wynkoop's orders to the chiefs and his assurances of safety. Lieutenant Soule said he heard Wynkoop tell them ''that, in case he got word from Curtis not to make peace with them, that he would let them know, so that they could remove out of the way and get to their tribe; then he should fight them if he had orders to, or words to that effect.''[11]

According to John Smith, the chiefs replied that they would do anything the Tall Chief (the name they had given Wynkoop), might choose to dictate, since they had ''perfect confidence'' in him.[12]

Following Wynkoop's orders, the chiefs set out for the Smoky Hill to collect their bands at about the same time the major's adjutant, Lt. W. W. Denison, left for Department Headquarters at Fort Leavenworth, a journey requiring about two weeks. Denison carried a full report for General Curtis on both the Smoky Hill and Camp Weld councils, as well as the message that the Southern Arapahos and Cheyennes were willing to cooperate with the military in every way, including fighting hostile Kiowas and Comanches. Black Kettle had also agreed to report any move-

---

[9] Testimony of John Smith, January 15, 1865, *WRR* series 1, vol. 41, pt. 1, p. 976.

[10] Ibid., p. 969.

[11] ''Sand Creek Massacre,'' p. 28.

[12] Testimony of John Smith, January 15, 1865, *WRR* series 1, vol. 41, pt. 1, p. 967.

[13] ''Sand Creek Massacre,'' p. 121.

ments of hostile Sioux, and One-Eye had already left for the Sioux camps to gather information on their plans.[13]

When Left Hand and Black Kettle reached the Smoky Hill, they found the villages still smarting from Blunt's attack on the warriors and ripe with opposition to placing any trust in whites or moving close to a military post. Less than half of the Southern Arapahos, in fact, indicated a willingness to follow Left Hand to the Arkansas River.

Among those who were willing was Little Raven. Although the principal Southern Arapaho chief remained wary of white motives, Blunt's attack had increased his fear that the Smoky Hill camps would eventually be hit by troops from Fort Larned. It had also become more difficult for the hunting parties—always in danger from scouting troops—to supply enough food for the large camps, and hunger continued to be a part of daily life. Although Little Raven disliked moving his band close to troops, he had reluctantly concluded that his people at least would receive the provisions and annuities they desperately needed.

About October 18, Left Hand, Little Raven, Neva, Storm, and No-Ta-Nee brought 652 Southern Arapahos to a campsite across the Arkansas River about two miles east of Fort Lyon. Colley and several officers at the fort who watched the Indians coming in said later that they were destitute.[14]

Although Evans had directed that no annuities or rations be issued to the tribes, and Curtis had issued a similar order to Chivington, Wynkoop believed himself honor-bound to feed the Indians who had come to the vicinity of the fort at his request. He began issuing rations daily from the post commissary and allowed the Southern Arapahos to come into the fort itself to trade robes for food and other necessary items. Colley, however, adhered to Evans' instructions, refusing to issue any part of the annuities, even though they legally belonged to the tribes.[15]

A kind of calmness settled over Fort Lyon during the last days of October, 1864. Wynkoop and the Southern Arapahos waited for Lieutenant Denison to deliver the report and return with

[14] Ibid., pp. 101–17.
[15] Ibid; "Report of Major Anthony," November 6, 1864, *WRR* series 1, vol 41, pt. 1, p. 912; "Cheyenne Massacre," p. 7; "Sand Creek Massacre," p. 124; "Chivington Massacre," pp. 35–36.

orders from Curtis regarding a peace treaty. Both the major and the chiefs were now convinced that peace had already returned to the plains and that a treaty would be only a formality. On November 5, however, a set of orders arrived at Fort Lyon that Wynkoop had not been expecting. Maj. Scott Anthony rode into the post on that date with Special Orders from District Headquarters, dated October 17, 1864, and signed by "A. Hellwick, AAA General," one of Curtis's aides, relieving Wynkoop of command and assigning Anthony to replace him. Wynkoop was also ordered to Fort Leavenworth to explain his dealings with the Indians, and from there he was to proceed to a new post, Fort Riley.

Leaving no doubt of the reason for Wynkoop's dismissal, the orders authorized Anthony "to investigate and report upon the unofficial rumors that certain officers have issued goods, stores and supplies to hostile Indians in direct violations of orders from General Commanding the Department."[16]

One of the continuing mysteries of this period is the question of who was responsible for the rumors that resulted in Wynkoop's dismissal just when a formal peace treaty was within reach. Not a few historians, including George Bird Grinnell, have blamed Chivington. Certainly Chivington and Evans made no effort to conceal their contempt for the humane treatment Wynkoop had given the Indians who, in their view, were enemies marked for punishment. Evans's letters to Dole, Colley, and Stanton that autumn leave no doubt of his intentions to bring the tribes to heel by military force, intentions Chivington whole-heartedly supported. According to U.S. Attorney Browne, Chivington's attitude toward the Indians was widely known in the territory at this time. Earlier in the summer he had made a public speech in which he stated that his policy was "to kill and scalp all Indians, little and big. . .nits make lice."[17]

Although no direct evidence links Chivington to the rumors that led to Wynkoop's dismissal, it is very likely that sometime in

[16] "Special Orders," Hellwick to Wynkoop, October 17, 1864, in Scott J. Anthony Letters, Colorado Historical Society, Denver, Colo.; "Cheyenne Massacre," p. 70

[17] George B. Grinnell, *Fighting Cheyennes*, p. 161; "Chivington Massacre," p. 71.

September, when the chiefs' peace overtures threatened to disrupt his military plans, Chivington complained to Curtis about Wynkoop's meddling, either by letter or through a personal messenger. It is curious that when Anthony arrived at Fort Lyon he made nearly the same comment on affairs at the post that the colonel would make later. Anthony said that it was believed at headquarters that "the Indians were running things at Fort Lyon." Chivington later made the statement that "Left Hand was in command" at the fort. The similarity of these remarks strongly suggests that one was the source of the other.[18]

Wynkoop blamed himself for his dismissal, however, saying later that he should have taken the chiefs to Fort Riley to confer with the military authorities rather than to Denver for a meeting with Evans.[19] In this, Wynkoop accepted the judgment of Curtis, Evans, and Chivington, that only the military commander had authority to deal with the tribes, a judgment disputed by Commissioner Dole. Dole's reprimand to Evans indicates that the governor had both the authority and the responsibility to work with the military in negotiating peace. Evans could have influenced a peace treaty if he had desired to do so.

Settling into his new command, Anthony was horrified to find the Southern Arapahos wandering about the fort receiving rations and trading robes. He immediately arranged a meeting with the chiefs and issued orders to the guards to arrest all Indians coming within the post until, as he put it, "I . . . learn something more about them."[20]

Taking several troops, Anthony and Wynkoop rode along the Arkansas River to a point halfway between the fort and the Indian camp where Left Hand and Little Raven had agreed to meet them. Anthony demanded "by what authority and for what pur-

---

[18] "Sand Creek Massacre" pp. 116, 122. Chivington and Evans, having laid plans for an attack, were motivated to have Wynkoop removed from Fort Lyon. There is no evidence to suggest that, without their influence, Curtis had any reason to remove Wynkoop. Wynkoop himself said that rumors reaching headquarters caused his dismissal. See Wynkoop to Tappan, January 15, 1865, *WRR* series 1, vol. 41, pt. 1, p. 959-62.

[19] "Sand Creek Massacre," p. 123.

[20] Anthony to Curtis, November 6, 1864, *WRR* series 1, vol. 41, pt. 1, p. 912.

pose'' the Indians were encamped there. According to Anthony's letter to General Curtis of November 6, 1864, the chiefs replied that they had brought in their people for several reasons: ''to show that they desired peace... to be where the traveling public would not be frightened by them, or the Indians be harmed by travelers or soldiers on the road.''[21]

Once again, Left Hand took the opportunity to assure white leaders that his people had always been friendly and still desired nothing but peace. The Southern Arapahos, he said, would not join a war against whites, and nothing could compel them to do so. Nevertheless, Anthony informed the chiefs, he could not permit armed Indians to remain in the vicinity or come into the post except as prisoners of war. He had orders to keep them away, he said, and could not issue rations.[22] This confused the chiefs. They had been told to come into the post, and now this new commander wanted them to stay away. When they asked what they should do, Anthony replied that they would have to give up all arms and stolen stock in their possession. The chiefs readily agreed.

That matter settled, Anthony, Wynkoop, and the guard followed Left Hand and Little Raven across the Arkansas to their camp. Before ordering his warriors to turn over their arms, however, Left Hand asked Anthony if his ''boys,'' as he called them, could keep their bows and arrows to shoot dogs and jackrabbits for food, saying ''it would be a great help because of the destitute situation.'' Anthony denied the request. Signaling his men to lay their arms in a pile, Left Hand turned to Wynkoop and said he would submit to this because his people had to have peace. The whites could imprison him, he said, or kill him, but he would not fight.[23]

When the arms had been collected, Anthony counted three rifles, one pistol, and sixty bows with quivers. A soldier, ordered to scout the Indian herd, found ten mules and four horses belonging to whites. Later, Anthony reported to Curtis that ''these

[21] Ibid.
[22] ''Sand Creek Massacre,'' pp. 122–23.
[23] ''Cheyenne Massacre,'' p. 77; ''Sand Creek Massacre,'' p. 87.

arms are in very poor condition and but few, with little ammunition. Their horses far below the average grade of Indians' horses. In fact these [Southern Arapahos] that are here could make but a feeble fight if they desired war."[24]

Anthony also probably ordered the chiefs to turn over any warriors who had taken part in raids, since he had written Curtis that he would demand the "perpetrators of depredations." If he did make this demand, the chiefs refused to comply, although Little Raven's son and the other Southern Arapahos who attacked the Snyder wagon were in camp; in fact, some of the mules taken in that attack were among those confiscated by Anthony.[25]

Left Hand had made it no secret that a few hostiles had joined the camp, and had agreed to abide by his and Little Raven's regulations. One of the soldiers at Fort Lyon said later that he had spoken with Left Hand before Anthony's arrival at the post: "I pointed out two or three Indians that stood on the parade ground and asked him if those were the ones that killed the soldier and blacksmith beyond Spring Bottom." Left Hand had replied, "They are the Indians."[26]

That these guilty Indians were in camp suggests a rift in Left Hand and Little Raven's long relationship. While Left Hand was trying to comply with Wynkoop's instructions and with those given at Camp Weld, hoping for a peace agreement, Little Raven was harboring hostiles, no doubt because one of them was his son. Neither chief would turn them over to the military, but their presence in camp was a source of concern to Left Hand. It would have been better for the innocent men, women, and children in camp if the guilty warriors had stayed in the hostile camps on the Solomon.

Anthony told the chiefs they could remain camped near the fort and consider themselves prisoners until he had heard from General Curtis. He also promised them, as Wynkoop had done, that he would let them know when Curtis's orders arrived. Having taken their arms, the new commander now found that he had

[24] Report of Major Anthony, November 6, 1864, *WRR* series 1, vol. 41, pt. 1, p. 913.
[25] "Sand Creek Massacre," p. 225–26.
[26] Ibid., p. 225.

no choice but to continue Wynkoop's policies and issue rations, despite orders to the contrary.[27]

On the following day, November 6, a delegation of nine Cheyennes, led by Black Kettle, approached Fort Lyon and requested permission to speak with the commander. According to some of the officers, Left Hand was with them. Black Kettle probably had stopped at the Southern Arapaho camp to ask the English-speaking chief to accompany the Cheyennes to the fort.[28]

Anthony agreed to meet with the delegation in the commissary, the low, flat-stone building, originally part of Bent's New Fort, that was located one mile from the post. When the meeting got under way, Black Kettle informed Anthony that six hundred Cheyennes were camped at Sand Creek, forty miles northeast of Fort Lyon, ready to move into the post. Another two hundred, still in the Smoky Hill camps, had agreed to move south and were waiting for better weather. The chiefs had complied with instructions to bring their people, he said, and now they were eager to surrender them to the safety of the fort.[29]

Alarmed, Anthony said that he could not permit the Indians to approach Fort Lyon, that he was under orders not to issue rations, and that, in any case, he could not provide for such large numbers. He told Black Kettle to keep them at Sand Creek "until the pleasure of the commanding officer of the district could be learned."

Black Kettle saw the understanding he believed had been reached at Camp Weld collapsing about him. He angrily accused Anthony of not following the previous agreement to allow the Indians to surrender at the fort. On their part, the Indians had now left the relative safety of the large Smoky Hill camps for the gameless area of Sand Creek, where they were in danger of meeting troops from Larned or Denver. Black Kettle warned Anthony that if troopers should molest any of his people he would not be able to restrain his warriors. Provisions were low, he said; they could not wait at Sand Creek long. Anthony assured Black Kettle

[27] "Report of Major Anthony," November 6, 1864, *WRR* series 1, vol. 41, pt. 1, p. 93; "Cheyenne Massacre," pp. 17–18.
[28] "Sand Creek Massacre," p. 146.
[29] "Sand Creek Massacre," pp. 46, 105.

that they would not have to wait long. He expected to hear from Curtis by the next mail, he said, and, whether the news was good or bad, he would let the chiefs know.[30]

Wynkoop and Smith, both of whom were present at the meeting, said later that Anthony told the Cheyennes he would not depart from Wynkoop's course and that the Indians would be under the protection of Fort Lyon while they were at Sand Creek.[31]

In his report of this meeting to Curtis on November 16, 1864, Anthony affirmed that he had told the chiefs they need not worry about their safety at Sand Creek:

> They appear to want peace, and want someone authorized to make a permanent settlement of all troubles with them to meet them and agree upon terms. I told them that I was not authorized as yet to say that any permanent peace could be established, but that no war would be waged against them until your pleasure was heard . . . they cannot understand why I will not make peace with them."[32]

The reason, as Anthony went on to explain to Curtis, was simply that he had no intention of making peace, although he deliberately led the chiefs to believe otherwise:

> I have been trying to let the Indians that I have talked with think that I have no desire for trouble with them, but that I could not agree upon a permanent peace until I was authorized by you, thus keeping matters quiet for the present, and until troops enough are sent out to enforce any demand we may choose to make.

It would be an easy matter to attack the bands surrendering at the fort, Anthony continued, "but that would only lead to more Indian hostilities, travel cut off, settlements attacked." Anthony's plan was to wait until enough government troops had ar-

[30] Ibid.
[31] "Sand Creek Massacre," pp. 46, 87, 105–106, 146; "Cheyenne Massacre," pp. 17–18; Testimony of John Smith, January 15, 1864, *WRR* series 1, vol. 41, pt. 1, p. 968.
[32] Anthony to Helliwell, November 16, 1864, *WRR* series 1, vol. 41, pt. 1, p. 914.

rived to attack the main Indian camps in the vicinity of the Republican, Solomon, and Smoky Hill rivers: "My intention, however, is to let matters remain dormant until troops can be sent out to take the field against all the tribes."[33]

Black Kettle and the other Cheyenne leaders sensed Anthony's duplicity. They left Fort Lyon deeply concerned about the change in command, fearing, as John Smith said later, "that it boded them no good,"[34] Before returning to Sand Creek, they stopped at John Prowers' ranch near Big Timbers. Prowers, a trader who had come to the plains in the 1850s with Agent Robert Miller and stayed to work for William Bent, had married Amache, One-Eye's daughter. Always friendly with his wife's people, he warmly welcomed the Indian visitors, as he had often done in the past, giving them dinner and putting them up for the night. Before they left on the following morning, John Smith arrived with a message from Anthony that they should not fear returning to Sand Creek because "they would be perfectly safe."[35]

With the Cheyennes out of the way, Anthony turned his attention to the Southern Arapahos. Meeting again with Left Hand and Little Raven, he told them they could expect no more rations. This abrupt announcement was no doubt prompted by the directive of November 10 from Evans to Colley (who, as agent to the Indians, was in residence at the fort), which prohibited him from giving food to the Indians. In any case, he ordered Lieutenant Soule to return the Southern Arapaho arms and advised the chiefs to move toward the buffalo country where the warriors could hunt.[36]

Following this meeting, Anthony confided to Lieutenant Soule his real intentions. "He was for killing all Indians," Soule said later, "and was only acting friendly until he had a force large enough for the job." Anthony admitted, however, that some In-

[33] Ibid.

[34] Testimony of John Smith, January 15, 1865, *WRR* series 1, vol. 41, pt. 1, p. 968.

[35] Mary Prowers Hudnall, "Early History of Bent County," *Colorado Magazine* 22 (1945):237.

[36] Evans to Colley, November 10, 1864, Evans Letters, CSA; "Sand Creek Massacre," pp. 19, 20, 27.

dians, Black Kettle, One-Eye, White Antelope, and Left Hand, should probably be saved.[37]

These same intentions were passed on to Chivington at this time. Anthony sent the colonel a letter stating that after he got some of the few friendly Indians "out of their camp," he would, if he had one thousand men ready for the field, "kill the balance."[38]

Anthony was busy dispersing the Indians that Wynkoop had brought in to surrender while Wynkoop was preparing to leave for Fort Leavenworth. On November 25, he boarded the eastbound stage for the arduous 450-mile trip, carrying a satchel full of letters and statements from officers and civilians at the fort upholding his conduct toward the tribes. One letter in praise of his actions had been signed by every officer at the fort, including Anthony.[39]

Shortly before Wynkoop's departure, the Southern Arapaho women broke camp, preparing to move away from the vicinity of the fort as Anthony had directed. Little Raven, distrusting Anthony, decided to travel sixty-five miles down the Arkansas to a campsite out of the way, he hoped, of troops and hostiles. With him would go most of the Southern Arapahos in camp, about six hundred, including Neva.

Perhaps Left Hand planned to meet them there later. Having joined with Black Kettle in leading the peace movement, however, he chose to continue the work already begun and wait for Curtis's orders with the Cheyennes at Sand Creek. With him would go his family, numbering about fifty persons, including his wife and children; his sister MaHom and her fair-haired daughter Mary Poisal; and No-Ta-Nee, his cousin and aide.

When Left Hand's band started northward, soldiers at Fort Lyon said later, the chief was very ill.[40] He was also no doubt weary of the long struggle for peace, the white indecision and backtracking, and broken promises. With the increasing destitution of his people and the gray uncertainty of the future, he could only hope that Curtis's reply would arrive soon and that the mat-

[37] "Sand Creek Massacre," pp. 13, 25, 182.
[38] Ibid., p. 140.
[39] Ibid., pp. 93-94.
[40] Ibid., p. 117.

ter of peace would be settled. At least the wait at Sand Creek would give him time to rest and recuperate from the illness that had taken hold of him.

Left Hand and his band reached Sand Creek about the same time that One-Eye returned from the Sioux camp near the Solomon with word that two hundred hostile Sioux were ranging near the road connecting Forts Lyon and Larned. Knowing that Wynkoop was traveling on that road, Black Kettle and Left Hand immediately sent No-Ta-Nee to warn him.

When the lone Southern Arapaho overtook the stage, Wynkoop recognized Left Hand's cousin and ordered his escort to stand at ease. In sign language No-Ta-Nee told the major that the chiefs had sent the message that a large band of Sioux were in the area and that he should turn back to Lyon if he did not have a sufficient number of men to ward off an attack.

Although Wynkoop's escort consisted of only twenty-eight men, he decided to continue toward Fort Larned, eager to complete the first leg of a long journey that would bring him closer to straightening out matters with Curtis. He reached the post without seeing any hostiles, but officers there expressed surprise that he had made it through safely. They told him that a large party of Sioux were roving the nearby country.

It was then that Wynkoop understood that Left Hand and Black Kettle, the chiefs he had befriended, had repaid him for his efforts on behalf of their people by trying to protect his life.[41]

41 Ibid., p. 87; Wynkoop manuscript, p. 36.

Nothing lives long,
except the earth
and the mountains.

18

White Antelope,
Southern Cheyenne

Denver was torn apart during the summer and fall of 1864. Indian troubles, as Wynkoop had correctly noted, had split the citizens into two bitterly opposed camps, and as September opened, those camps faced each other in a showdown over the question of statehood.

The faction led by Evans and Chivington supported both a campaign against the Indians and statehood for the territory, believing that Colorado's admittance to the Union would guarantee adequate military protection and, at the same time, somehow give whites title to lands that still legally belonged to the Southern Arapahos and Cheyennes.

It would also give Colorado a stronger voice in Washington, the lack of which, in Evans's view, seemed likely to result in the Union Pacific Railway Company settling on a transcontinental route through Wyoming. The selection of a route that would bypass Colorado Territory would be a harsh blow to the governor's plan for the economic future of the area. He was eager to go to Washington as a senator, confident that once he was there he would be able to use his considerable influence among politicians and fellow businessmen to have a route through Colorado selected.[1]

The second faction opposed both an Indian campaign and statehood and accused Evans and Chivington of "getting up a war" to further their own political ambitions. To make matters worse, companies of the Third Colorado Regiment, quartered at Camp Weld and scattered at stations along the South Platte, eager to get on with the job of fighting Indians, were becoming

[1] Elmer Ellis, "Colorado's First Fight for Statehood: 1865–1868," *Colorado Magazine* 8 (1931):25–26.

restless and bored. Lacking basic military discipline, they began to make drunken forays through the streets of Denver, attacking and intimidating respectable citizens, which only increased the public's dissatisfaction with the governor and colonel.

Feelings against the two leaders became so bitter and widespread, in fact, that Evans began to fear that the question of statehood would go down in defeat out of opposition to him personally. He reluctantly decided to withdraw his bid for the Senate before the election date, September 13. Nevertheless, voters soundly defeated statehood by a margin of nearly three to one: 4,762 to 1,520. They also handed Chivington a decisive defeat in his bid for a congressional seat from the territory.[2]

The election marked a low point in the popularity of the two territorial leaders. Instead of reassessing their policies, however, they cast about for scapegoats to explain the downward plunge of their political appeal. On November 11, Evans wrote President Lincoln that statehood had been defeated because of the "discouragement caused by the Indians and the floods."[3]

Their defeat at the polls strengthened Evans and Chivington's resolve to settle Indian affairs. There would be no more attempts to get the tribes to agree to move to the reservation peacefully. Neither would there be any more Indian raids on white settlements, nor fears of an uprising such as New Ulm's, if they could help it. With the approach of winter—that time when the governor had told the chiefs he could make war best—he and Chivington laid the plains for a decisive Indian defeat.

In early October those plans were abetted by some skirmishes along the South Platte. Although the hostile warriors had remained quiet, waiting on the outcome of Left Hand and Black Kettle's peace efforts, new trouble had been caused by Chivington's troops. Capt. David H. Nichols, at Valley Station on the South Platte, had received word that an Indian in war paint had been seen lurking near a ranch. Nichols immediately ordered forty troopers into the field, he said later, to give the Indians a "little surprise party." What he did was attack two Cheyenne

² Ibid; "Chivington Massacre," p. 96
³ Evans to Lincoln, November 11, 1864, Evans Letters, CSA.

lodges, killing six men, three women, and one fifteen-year-old boy.[4]

To justify his actions, Nichols claimed that he found a white man's scalp, his clothing, and several freight bills in the lodges, and that he had accepted these as evidence that the warriors had taken part in earlier raids along the Overland Road. Chivington issued no reprimand to Nichols for killing the women and boy, however. In fact, he congratulated the captain on his bold attack, reaffirming his previous orders to "kill all the Indians you come across."[5]

Not surprisingly, Nichols's attack caused Cheyenne warriors to make retaliatory raids along the Overland. On October 14 they attacked a small detachment of cavalry west of Fort Kearny, killing two and wounding two others. Alarmed that the road could once again be closed by hostiles, the owners of the Overland Stage bombarded Curtis with pleas for troops to quiet the Indians.[6]

The army had no intention of allowing the Indians to take control of the roads again, however, and to make certain they remained open, Maj. Gen. Henry W. Halleck dispatched an order from Washington to Brig. Gen. Patrick Edward Connor in Salt Lake City to guard the Overland between Salt Lake and Fort Kearny, "without regard to department lines." The part of the road most vulnerable to Indian attack, of course, lay in Chivington's jurisdiction, where companies of the Third were wantonly attacking Indian camps. Halleck's order is a clear indication of his lack of confidence in Chivington and the volunteer troops and his desire to put a seasoned military officer in charge.

Chivington took Connor's appointment as a personal affront and a reflection on his competence, which, in fact, it was. He wired Curtis immediately: "Have department lines been changed; if not will I allow him to give direction to matters within

[4] Nichols to Chivington, October 11, 1864, *WRR* series 1, vol. 41, pt. 3, p. 798-99.

[5] Chivington to Nichols, October 14, 1864, *WRR* series 1, vol. 41, pt. 3, p. 876.

[6] Holliday to Curtis, October 1, 1864, *WRR* series 1, vol. 41, pt. 3, pp. 549-50, 758.

this district? Line perfectly protected to Julesburg, the line this side of Julesburg ought to be in this district, as my troops are taking care of it."[7]

Chivington had reason to worry about Connor's move into his jurisdiction. In January, 1863, Connor had forced his troops on a 140-mile march and launched a surprise attack at daybreak on a camp of Shoshonis and Bannocks near present-day Preston, Idaho. When the attack ended, 240 men, women, and children lay dead and General Halleck himself congratulated Connor for his "heroic conduct and brilliant victory" and promoted him to brigadier general.[8] Should Connor hand the same kind of defeat to the Plains Indians in Chivington's jurisdiction, it would stamp the colonel as a failure before his superiors and stop his own advance toward the rank of brigadier general.[8]

Evans cheered Connor's appointment heartily enough to suggest the governor's disgust that Chivington and Colorado troops had not yet settled matters with the Indians. In a congratulatory letter to Connor dated October 24, the governor wrote: "I am glad that you are coming. I have no doubt the Indians may be chastised during the winter, which they very much need. Bring all the forces you can; then pursue, kill and destroy them, until which we will have no permanent peace on the plains."[9]

Faced with the loss of Evans's support at the moment when his popularity in the territory had greatly declined, Chivington found himself desperately in need of some dramatic victory that would restore both the governor's confidence in him and his public stature as a hero. Casting about for a way to turn Connor's orders to his advantage, the colonel decided to leave the South Platte in the general's hands and march the Third to the vicinity of the Arkansas River where he knew Left Hand and Black Kettle's bands were camped. With this in mind, he denied the general's request for a loan of troops to patrol the South Platte and ordered Colonel Shoup to begin moving the Third to Bijou Basin, sixty miles southeast of Denver. To Curtis, he wrote:

[7] Raymond G. Carey, "The Puzzle of Sand Creek," *Colorado Magazine* 41 (1964):293; Chivington to Curtis, October 26, 1864, *WRR* series 1, vol. 41, pt. 4, p. 259.

[8] Carey, "Puzzle of Sand Creek," p. 293.

[9] Evans to Connor, October 24, 1864, Evans Letters, CSA.

"Having ascertained that the hostile Indians had proceeded south from the Platte and were almost in striking distance of Fort Lyon, I ordered Shoup to move south."[10]

Connor arrived in Denver November 14, welcomed by a rousing performance from the Colorado First's regimental band. That same day Chivington issued marching orders to the Third. Much later, Chivington recounted how Connor had strode over to him just as he was mounting his horse, about to ride off, and inquired about the location of Indian camps on the plains. "Colonel," he asked, "where are these Indians?" Chivington answered: "General, that is the trick that wins in this game, if the game is won. There are but two persons who know their exact location, and they are myself and Col. George L. Shoup."[11]

There was also a third person. Governor Evans had made it his business throughout the summer and fall to keep close track of Indian movements and had passed the information along to Chivington. Two days after Chivington had issued orders to the Third, Evans, confident that matters would now take their course, left Denver for an extended stay in Washington "to attend to duties as Superintendent of Indian Affairs."[12]

Toward late November, companies of the Third began rendezvousing at Spring Bottom near Booneville, five miles east of Pueblo. They had marched through bitter cold and through snow that was at times two feet deep. As they neared the Arkansas River, however, the weather became milder and the ground clear.[13]

On November 24, Chivington joined them. With him were three companies of the Colorado First from Denver, as well as Jim Beckwourth, the trader and longtime friend of the Indians, who had been hired by Colonel Shoup to act as guide.

Irving Howbert, who was with the Third, later described the

[10] Chivington to Curtis, November 29, 1864, *WRR* series 1, vol. 41, pt. 1, p. 948-50. The letter to Curtis was written on December 16, 1864.

[11] *Denver Republican*, May 18, 1890.

[12] Evans to Seward, (requesting leave to go to Washington), October 18, 1864, Evans Letters, CSA.

[13] For details of troop movement see Lynn I. Perrigo, ed., "Major Hal Sayre's Diary of the Sand Creek Campaign," *Colorado Magazine* 15 (1938) 41-57.

regiment of miners, farmers, shopkeepers, adventurers, and ruffians camped at Spring Bottom. Their army uniforms and long
blue overcoats were wrinkled and disheveled from weeks in camp
and the long march south, he said. Only a third of the men were
mounted, and those on a motley assortment of ponies and plow
horses. Their guns were outdated Austrian muzzle-loading muskets which, according to Howbert, "sent a bullet viciously, but
one could never tell where it would hit."[14] Ammunition consisted of paper cartridges, one end of which had to be bitten off
before loading. All in all, there is no doubt but that the troops
looked the part of the raw recruits and amateur soldiers that they
were.[15]

Before the troops pulled out of Spring Bottom, James M.
Combs, a Fort Lyon employee on his way to Pueblo, stopped at
the camp for the night. Chivington took advantage of the opportunity to question him closely about the situation at the fort,
wanting to know, in particular, who was in command, a surprising question unless he had anticipated Wynkoop's peremptory
removal. Combs replied, "Major Anthony," and Chivington
guffawed, making the remark similar to that made by Anthony at
Fort Lyon: "Oh, you must be mistaken; I think that Left Hand
was in command before Major Anthony came here."[16]

Combs said later that he told Chivington the Cheyennes and
Arapahos had given up their arms, had returned stolen horses
and mules, and were considered prisoners of war.[17] Only part of
this information was correct, however, Anthony had never
disarmed the Cheyennes, and he had already returned the poor
assortment of arms to the Southern Arapahos. Combs also told
the colonel that Anthony had allowed the warriors to go hunting,
but not all had gone. Chief Left Hand, he said, was very sick, and
most of his party had stayed with him.

To this, Chivington remarked that he "would give them a very
lively buffalo hunt." The other officers made similar remarks.
"It was a general conversation with all present," Combs said. "I

[14] Irving Howbert, *Memories of a Lifetime in the Pike's Peak Region*, pp.
118–20.
[15] George B. Grinnell, *Fighting Cheyennes*, p. 169.
[16] "Sand Creek Massacre," p. 116.
[17] Ibid., pp. 116–17.

think that Major Downing had as much to say as any of them. Some said they were going to have Neva's [scalp], some Left Hand, etc."[18]

At 4:00 a.m. on November 25, Chivington's troops left Spring Bottom for the three-day march down the Arkansas to Fort Lyon. The weather remained mild, skies clear, and the midday sun warm. The troops were on the move eleven or twelve hours a day before stopping to camp at night.

Taking no chances that the Southern Arapahos and Cheyennes would get word of his advance, Chivington threw guards around the ranches, including William Bent's, at the mouth of the Purgatoire River, and Prowers's, seven miles above Lyon at Caddo. For two and a half days, no one at Prowers's ranch was allowed to leave the house.[19]

Chivington also stopped all travelers along the road between Denver and Lyon, even the mail wagons. His approach was such a well-kept secret, in fact, that not even Major Anthony knew that troops were on the way.

On the evening of November 27, a guard at Fort Lyon notified Anthony that campfires were flickering in the distance above the fort. Thinking the fires were those of Kiowas, Anthony ordered Lieutenant Soule to take a detail and identify the camp. As Soule moved west, he met a wagoneer heading toward Lyon and inquired if he had seen any Indian camps. The wagoneer replied in the negative, but added that "Chivington's hundred-daysers are back there."[20]

Soule then continued on to Chivington's camp. Once again the colonel seized the opportunity to gather information on the Indians in the vicinity. Soule, in response to the colonel's questions, told him frankly that the Southern Arapahos and Cheyennes were camped on Sand Creek, waiting for word from Curtis. They presented no danger, he said, and were considered prisoners of war. One of Chivington's officers remarked: "They won't be prisoners after we get there."[21]

[18] Ibid., pp. 117, 134.
[19] Ibid., pp. 51, 107.
[20] Ibid., pp. 10–11.
[21] Ibid., pp. 11, 15, 165.

The following day, November 28, Chivington's command moved into Fort Lyon and the colonel immediately posted a guard with orders to kill anyone attempting to leave.[22] He also set up a meeting with the fort's officers, at which he laid out his plan to attack the camp at Sand Creek. Major Anthony voiced no opposition, despite the assurances of safety he had given the chiefs, believing that here, at last, were the troops he had been awaiting and that the attack would be part of a full-scale war against the tribes.[23]

In a later letter to his brother, Anthony admitted that he had gone along with Chivington's plan, thinking the colonel "would go further."[24] He expressed the same opinion to his officers—that the attack would be part of a battle continuing on to the Smoky Hill and Republican camps—but privately he expressed misgivings to Lt. James Cannon, saying he feared that Chivington's attack "would only be on the Indians we had corraled." Despite these misgivings, Anthony himself ordered 125 Fort Lyon troops to prepare for the field.[25]

The order did not sit well with the officers who had served under Wynkoop, nor with the civilians at the fort, including Agent Colley, and they took issue directly with Chivington. Lt. Joseph Cramer said later that he told the colonel that the officers at the fort were honor-bound to uphold Major Wynkoop's pledges to the Indians, as well as Major Anthony's, and that "it would be murder in every sense of the word, if he attacked those Indians." In reply, Chivington brought down his fist close to Cramer's face, shouting, "Damn any man who sympathizes with the Indians." Still Cramer persisted. "I told him what pledges were given the Indians. He replied that he had come to kill Indians and believed it to be honorable to kill Indians under any and all circumstances."[26]

Other officers joined Cramer in opposition to the plan, and

[22] Ibid., p. 11, 165.
[23] Ibid., pp. 179, 182, 208, 212; "Cheyenne Massacre," p. 108; "Chivington Massacre," pp. 69–70.
[24] December 23, 1864, Scott J. Anthony Letters, Colorado Historical Society, Denver, Colo.
[25] "Sand Creek Massacre," pp. 62, 110.
[26] "Chivington Massacre," p. 74.

following the meeting they went to Chivington privately, reiterating their belief that the Indians at Sand Creek were friendly, with no hostile intentions. Only two days before, they told the colonel, Anthony had given a group of whites—John Smith, his son Jack, another trader R. Watson Clarke, and Pvt. David Louderback—permission to go to Sand Creek to trade with them.[27]

Later that day Chivington convened another meeting with the officers. They remained adamantly set against his plan, however, contending that it would be a crime to attack Indians who were prisoners. Lieutenant Cannon said later that he spoke out because he was "aware that they were resting in fancied security under promises of safety by Major Wynkoop and Major Anthony."[28] Chivington prowled the room as the officers protested, disgusted and angry with men who, he said, ought to get out of the service.[29] At last the long argument came to an abrupt end, according to Colley, when Chivington shouted that he would arrest anyone opposed to going against the Sand Creek Indians.[30]

Lieutenant Soule remained deeply troubled. That evening he sought out Anthony, reminding him of the pledges he had given Black Kettle and Left Hand. Anthony assured him, Soule said later, "that Colonel Chivington had told him that those Indians he had pledged, the soldiers and the white men in camp should not be killed; that the object of the expedition was to go out to the Smokey Hill and follow the Indians up...that I would not compromise myself by going out, as I was opposed to going."[31]

At 8:00 P.M. that November 28, Chivington's command left Fort Lyon and marched northeastward. In the lead rode the massive colonel, and close behind him followed the guides, Jim Beckwourth from Denver and Robert Bent. Bent had been pressed into service at the fort, where he worked as an interpreter and guide. In addition to their arms, the command brought four

[27] Ibid., p. 34.
[28] "Sand Creek Massacre," p. 129.
[29] Ibid., pp. 147, 153, 156; "Cheyenne Massacre," p. 15; "Chivington Massacre," pp. 34, 52, 62.
[30] "Chivington Massacre," p. 34.
[31] "Sand Creek Massacre," pp. 25, 28.

twelve-pound mountain howitzers, and each trooper carried a four-day supply of hardtack in his saddlebag or haversack, hardly enough for a campaign on the central plains, despite Anthony's professed belief that Chivington meant to go farther than Sand Creek.

The number of men marching with Chivington that night has long been a matter of controversy. Historians generally put the number at 650 or 700, but that estimate is based on Chivington's report to Curtis, dated December 16, in which he said that his command consisted of 450 men of the Colorado Third, 125 of the First from Denver, and another 125 of the First from Fort Lyon[32]

Other sources estimate the number of soldiers to have been much higher. Major Anthony reported to Curtis that Chivington had arrived at Fort Lyon with nearly 1,000 men and that he had added 125. Robert Bent and John Smith also said that Chivington had between 900 and 1,000 troopers, and Lieutenant Cramer claimed that the colonel had brought 800 to 900, and took 100 more from Fort Lyon.[33]

The discrepancy rests in the number of men Chivington had brought from Denver. If there were more than the 575 he claimed, the command could have totaled 800 to 900 men after he took on additional troops from Fort Lyon. Chivington had altered numbers in the past—and would do so again—to make his victories appear more glorious, and it is likely that he deliberately understated the strength of his command to Curtis.[34]

That command pushed forward through the night across the desolate landscape. Howbert remembered later that the night was cool but the sky was bright and clear, lit by "thousands of stars." Anthony also remembered that the weather was so mild that he had felt no need to wear his overcoat.

[32] Ibid., pp. 48-50; Stan Hoig, *The Sand Creek Massacre*, p. 142, 143; Donald J. Berthrong, *The Southern Cheyennes*, p. 216, Grinnell, *Fighting Cheyennes*, p. 169; Carey, "*Puzzle of Sand Creek*," *p. 279*.

[33] Anthony to Helliwell, November 28, 1864, *WRR* series 1, vol. 41, pt. 4, p. 708; Testimony of John Smith, January 15, 1865, ibid., pt. 1, p. 968; Testimony of Clark and Louderback, January 27, 1865, ibid., p. 972; "Sand Creek Massacre," p. 142; "Chivington Massacre," p. 96.

[34] Virginia Cole Trenholm in *The Arapahos, Our People*, p. 194, believes that he did.

The elderly Beckwourth was numbed by cold, however, or so he said, protesting he could no longer make out the course. At this, Chivington ordered Bent to take over as guide, but when the half-blood Cheyenne led the troops through a shallow pool—deliberately, some believed, in order to wet the ammunition and render it unusable—Chivington barked a reprimand. "I haven't had an Indian to eat for a long time," he said. If you fool with me, and don't lead me to that camp, I'll have you for breakfast."[35]

The troops marched without rest for about ten hours, covering four miles an hour. Later Chivington would refer to the "noble, heroic efforts" of his men on this "forced march," similar in his view, no doubt, to another forced march two and a half years earlier into New Mexico.[36]

By the time the sun began to rise, Chivington and his troops had topped a ridge on the southeast of Sand Creek. Spread before them was the sleeping Indian camp, its white lodges scattered through the area known as the Big Bend where the southerly course of the creek arcs to the east. Here and there among the lodges stood large old cottonwoods rooted in the sandy, dry creek bed among scatterings of underbrush, giving Big Bend the look of a desert oasis.

The number of persons in Black Kettle and Left Hand's camp is also a matter of controversy. Most sources place the number between five hundred and six hundred, including eighty to one hundred lodges of Cheyennes and eight to ten lodges of Southern Arapahos. Both John Smith and David Louderback, who were there, said later that five hundred persons were in the camp and that two-thirds of them were women and children. George Bent, who was also there, gave the same number.[37]

That number is close to the information Black Kettle had given Major Anthony at Fort Lyon three days earlier, when he said six hundred Cheyennes were at Sand Creek waiting to come into the

[35] Jacob P. Dunn, *"Massacres of the Mountains,"* p. 342.
[36] "Cheyenne Massacre," pp. 48–50; Howbert, *Memories of a Lifetime,* p. 122.
[37] Testimony of John Smith, January 15, 1865, *WRR* series 1, vol. 41, pt. 1, p. 968; "Sand Creek Massacre," p. 131; Frank Hall, *History of the State of Colorado,* 1:347; George Hyde, *Life of George Bent,* p. 149.

fort. Within those three days Left Hand had moved in with another fifty persons, but during the same time many warriors had gone out in hunting parties. All in all, the total population was probably about six hundred.

How many of that number were warriors is another controversial issue. John Smith estimated later that only sixty warriors were still in the camp. Even if there were more, the figure probably did not exceed 130, since the estimated ratio of warriors in a tribal population is generally given as one in five.

From the ridgetop Chivington surveyed the quiet camp. The circumstances were strikingly similar to those of La Glorieta Pass: below him lay an unsuspecting enemy, smaller in number than his command; the elements of surprise and strength were with him.

Yet the circumstances were also different. At La Glorieta Pass the enemy consisted of trained, well-equipped troops. Here the enemy consisted of families, of men, women, and children, only some of whom were trained and equipped to fight a battle—and these would be encumbered by the helplessness of the others.

Chivington, who was far from a creative military strategist, fell back upon the maneuver that had won the day at Apache Canyon and Johnson's Ranch—he would outflank the enemy camp on both sides while charging headlong through the center. He later reported the strategy to Curtis: "My line of battle was formed with Lieutenant Wilson's battalion of the First Regiment on the right, Colonel Shoup's Third Regiment in the centre, and Major Anthony's battalion of the First Regiment on the left."[38]

Chivington quietly rode among his troops, giving last-minute instructions. According to Beckwourth, the colonel said, as he moved through the lines, "Men, strip for action. I don't tell you to kill all ages and sex, but look back on the plains of the Platte, where your mothers, fathers, brothers, sisters have been slain, and their blood saturating the sand of the Platte."[39]

With those final words, Colonel Chivington gave the order to attack.

[38] Chivington to Curtis, December 16, 1864, *WRR* series 1, vol. 41, pt. 1, pp. 948–50; Chivington Report, December 16, 1864, in "Cheyenne Massacre," pp. 48–50.

[39] "Sand Creek Massacre," p. 69.

My shame is as big as the earth.

Black Kettle, Southern Cheyenne **19**

As day broke across the plains on November 29, 1864, several Southern Arapaho and Cheyenne women made their way toward the pony herds picketed along the southwestern edge of Sand Creek. At first they thought the black shadows rolling across the ridge to the southeast were buffalo, but, as line after line of the troops began to move toward the village, the women realized that soldiers were advancing. Terrified, they ran back to sound the alarm.

The traders John Smith and R. Watson Clarke were having breakfast in one of the lodges with Pvt. David Louderback when the women burst inside, shouting and crying, "Soldiers are coming. What does it mean? What does it mean?"[1] Smith and the others jumped up and ran outdoors in time to see that some of the troops were outflanking the camp while others were heading toward its center. Lieutenant Wilson's troops on the eastern edge of the arena fired the first shots. These were followed by countless volleys from other troops. Bullets began hitting the ground everywhere, Smith said, and pelting the lodges like hailstones.

Always quick to size up a situation and know which way to jump, Smith ran toward the troops with Louderback and Clarke close on his heels. To his horror, one soldier yelled, "Shoot the old son of a bitch," and others began firing. Another soldier, George Pierce, seeing what was taking place, hastily turned his horse toward Smith to give him cover and, in so doing, was shot out of his saddle, the first white casualty of the attack.[2] At that moment Chivington caught sight of the trader's predicament and shouted, "Old man, over here." Smith scurried for safety

---

[1] "Sand Creek Massacre," pp. 48–49, 128; "Cheyenne Massacre," p. 5; Testimony of John Smith, January 15, 1865, *WRR* series 1, vol. 41, pt. 1, p. 968.

[2] "Sand Creek Massacre," pp. 48–49.

near Chivington and stayed with the troops as the attack burst forward.

George Bent was still in bed when he heard the women screaming and footsteps pounding through camp. Pulling a blanket around him, he ran outside just as the troops swept toward camp, some circling to the east, others to the west. "All was confusion and noise," he wrote later,

> men, women and children rushing out of the lodges partly dressed; women and children screaming at the sight of the troops, men running back into the lodges for their arms, other men, already armed, or with lassos and bridles in their hands, running for the herds to attempt to get some of the ponies before the troops could reach the animals and drive them off.[3]

Bent dove back into his lodge, grabbed a gun, and joined some middle-aged Cheyenne men who were running toward the west, trying to get out of the range of fire.

When Black Kettle heard the women's screams, he rushed out of his lodge and stared at the wave of approaching soldiers in stunned disbelief. Certain that some terrible mistake had been made "as to who [the Indians] were," the chief grabbed an American flag and a white flag from his lodge, both of which had been given him at the Fort Wise Treaty Council by Commissioner Greenwood, who had advised him to hoist the flags as a sign of peace and friendliness should troops ever approach his village.[4]

Working as fast as he could, Black Kettle tied the flags to the top of a lodgepole and hoisted it upright. Robert Bent, approaching with the troops, said later that he saw the hoisted flags when the soldiers came within fifty yards of camp and that Black Kettle stood holding the lodgepole, frantically shouting and waving for the women and children, who were running wildly about, to gather around the flags. The troops turned their fire on them.[5]

[3] Bent to Hyde, March 14, 1905, George Bent Letters, Colorado State Historical Society, Denver, Colo.; George Hyde, *Life of George Bent,* pp. 151-52.

[4] "Sand Creek Massacre," p. 128.

[5] "Cheyenne Massacre," p. 5; "Sand Creek Massacre," p. 128; Hyde,

At the same time, White Antelope was pushing through the milling crowd toward his brother, and together the two chiefs, understanding now that the attack was no mistake, shouted to the people to run for cover. Then, according to Louderback, they and another Cheyenne leader, Standing in the Water, ran toward the soldiers, holding out their hands to show they were unarmed and that this was a friendly camp, White Antelope shouting in English, "Stop. Stop."[6]

Some of the Cheyennes followed them, and later Lieutenant Cramer said that "a great many started towards our lines with hands raised, as if begging for us to spare them." Instead, a rain of bullets scattered about them until all of them, including the chiefs, were forced to break and run. Black Kettle found his wife, Woman to be Hereafter, and together they headed northward up the creek bed, running and stumbling with the throngs of fleeing men, women, and children.[7]

Different sources provide accounts of White Antelope's reaction to the attack. According to Louderback, both White Antelope and Standing in the Water went to their lodges, got their guns, and came out firing. Both were shot down. George Bent, however, said that White Antelope, seeing his people falling about him, chose to die with them, and, standing with his arms folded across his breast, he sang his death song: "Nothing lives long, except the earth and the mountains," until the soldiers' bullets finally found their mark.[8]

The troops pushed forward, driving scattered groups of Indians into the creek bed. Those warriors who had reached the ponies rode off, instead of turning back to defend the camp. Among them was Edmund Guerrier, the half-blood Cheyenne, who said later that when he saw the great number of troops he realized defense was impossible. The escape of these warriors, however, laid a crushing burden on those who were still in camp. Pushing the women and children behind them, they frantically

---

Life of George Bent, p. 152; "Chivington Massacre," p. 96; George B. Grinnell, *Fighting Cheyennes,* pp. 177–78.

[6] "Sand Creek Massacre," pp. 6, 70.

[7] Ibid., pp. 50–51.

[8] Ibid., p. 138; Hyde, *Life of George Bent,* p. 155.

attempted to place themselves between the fleeing villagers and troops, fighting a rear-guard action. "They fought desperately," Lieutenant Cramer said later. "They fought singly or a few in a place where the ground would give them shelter from our fire, and fought bravely."[9] Major Anthony also said later that he had never seen men fight so bravely. "I saw at one time three Indians charge not less than 150 men. They came within four yards, firing their revolvers and arrows until they were shot down."[10]

But courage could not compensate for the lack of fighting strength. As a result, the very thing the chiefs had most feared took place: the old, the young, and the women took the full force of Chivington's attack. It was out of concern for those who could not defend themsleves, or escape like the fleet young warriors who were riding away on their ponies, that Left Hand and Black Kettle had worked for peace and had endeavored for years to hold their young men in check. In panic and confusion, those who were helpless now huddled together or ran this way and that, and, Cramer said, "most of our fire was concentrated on them."[11]

Left Hand's camp was hit especially hard. Located in the center of the lodges, it caught the brunt of the attack by Chivington's troops. Later, Captain Nichols, one of the officers with Chivington who led the forty-six volunteers from Boulder, said that only moments after the attack began his men had routed the Arapahos, killing twenty-five to thirty persons.[12]

Circling the northern edge of the Indian camp, Lieutenant Wilson's troops moved toward the creek bed, now filled with fleeing Indians, and formed a line to block their path. At this point the Indians began digging pits in the steep, sandy southern bank, desperately trying to find cover. The troops dismounted, poured a barrage of fire into the creek bed and along the banks, and engaged some of the Indians in hand-to-hand combat. One of the men in the Third said later than an Indian hidden in a pit

[9] "Sand Creek Massacre," pp. 50–51.
[10] Anthony to Tappan, December 15, 1864, *WRR* series 1, vol. 41, pt. 1, p. 953.
[11] "Sand Creek Massacre," pp. 50–51.
[12] Anthony to Tappan, December 15, 1864, *WRR* series 1, vol. 41, pt. 1, p. 953.

yelled to him in English: "Come on, you God damn white sons of bitches, and kill me if you are a brave man."[13] That Indian was probably George Bent, who by this time had reached the creek and was huddled in a hastily dug pit with Black Kettle and his wife.[13]

The pits were all that saved some of the Indians, according to an account given later by Little Bear, one of the Cheyennes. "After we got into holes [in the bank] not many were killed, but all who did not reach the holes were killed." And Irving Howbert said later that the soldiers kept firing up and down the banks, but that the pits gave the Indians some protection.[14]

Much later Chivington claimed that these pits were "entrenchments" prepared ahead of time by the Indians as a defense, a claim that displays the colonel's profound ignorance of the Southern Arapaho and Cheyenne people in his jurisdiction.[15] These tribes never dug trenches around their camps or villages. Neither did they move women and children into a camp if they feared an attack; in fact, during the summer conflicts, the Cheyennes had moved many of their women and children to the vicinity of Medicine Lodge Creek in southern Kansas, as far away from the hostilities as possible.[16] One of the soldiers with the First, Amos C. Miksch, disputed Chivington's claim: "There were no rifle pits except what the Indians dug into the sand bank after we commenced firing. I saw them digging out sand with their hands, while firing was going on; the water came into the trenches as they dug in this manner."[17]

The fighting raged on for six more hours, into the afternoon, when, according to Chivington, the Indians "abandoned resistance and dispersed in all directions, and were pursued by my troops until nightfall." By that time the Indians had reached a ravine ten miles north, and pockets of troops were returning to

---

[13] "Sand Creek Massacre," p. 195.

[14] Bent to Hyde, Bent-Hyde Papers, Western History Division, University of Colorado Library, Boulder, Colo.; Irving Howbert, *Memories of a Lifetime in the Pike's Peak Region,* pp. 124-27, 128.

[15] "Cheyenne Massacre," p. 102.

[16] Donald J. Berthrong, *The Southern Cheyennes,* p. 189.

[17] "Chivington Massacre," p. 75.

the Sand Creek camp.[18] The entire length of the creek bed was littered with bodies, mostly those of women and children who were either dead or dying.[19] As Beckwourth put it later, "all sexes and ages were killed, women and children and warriors, all ages from one week to 80 years."[20]

From the moment the attack began, evidence indicates that Chivington, the untrained commander, was unable to maintain discipline among his troops or to control their actions. No sooner had the men in G Company from Fort Lyon mounted two howitzers, for example, than they began lobbing grapeshot into the midst of Indians and troops alike. Major Anthony railed against Chivington for allowing the Third to fire over and through his men, and Lieutenant Cramer, whose detachment followed Anthony's into the camp, also said he was compelled to move his company "to get out of the fire of our own men."[21]

By the time the soldiers began falling back along the creek toward the camp that afternoon, all semblance of control had disappeared. In an outburst of savagery, they began scalping and mutilating the Indian bodies, cutting off fingers, noses, ears, the genitals of both men and women, and women's breasts. Even the bodies of children were scalped. The savagery continued as the soldiers worked their way back to camp where they came upon White Antelope's body. First they cut off White Antelope's nose and ears; then he was scalped and castrated.[22]

Some sources claimed that most atrocities were committed by the Third, the undisciplined, ill-trained volunteer army gone berserk in the field. But John Smith said he also saw men of the First "at the same manner of work," and Agent Colley said later that when the soldiers returned to Fort Lyon, "none denied that [the Indians' bodies] were butchered in a brutal manner and scalped and mutilated, as bad as an Indian ever did to a white

[18] Chivington to Curtis, December 16, 1864, *WRR* series 1, vol. 41, pt. 1, pp. 948–51; Jacob P. Dunn, *Massacres of the Mountains,* p. 343.

[19] Hyde, *Life of George Bent,* p. 154.

[20] "Sand Creek Massacre," p. 69.

[21] Ibid., pp. 48–49; "Chivington Massacre," p. 73.

[22] "Chivington Massacre," pp. 11, 42, 53, 73, 74; "Sand Creek Massacre," pp. 11, 53, 59, 111–13, 137–38; "Cheyenne Massacre," p. 29.

man. That is admitted by the parties who did it. They were cut to pieces in almost every manner and form."[23]

There is no evidence that Chivington attempted to stop the carnage, some of which took place under his eye, according to information given Wynkoop later by the men of the First.[24] Had the colonel wanted to rein in the troops, however, it would have been difficult, so general was the rampage over an extended area. Nevertheless, his later attitude suggests that, in fact, he had not disapproved his men's actions. During the military investigation into Sand Creek held in Denver, Chivington crossexamined one of the soldiers, Corp. James J. Adams of the First, about the atrocities. Chivington asked, "Did not the men who were cutting the fingers off the dead Indians for rings tell you that they were simply obtaining trophies, to preserve as reminiscences, to bequeath to their children, of the glorious field of Sand Creek?" Adams answered simply, "No, Sir." [25]

The actions of another officer, Capt. Silas S. Soule, the man who had been greatly concerned about the campaign, proved that a resolute commander could keep his men under control, even during the hysteria of Sand Creek. Through the hours of battle and butchery, Soule kept his men to one side, away from the camp, refusing to obey Chivington's orders to attack and refusing to order his men to fire. Wynkoop later said that Soule told him his men sat on their horses, apart from the battle, like statues. It was an act of defiance for which Soule would later pay with his life.[26]

In the afternoon lull of the bloody day, with scattered shots still heard along the creek bed, John Smith, his son Jack, and Beckwourth sat in one of the lodges under guard. Knots of soldiers milling about camp began insisting that Jack Smith should die. Why they wished him dead has never been explained, although one early historian claims, without evidence,

[23] "Chivington Massacre," p. 29, 42. For details of these atrocities, see "Sand Creek Massacre," p. 53n. Diary of S. F. Tappan, January 1, 1865, Colorado State Historical Society.

[24] Wynkoop to Tappan, January 15, 1865, WRR series 1, vol. 41, pt. 1, p. 961.

[25] "Sand Creek Massacre," p. 152; Wynkoop manuscript, p. 38.

[26] Wynkoop manuscript, p. 38.

that he had earlier taken part in a stage raid.[27] Lt. Clark Dunn approached Chivington to ask if he had any objections to having the young Smith executed. The colonel replied: "Don't ask me; you know my orders; I want no prisoners."[28]

According to Beckwourth, ten to fifteen soldiers entered the prisoners' lodge and ordered John Smith outside. Someone said to the old trader, "They are going to kill your boy," but he only shrugged, replying, "It cannot be helped." George Bent, who was not himself an eyewitness, said later that he had heard that Smith ran over to Chivington, pleading with him to spare his son's life. Chivington said he could not.[29]

When the trader had left, Beckwourth said, one of the soldiers poked his gun through the lodge flap, trained it on Jack Smith, and fired. "I went out and met the man with a pistol in his hand," Beckwourth recounted. "He said, 'I am afraid the damn son of a bitch is not dead, and I will finish him.' Says I, 'Let him go to rest; he is dead.'"[30]

Major Anthony wrote to his brother on December 1, 1864, that no prisoners had been taken except Jack Smith, but that "he was suddenly taken ill in the night and died by morning."[31] It is possible, however, that Anthony, who had been ordered to take the dead and wounded troops back to Lyon that afternoon, was merely echoing Chivington's explanation and did not learn until later how Smith had actually died.

Following the young man's execution, Chivington set about mopping up. Eager to know which chiefs had been killed, he ordered John Smith out over the field to look for the bodies of leaders. "The bodies were so badly mutilated," Smith said later, "that it was hard for me to tell one from the other."[32] Yet he fulfilled his grim task, moving from body to body trying to identify the leading men. Nine Cheyenne chiefs who had supported

[27] Dunn, *Massacres of the Mountains,* p. 372.

[28] "Cheyenne Massacre," p. 10; "Chivington Massacre," p. 74; "Sand Creek Massacre," p. 28.

[29] George Bent Letters, March 9, 1905, Colorado State Historical Society; "Sand Creek Massacre," p. 71.

[30] "Sand Creek Massacre," p. 71.

[31] Scott J. Anthony Letters, December 1, 1864, Colorado State Historical Society; "Chivington Massacre," p. 92.

[32] "Cheyenne Massacre," p. 8.

peace were dead. Among them were White Antelope, the dignified Cheyenne statesman and brother of Black Kettle who had met with Evans and Chivington at Camp Weld; Standing in the Water and War Bonnet, who had visited Washington with Lean Bear in 1863; and One-Eye, who had put his life in danger to bring the chiefs' plea for peace to Fort Lyon. Although Black Kettle and No-Ta-Nee were also believed killed at first, they had escaped. No one was sure what had happened to Left Hand, but his body was not on the field.

Chivington also ordered the Indian ponies and mules rounded up and placed under guard. Later, the assistant quartermaster at Lyon said he counted 450 head of captured animals. Other sources placed the total at around 600, still a low figure since the Southern Arapahos and Cheyennes kept between six and fifteen animals for each lodge.[33]

After the ponies and mules were secured, Chivington ordered Lieutenant Cramer to take a detail through the lodges. Buffalo robes, finely tanned and embroidered deerskin dresses and shirts, food, utensils, tools—everything of value was taken and packed onto the animals. The lodges were then torched.[34]

In the settling darkness, soldiers straggled back to camp and huddled around bonfires, eating hardtack and preparing for a night on the plains that had turned ominously cold. Howbert later remembered the eeriness of the evening, with the blazing lodges casting strange, flickering light all about and the soldiers feeling jumpy and irritable. Some of the men, thinking they had spotted ponies running about on a ridge, leaped to their feet and grabbed their guns, fearing that warriors had returned. But the ponies seemed to be without riders, and the soldiers then realized that what they had seen were not ponies but Indian dogs, "running about wildly, looking for their masters."[35]

That evening Chivington dispatched his first report on Sand Creek to Curtis:

In the last 10 days, my command has marched 300 miles, one

[33] "Sand Creek Massacre," pp. 108, 154; "Chivington Massacre," p. 30.
[34] "Chivington Massacre," p. 30.
[35] Howbert, *Memories of a Lifetime,* pp. 129–30.

hundred of which the snow was two feet deep. After a march of 40
miles last night, I, at daylight attacked Cheyenne villages of one
hundred and thirty lodges, from nine to ten hundred warriors
strong, killed chiefs Black Kettle, White Antelope, Knock Kno
[No-Ta-Nee], and Little Robe, and between four and five hundred
other Indians, and captured many ponies and mules. Our loss
nine killed, 38 wounded. All did nobly. Think I will catch some
more of them. Eighty miles on Smokey Hill, found white man's
scalp, not more than three days old in one of the lodges."[36]

Once again Chivington had altered figures to his advantage,
claiming that his troops had gone against nine hundred to one
thousand warriors and had killed between four and five hundred.
In another report, sent later from Denver, he increased the
number of Indians killed to between five and six hundred and
put his own losses at eight dead, forty wounded.[37]

In fact, Chivington's command of around nine hundred men
had met a fighting force of not more than one hundred. Robert
Bent said later that only about sixty men defended the camp,
thirty-five warriors and twenty-five old men. Smith agreed:
"From my observation I do not think there were over sixty Indians that made any defense." And Lieutenant Cramer testified
later that not more than one hundred Indian men engaged in the
fighting.[38]

Major Anthony's remarks on the Indian strength, made in a
letter to his brother dated December 23, 1864, are especially
damning to Chivington's claim: "Our loss in killed and
wounded in the 'great battle' was very near as many as there were
armed Indians in the camp," he wrote. The loss of troops was
slightly greater than the colonel had claimed: thirteen dead and
thirty-eight wounded. If Anthony's remark is to be taken, only
about fifty Indians put up a defense at Sand Creek.[39]

---

[36] Chivington to Curtis, December 16, 1864, *WRR* series 1, vol. 41, pt. 1,
p. 948.
[37] "Cheyenne Massacre," pp. 48–50.
[38] "Chivington Massacre," pp. 73, 96; Chivington to Curtis, December
16, 1864, *WRR* series 1, vol. 41, pt. 1, p. 968.
[39] Scott J. Anthony Letters, December 23, 1864, Colorado State
Historical Society.

Rather than 500 to 600 warriors dead on the field, as Chivington bragged, the number of dead was 148, and two-thirds of those were women and children. Again, different sources provided different estimates of fatalities. Smith testified that he rode over the field and counted 60 to 70 dead bodies, "the majority women and children, all of whose bodies had been mutilated in the most horrible manner." Anthony said that he believed 120 Indians had been killed, but Lieutenannt Cramer put the figure higher, at around 175 or 180. Probably the most accuate figure, however, came from the Cheyennes themselves, who said later that 148 persons had died at Sand Creek. Of these, only 60 were men.[40]

Left Hand's camp had been annihilated. Caught in heavy fire early in the attack, only four Southern Arapahos out of fifty or sixty had managed to escape. One was MaHom, Left Hand's sister, and another was her daughter Mary.[41]

Early in the morning of November 30, Chivington's command left the burned-out village of Sand Creek and marched south. The colonel's destination was Little Raven's camp on the Arkansas River, although he had dispatched a report to Curtis the previous evening saying that he intended to push northward to attack the Smoky Hill camps. He had also led Anthony to believe that Sand Creek would be merely the jumping off place to the main battleground.

All evidence suggests, however, that Chivington never had any intention of moving against the camps in the area of the Smoky Hill or Solomon rivers. He had issued his men only four days of rations, for example, when at least a ten-day supply was required to reach the central plains, launch an attack, and return to Lyon. In addition, a march deeper into the plains would have isolated his command, dangerously lengthening his supply line from the fort.

Another persuasive reason against such a campaign, of course, was the presence in these camps of warriors capable of mounting a

---

[40] Chivington to Curtis, December 16, 1864, *WRR* series 1, vol. 41, pt. 1, p. 968; "Cheyenne Massacre," p. 12; "Sand Creek Massacre," p. 50; "Chivington Massacre," p. 66.

[41] "Early Far West Notebook," vol. 3, p. 40, Cragin Collection, Pioneers Museum, Colorado Springs, Colo.

strong defense. Such opposition would have seriously taxed the capacities of an untrained commander, and Chivington meant to avoid a situation like that. Although he had deliberately led Anthony to believe otherwise, in order to obtain his assistance, his plan had always been to hit the underprotected camps of those Indians who had surrendered at Fort Lyon. Chivington, now running on borrowed time, had been desperate for a quick, dramatic victory that would justify the Third's existence—the one-hundred-day enlistment period of the regiment had expired on November 21—restore his own honor, and bring him a promotion.

After reaching the Arkansas, Chivington turned eastward, following Little Raven's tracks. Twice the troops came upon hastily abandoned campsites, their fires still smoldering, buffalo robes and camp kettles strewn over the ground. Finally the colonel ordered three hundred men to scout ahead, but they failed to discover the fleeing Southern Arapahos. On December 7 he ordered the command back to Fort Lyon because he feared the horses were about to give out.[42]

The hasty manner in which Little Raven retreated down the Arkansas suggests that he somehow had been warned of Chivington's plans in advance. Lieutenant Cramer said later, however, that he knew of no such warning,[43] and since the colonel had posted guards around Lyon with orders to shoot anyone attempting to leave, it is unlikely that a civilian or soldier got away to warn Little Raven before the evening of November 28. After Chivington left the fort, however, it is possible that someone rode hurriedly to the Southern Arapaho camp downriver. Given the strong objection raised at the fort to Chivington's plans, such was probably the case, and might account for Little Raven heading for the safety of the large Kiowa and Comanche camps south of the Arkansas instead of turning north toward the Smoky Hill camps, where he might otherwise have gone.

On December 11, Chivington arrived at Fort Lyon, flushed with victory despite his failure to find Little Raven. An officer in

---

[42] Howbert, *Memories of a Lifetime*, p. 132; "Sand Creek Massacre," p. 77. By traveling south down the Arkansas, Chivington could maintain supply lines from Fort Lyon.

[43] "Sand Creek Massacre," p. 63.

the First, Lt. C. M. Cossitt, said later that the colonel bragged about the defeat he had handed the Cheyennes and Southern Arapahos at Sand Creek, calling it a "brilliant thing" which would make him a brigadier general, or, as he said, "put a star on my shoulders."[44]

But officers and civilians at the fort did not share that assessment. When the men with Anthony had returned with the dead and wounded, they told the other soldiers who had remained at Lyon about the attack and the atrocities. Gradually the realization of what had happened at Sand Creek began to settle over the fort, sickening both the men who had taken part in the massacre and those who had stayed behind, as their testimony later would show.

A measure of this feeling of revulsion can be judged from a letter Anthony wrote to his brother on December 23, 1864. The major had not opposed any attack on Sand Creek which was part of a drive against the Plains Indians, he said, but then he had realized that the "corralled" Indians were Chivington's final goal.

> I am inclined to think the colonel dared not risk a longer trip into the hostile Indian country for fear he could not get promoted before reports in detail were published, showing his foolish action in that affair.... One thing is certain: we here feel wronged by his action; he has whipped the only peaceable Indians in the country, (which I wanted him to do if he would go further)...He has, within sight of them, turned back with the largest and best outfitted command that ever went against Indians in this locality, while everything was favorable...for a campaign that would have been a credit to everyone in it, if he entered it for other than selfish reasons.[45]

In the same letter Anthony described the Sand Creek attack as "the most miserable management that ever was known upon a battlefield....Anyone not desiring to make himself Brigadier general could have gone to that 'peaceable Indian camp' with 200 men and killed the last Indian there without losing in killed and

[44] "Chivington Massacre," p. 74.

[45] Scott J. Anthony Letters, December 23, 1864, and following, Colorado State Historical Society.

wounded two persons.'' As for Chivington's claim that soldiers
had found a white scalp in camp, Anthony told his brother: ''I
have reported to the Commanding General the facts just as they
occurred, I did not state that a white man's scalp only two days old
was found for the reason that no such thing was ever heard of by
any one at this post.''[46]

Anthony concluded this letter by surmising that Chivington
would have him dismissed for his report to Curtis. He did not
care, he said. Sick at heart, his only thought was to get out of the
army and as far away from the plains as he could.

In a second letter to his brother, written a few days later, Sand
Creek still weighed heavily on Anthony's mind. ''Everyone in
Colorado will be the loser by Old Chivington's disgraceful Indian
campaign,'' he predicted. He also said that he was concerned that
other officers, his family, and his friends would not think him
human when they learned that he had been engaged in the Sand
Creek battle.[47]

About the same time that Anthony was pouring out his feelings to his brother, Chivington and the Third marched toward
Denver. There a tumultuous welcome awaited them, not unlike
the one that Chivington was accorded on his return from New
Mexico. The colonel was once again the man of the hour, a hero.
He and his men paraded through Denver's streets, Chivington in
the lead holding aloft a live eagle tied to a pole, the townspeople
cheering wildly. ''A high old time there was last night,'' the
Rocky Mountain News reported. ''Our streets, hotels, saloons
and stores today were thronged with strangers, chiefly Indian
killers.'' On December 28 the regiment, which was now called
the ''Bloody Third,'' a term of approbation, was mustered out.[48]

They were mustered out with an assortment of trophies, however. Chivington distributed among the men some of the captured Indian ponies which, according to Colley, the colonel had
brought to Denver loaded with plunder. Still other animals be-

---

[46] Ibid. Lieutenant Cramer also denied that any scalps had been found at
Sand Creek—he had been charged with checking each lodge—except for one
which he said was ''very old''; ''Chivington Massacre,'' p. 73.

[47] Scott J. Anthony Letters, December, 1864, Colorado State Historical
Society.

[48] *Rocky Mountain News*, December 23, 1864.

longing to the Indians had been sold by the colonel before he left the Arkansas and only a hundred animals were eventually turned in to the military quartermaster.[49] Other trophies included finely beaded and embroidered Indian dresses and shirts which the men of the Third sold to Denverites for twenty dollars each. And, following a theater performance one evening, some of the Third jumped onto the stage where, as the audience cheered, they displayed the Indian scalps they were carrying with them. Still other "curiosities" put on exhibit in town were three frightened Indian children whom soldiers had found wandering near Sand Creek after the attack.[50]

In Boulder the Indian fighters received another rowdy welcome before they returned to their ranches, farms, and mining claims. Captain Nichols and his men boasted that they had brought down the great Southern Arapaho, Chief Left Hand. For a long time a friend of Left Hand's, who lived near Boulder, Bob Hauck, hoped they were mistaken.[51]

Wynkoop's stage pulled into Fort Riley, in eastern Kansas, in early December, shortly after Chivington's first dispatch reached Curtis. When the general informed him of Chivington's attack on Left Hand and Black Kettle's camps at Sand Creek, Wynkoop went wild with rage.[52]

[49] George W. Thompson, "Experiences in the West," *Colorado Magazine* 4 (1927):175-79; "Chivington Massacre," p. 30.

[50] Virginia Cole Trenholm, *The Arapahoes, Our People*, p. 195.

[51] Augusta Hauck Block, "Lower Boulder and St. Vrain Valley Home Guards and Fort Junction," *Colorado Magazine* 16 (1939):189.

[52] Wynkoop to Tappan, January 15, 1865, *WRR* series 1, vol. 41, pt. 1, pp. 959-62.

20

My Father, have pity on me!
I have nothing to eat,
I am dying of thirst,
Everything is gone.

Southern Arapaho prayer

Because Left Hand's body was not found at Sand Creek, it was widely believed at the time that he had escaped. Major Anthony was certain that he had. In the December 23 letter to his brother he wrote: "Black Kettle, Knock-Knee [No-Ta-Nee], Left Hand, Little Robe and Neewah [Neva] are alive and well."[1]

Anthony gave the same information to Julia Lambert, the wife of the Fort Lyon stationmaster who would later chronicle the events of her life on the plains. Mrs. Lambert had been traveling by stage from Fort Leavenworth to Lyon on November 29, and arrived there shortly after Anthony had pulled into the fort with the dead and wounded. She inquired immediately about the fate of the Southern Arapaho chief whose dignity and intelligence had impressed her earlier, and was told that Left Hand had not been killed. Much later, in her account of Chivington's attack, she wrote that Left Hand and Black Kettle had both "escaped Sand Creek."[2] Private Lauderback agreed. He had seen Left Hand at Sand Creek, he said later, and he was certain that "Left Hand, War Bonnet and Little Robe had all got away."[3]

Chivington also believed Left Hand had escaped, according to a *Rocky Mountain News* report of December 14. "Among the killed were all the Cheyenne chiefs, Black Kettle, White Antelope, Little Robe, Left Hand, Knock Knee, One Eye and another, name unknown. . . . The Arapahoes probably suffered but little. It has been reported that the chief, Left Hand, of that tribe, was killed, but Colonel Chivington is of the opinion that he was not."[4] Neither, as it turned out, was Black Kettle or No-Ta-Nee.

---

[1] Scott J. Anthony Letters, December 23, 1864, Colorado State Historical Society, Denver, Colo.

[2] Julia S. Lambert, "Plain Tales of the Plains," *The Trail* 8 (1916):5–13.

[3] "Sand Creek Massacre," p. 138.

Yet there were others at the time who believed just as strongly that Left Hand had been killed. During one of the later investigations into Sand Creek,* Agent Colley was asked if the Indians who had given up the prisoners (Laura Roper and the other children) had been in the camp. He replied: "One was there and was killed. The other was in the employ of the government at the time." Colley was referring to Left Hand and to One-Eye, who had gathered information on the Sioux.[5] William Bent, the old trader who had known Left Hand most of his life, testified in another investigation that he believed Left Hand "was killed in the massacre on Sand Creek. From information I know of what occurred in the Sand Creek fight. I had two sons [George and Robert] in the village."[6]

The most definitive evidence, however, was provided forty years later in a series of letters written by George Bent to the historian George Hyde. In one letter, which is undated, Bent stated: "Left Hand was killed with all but four of his people." In another, written March 15, 1905, he said: "I will give you the names of the principal chiefs killed at Sand Creek. . . . There was one Arapaho chief killed—Left Hand." The most important letter, however, is dated April 2, 1906. In this, Bent distinguishes between Left Hand and the man by the same name who later became principal chief of the Southern Arapahos. Hyde had sent Bent a photograph of the later chief, inquiring if it was the same man who had been at Sand Creek. Bent replied: "The Left Hand whose picture you sent is still living here [in Oklahoma]; he is no relation to Left Hand killed at Sand Creek."[7]

---

*Two congressional investigations and one military investigation of Sand Creek would be held between January and March, 1865.

[4] *Rocky Mountain News*, December 14, 1864; "Cheyenne Massacre," p. 57.

[5] "Chivington Massacre," p. 29.

[6] Ibid., p. 94.

[7] Bent to Hyde, Bent-Hyde Papers, pp. 6–7, Western History Division, University of Colorado Library, Boulder, Colo.; Bent to Hyde, March 14, 1905, April 2, 1906, George Bent Letters to George Hyde, Western History Division, Denver Public Library, Denver, Colo. George Bent lists the principal chiefs killed as: White Antelope, Standing in the Water, One-Eye, War Bonnet, Spotted Crow, Two Thighs, Bear Man, Yellow Shield, and Yellow Wolf, all Cheyennes, and Left Hand, Arapaho (March 14, 1905, Bent to Hyde).

Shortly after the attack itself, Bent had given Colley some information which explains why Left Hand's body had not been found. "A half breed told me," the agent testified during one of the investigations, "Black Kettle was not killed, but Left Hand was wounded and died after he got over there, to the Sioux."[8] This information, added to other eyewitness accounts of Sand Creek, make it possible to piece together what happened to Left Hand and his band of fifty or sixty people on that chilly November 29, 1864.

When Left Hand had left the Arkansas River three days earlier, he was, according to one source very ill. In the winter of 1859 he had also been ill,[9] reportedly with mountain fever, and at that time had retired for several months to his village on the St. Vrain River north of Boulder. There he remained, apart from the hordes of whites and their burgeoning settlements which threatened to impose new and unknown changes upon the Southern Arapaho pattern of life. By November of 1864 those changes had occurred: Southern Arapaho and Cheyenne land no longer belonged to them, although a treaty signed long before still said otherwise; the large buffalo ranges had disappeared in the wake of heavily trafficked roads, stage stations, and telegraph lines; and ranches, towns, and settlements grew and prospered across the central plains while Southern Arapaho villages became increasingly impoverished, increasingly haunted by hunger and disease.

The Southern Arapahos and their allies the Southern Cheyennes had in fact been defeated by the sheer number of whites in a long, ongoing war that had occasioned outbursts of violence only during its last few years. The spoils of that war, the land, had gone to the victors.

In a world that was rapidly disintegrating, Left Hand had called upon his long experience with whites, his gift for speaking their language, and his skills as a leader of men to bring about an agreement that would restore peace to the central plains and ensure, at the least, that his people could survive. Rather than mov-

---

[8] "Cheyenne Massacre," p. 32; Jacob P. Dunn, *Massacres of the Mountains*, p. 417.

[9] "Sand Creek Massacre," pp. 116–17.

ing down the Arkansas River with Little Raven and the other Southern Arapahos, where he might have found time to recuperate, he followed Black Kettle to Sand Creek, there to await word from General Curtis and, he had hoped, to conclude the long work for peace.

When the women and children began wailing and running through camp early on the morning of November 29, Left Hand probably rushed from his lodge, just as Black Kettle had done, and was stunned to see the long lines of soldiers pouring over the ridge toward the village.

From the location of the Southern Arapaho lodges Left Hand was able to look toward Black Kettle's lodge where the Cheyenne chief had frantically hoisted his two flags aloft. Perhaps he also spotted White Antelope running through the milling crowds toward his brother.

Within moments a column of cavalry had begun tracing a half-circle around Left Hand's camp while another, with most of the soldiers on foot, knifed across the southern edge of the village toward its center. In the lead, his pistol raised high, rode a colossal man, red-bearded and garbed in the blue of a colonel's uniform. Left Hand must have recognized Chivington.

There is no evidence that the two men had ever met, but for six years both their paths had crossed the central plains—from the Missouri River to Denver and from the South Platte to the Arkansas—and they knew of each other. Chivington's remark that he thought Left Hand had been in charge at Fort Lyon was a grudging acknowledgment of the Southern Arapaho chief's leadership during a time when he felt his own to be slipping.

For his part, Left Hand had attempted to gain some insight into the characters of Chivington and Evans, the men who held the reins of power in the territory. His visit to Bob Hauck's ranch was made for the purpose of understanding the white leaders he was up against. Certainly Neva and the other Indians who had taken part in the Camp Weld Council had reported to Left Hand, in detail, Chivington's words and demeanor.

When the paths of these two men finally met at Sand Creek, they had much in common. Both were fated to live out their lives in an unsettled world, and both had learned early in life to depend upon their own wit and energy for survival in a harsh, inhospitable environment. They were close in age; both were strong and in their prime: Chivington was forty-three, Left Hand about forty-one. Each had a wife and children.

They were also leaders of men. The lives and safety of Colorado settlers rested to a large extent upon the decisions of the commander of the military District of Colorado, just as the welfare of the Southern Arapahos was in many ways determined by the decisions of Left Hand. Both had the power to issue orders that greatly affected the lives of others.

They were also extraordinarily courageous, willing to stand for their beliefs. Chivington had preached Christianity on the rough Missouri waterfront and in the raucous Colorado mining camps, sometimes in peril of his life. As a military commander he had forced his troops on difficult marches and ordered them into battle, but he had always led the way.

From the beginning of the Colorado gold rush, Left Hand had stood firm for maintaining a peaceful relationship with whites. He had faced down his own warriors on this issue, even preferring to leave his village on one occasion rather than to condone their hostilities by his presence among them. He had steadfastly worked for an agreement with whites that would allow his people to move toward a better and more secure future. At Fort Larned he had placed his own life in danger by offering his services, and he had returned white prisoners to a military camp where he gave himself as a hostage.

The differences between these two men exceeded any similarities, however. Left Hand recognized the complexities of the world about him. He sought to understand other people, both Indian and white, by learning their languages and visiting their settlements. The good that he found in other societies he was willing, even eager, to adapt to the Southern Arapaho way if it did not mean letting go of all he knew to be good in his own culture. He never lost the hope that his people could benefit from the white man's technical knowledge, particularly his skill in ranching, and he believed that only in peace could his people thrive. For Left Hand life was a journey toward an ever-expanding horizon of possibilities.

Chivington saw the world in simple terms. It never seemed to have occurred to him that the white culture into which he had been born did not possess all that was good and valuable. To learn the Southern Arapaho or Cheyenne languages, to visit their villages in his jurisdiction and learn about their way of life, would have seemed preposterous in the extreme; he was a man with an unalterable belief in his own superiority and the superiority of those of his race. Chivington believed that only by destroying the Indians through war could his own culture thrive. He was a man who seemed to have arrived, early in life, at a fixed ideology without ever questioning his own motives or weighing his own experience.

Once set in motion, the events precipitated by Chivington at Sand Creek proceeded at lightning speed. Troops deploying to the north of Left Hand's village opened fire, which was followed swiftly by a barrage of fire from Chivington's charging troops. After the initial shock, Left Hand understood that the attack was no mistake and that there was no stopping it. As a chief, his main concern was for those who could not protect themselves and, like Black Kettle and White Antelope, he probably began shouting for the women and children to run for the creek bed, placing himself in front of the troops and trying to divert the fire from his people. By now the Southern Arapaho camp was pressed on three sides, with Captain Nichols and the volunteers from Boulder charging the center and firing volley after volley into the group of Indians who were trying to break for the creek bed.

Lieutenant Cramer said later that Left Hand was shot as he "stood with his arms folded, saying he would not fight the white man, as they were his friends."[10] But if Cramer was with his troops, who were moving along the southern flank of the village toward the pony herd, it seems unlikely that he saw Left Hand, much less that he could have heard him speak in the midst of the confusion and gunfire.

Another account of how Left Hand was shot was provided later by the historian Jerome C. Smiley, who probably based it on interviews with some survivors of the massacre. According to Smiley, Left Hand ran toward Chivington's troops with his arms outstretched, the palms of his hands turned outward in the Plains Indian sign of peace, and, as he ran, he was shot down.[11]

[10] "Chivington Massacre," p. 73; Frank Hall, *History of the State of Colorado*, 1:327; Wilbur Fisk Stone, ed., *History of Colorado*, 1:76.
[11] Jerome C. Smiley, *History of Denver*, p. 407.

Although he was wounded, Left Hand was able to reach the creek, probably with the help of others. George Bent was also wounded—he was shot in the hip—but he reached the creek and, eventually, the Smoky Hill camps. His account of that painful escape suggests the way in which Left Hand must have also made his way north.

Like Bent and the others who were wounded, Left Hand probably took cover in one of the pits in the creek bank. When the soldiers moved away, Bent wrote later,

> ...we crawled out of the holes, stiff and sore, with the blood frozen on our wounded and half-naked bodies. Slowly and painfully we retreated up the creek, men, women and children dragging themselves along, the women and children wailing and crying, but not too loudly, for they feared the return of the whites.[12]

As the tattered band moved northward, Bent said, the warriors who had cut off a few ponies and ridden out of camp when the attack began now made their way back under the cover of darkness to look for survivors. They came upon the wounded stragglers, hoisted them onto the ponies, and the party continued, moving slowly, until, according to Bent, ''the wounded and the women and children could go no further, we all bivouacked on the open plain for the night.''[13] It was a night, he said, that ''will never be forgotten.''

The temperature dropped to bitter cold, and gusts of wind swept the ground where the exhausted and wounded Indians lay. Many, according to Bent, had not yet dressed when Chivington attacked at dawn that morning, and were still half naked. Other had lost their clothing in the flight, but those who still had shirts or blankets removed them and covered the wounded and the children. Hurriedly they went about gathering bunchgrass by the handsful to pile over them, ''trying,'' as Bent said, ''to keep them from freezing to death.'' They also built small fires from clumps of dried grasses and ''all through the night, the Indians

---

[12] George Hyde, *Life of George Bent*, pp. 156–57.
[13] Ibid.; Bent to Tappan, February 23, 1889, George Bent Letters, Colorado State Historical Society.

kept halooing to attract the attention of those who had escaped from the village to the open plain and were wandering about in the dark, lost and freezing.''[14]

After doing what they could for others, some of the men started back toward camp along the creek bed looking for other survivors. Black Kettle was among them, searching for his wife, Woman to be Hereafter, who had been shot as they ran. He finally found her lying in the sand, still alive but badly wounded. Placing her on his back, he carried her several miles back to the campfires of the others. Later she said that a soldier had stood over her after she had fallen and continued to fire bullets into her.[15]

The survivors, fearful that the soldiers would pursue them, left camp before daybreak and started northeastward toward the Smoky Hill, fifty miles away. Bent wrote that some of the warriors who had reached their ponies had made a dash for the Smoky Hill camps, riding all day to sound the alarm. Large numbers of warriors had immediately set out for Sand Creek, leading extra ponies loaded with blankets, robes, and food. By daybreak this rescue party reached the straggling group making its way north. After being fed, clothed, and mounted, the survivors ''moved at a better pace and with revived hope,'' Bent said, and reached the Smoky Hill camps at sunset.[16]

Edmund Guerrier was one of the warriors who had raced toward the Smoky Hill with news of the attack. Later he said that when he saw there could be no resistance to Chivington's troops, he struck out and ran to the northeast where he met White Antelope's daughter, who had managed to cut off ten to fifteen ponies from the herd. The two then rode together to the main camps.[17]

All was confusion as the survivors arrived. Everyone in the Smoky Hill camps had friends or relatives at Sand Creek, Bent said, and the camps were filled with grief. Shrill screaming and

[14] Hyde, *Life of George Bent,* pp. 157-58.
[15] Bent to Tappan, February 23, 1889, George Bent Letters, Colorado State Historical Society.
[16] Hyde, *Life of George Bent,* p. 158.
[17] ''Chivington Massacre,'' p. 66.

wailing pierced the night, and women cut off their hair and slashed their arms and legs. Everyone was crying, even the warriors.[18] Left Hand was brought into the camp and was made as comfortable as possible in one of the lodges.

When Black Kettle came into the camp, the anger toward the white soldiers was turned upon him. The Cheyennes told him they no longer recognized him as chief. They taunted and insulted him, threatening his life because "his faith in the whites had led to the murder of women and children." They asked him why he had not stayed at Sand Creek and died with his brother. It was probably George Bent who said to the chief, "You are an old fool; you ought to have stood and been shot down as the rest of us."[19]

There was no longer any thought of peace. Those chiefs who had worked for an agreement with whites had fallen: Black Kettle was discredited; Left Hand was fatally wounded; and the others lay dead. According to Bent everyone in the camps, even the women, clamored for war, and those warriors who had always opposed peace assumed leadership. In a council held a few days later, the alliance was formed that Governor Evans had long insisted already existed. The Southern and Northern Cheyennes would join the hostile Dog Soldiers, the Sioux and Northern Arapaho bands in war against the whites. Some of the Southern Arapaho warriors would go with them.

Shortly afterward Black Kettle left the Smoky Hill camp, taking those Cheyennes too weary or grief-stricken to join in the coming battles. They moved south, searching for Little Raven's Southern Arapahos. There is no evidence that Left Hand was also taunted or discredited, although he and Black Kettle had been closely allied in the work for peace. He had probably escaped Black Kettle's fate, however, only because he was close to death.

Left Hand, a man of peace, had come to a village not his own, whose people were now allied in war. Except for MaHom and her daughter, most of the people closest to him—his wife, children,

---

[18] Hyde, *Life of George Bent*, pp. 158-59.
[19] "Chivington Massacre," pp. 30, 76. Colley testified that Black Kettle said so to Edmund Guerrier, but this would not make sense. It was probably George Bent, who was wounded, who made the statement to Black Kettle.

and other family members, his friends, and those who had supported his actions—had been killed at Sand Creek. The children of his family lay there alongside the fine young warriors who had believed in him, their promising lives unfulfilled. The long years of work toward peace and understanding between different peoples were lost. When death came to Left Hand shortly after he had reached the Smoky Hill, it was probably not unwelcome.

There is evidence that at least one family member was with him when he died. Many years later an elderly Southern Arapaho woman spoke of how she had been tanning a fine buffalo robe for her son-in-law, Left Hand, when he had unexpectedly died. She took the unfinished robe, she said, and carefully wrapped his body in it for burial.[20]

Afterwards some of the Cheyenne, Sioux, and Southern Arapaho warriors must have taken Left Hand's body out onto the plains near the Smoky Hill River and buried it in the earth, which was the Arapaho way.

Six weeks later Jim Beckwourth came to the Smoky Hill camps to talk with the Cheyennes and Sioux about a peace council with the whites. Leg in the Water and Little Robe, a son of the Little Robe killed at Sand Creek, were acting chiefs. When Beckwourth, who had guided Chivington to Sand Creek, entered Leg in the Water's lodge, the new leader taunted him, saying, "Medicine Calf, what have you come here for; have you fetched the white man to finish killing our families again?"

"I told him," Beckwourth said later, "I had come to talk, to fetch in the council. They [the other leading men] came in and I told them I had come to persuade them to make peace with the whites." Beckwourth said he told them that there were not enough of them to fight the whites, who were "as numerous as the leaves of the trees." Beckwourth reported their response:

We know it. But what do we want to live for? The white man has taken our country, killed all of our game; was not satisfied with that, but killed our wives and children. Now no peace. We want

[20] Alfred L. Kroeber, "The Arapaho," *American Museum of Natural History* bulletin 18, nos. 1-4 (1902-1907), pp. 29-30.

to go and meet our families in the spirit land. . . . We have raised
the battle-ax until death.

Then, Beckwourth said, the Cheyennes asked why he had
brought the soldiers to Sand Creek, ''I told them if I had not the
white chief would have hung me.'' They replied, ''Go and stay
with your white brothers.''[21]

[21] ''Sand Creek Massacre,'' pp. 73–74.

Listen...
All you creatures
    under the ground,
All you creatures
    above the ground
    and in the waters.
May this people
    be long in life,
    and increase.
May our boys and girls,
    our children of all ages...
May our grown men and women,
    and all our elders...
May they increase
    and be strengthened.

21

Arapaho prayer*

With Sand Creek had passed the chance for reasonable men to come to an agreement that would allow Indians and whites to live together on the central plains in peace and with tolerance for one another's differences.

On January 7, 1865, the war that Governor Evans had long been predicting finally erupted on the plains. One thousand warriors—Cheyennes, Brulé Sioux, and Northern Arapahos—struck the settlement of Julesburg on the South Platte near the Colorado-Nebraska line, killing fifteen or sixteen soldiers and looting stores and warehouses.[1] Three weeks later, war parties went on a five-day rampage up and down the South Platte, capturing wagon trains and destroying telegraph lines, before they attacked Julesburg for the second time.[2]

With these attacks began the longest war in United States

*Translated by Benjamin Friday and William Shakespeare of the Wind River Reservation and reprinted with permission of Saint Stephen's Indian Mission, Wind River Reservation, Wyoming.

[1] Eugene F. Ware, *The Indian War of 1864.*
[2] George B. Grinnell, *The Fighting Cheyennes*, p. 189.

history. The war between the Plains Indians and the United States was waged intermittently across the vast expanse of the plains for twenty-five years. It moved north across the prairie settlements of Nebraska and Wyoming and the gold-mining districts of Montana and South Dakota, and south over the ranches and farms of Kansas, Indian Territory, and into Texas. With the exception of the first strikes along the South Platte, however, few battles were fought in Colorado Territory.

The costs of the war were enormous. Within the first six months the government had spent forty million dollars to launch an army of eight thousand troops in an attempt to subdue the Plains Indians.[3] By the war's end countless millions more had been spent on armies, military posts, equipment, and supplies. Thousands of lives were lost, mostly those of the noncombatants, the women and children, the old and infirm, who were caught in a guerilla-style conflict.

Instead of settling affairs between the whites and the Indians, Sand Creek had driven a mighty wedge between the two peoples. Gen. Nelson A. Miles, one of the officers who took part in the subsequent battles, said "but for that horrible butchery it is a fair presumption that all subsequent wars with the Cheyennes and Arapahos and their kindred tribes might possibly have been averted."[4]

As a people the Southern Arapahos had not sought war and did not take part in it when it came, although knots of warriors occasionally rode northward to join the hostiles. Most of the tribe remained with Little Raven, who wandered the southern plains of Kansas and the Oklahoma Panhandle, remaining apart from the areas of conflict. After Sand Creek, they never returned to Colorado.

Sand Creek did not pass unnoticed.

On December 31, 1864, Major Wynkoop was reassigned to Fort Lyon with orders to investigate the Sand Creek attack. The

---

[3] U. S., Congress, Senate, "Letter of the Secretary of the Interior," Sen. Exec. Doc. 13, 40th Cong., 1st sess., 1868, p. 2.

[4] Nelson A. Miles, *Personal Recollections of General Nelson A. Miles*, p. 139.

affidavits that he obtained from officers, enlisted men, and civilians at the fort vehemently denounced Chivington's actions. These were sent to District Headquarters at Fort Riley, and on January 15, 1865, they were forwarded to Washington.[5] Before they arrived, however, Washington was alive with rumors that Sand Creek had not been the glorious field of battle its commander had claimed. The rumors were based on letters sent directly to government officials by men at Fort Lyon, among them Agent Colley.

On January 10, Congress authorized the Joint Committee on the Conduct of the War, which had been looking into aspects of the Civil War, to inquire into the facts of Sand Creek. The committee heard testimony from Governor Evans, who was still in Washington, and took depositions from military officers, including Chivington, and several civilians connected with Sand Creek. It then issued a report, "Massacre of the Cheyenne Indians," which scathingly denounced Evans and Chivington. The report contains the following characterization of the governor's demeanor during the hearings:

His testimony before your committee was characterized by such prevarications and shuffling as has been shown by no witness. . . examined during the four years [of] investigations; and for the evident purpose of avoiding the admission that he was fully aware that the Indians massacred so brutally at Sand Creek, were then, and had been, actuated by the most friendly feelings toward the whites, and had done all in their power to restrain those less friendly disposed.[6]

As for Chivington, the committee found that

He deliberately planned and executed a foul and dastardly massacre which would have disgraced the veriest savage among those who were the victims of his cruelty. Having full knowledge of their friendly character, having himself been instrumental to some extent in placing them in their position of fancied security

---

[5] Wynkoop to Tappan, January 15, 1865, *WRR* series 1, vol. 41, pt. 1, pp. 959–62.

[6] "Cheyenne Massacre," p. vi; see Evans's reply in "Chivington Massacre," pp. 77–87.

he took advantage of their inapprehension and defenceless condition to gratify the worst passions that ever cursed the heart of man. It is thought by some that desire for political preferment prompted him to this cowardly act; that he supposed by pandering to the inflamed passions of an excited population he could recommend himself to their regard and consideration . . . it is to be hoped that the authority of this government will never again be disgraced by acts such as he and those acting with him have been guilty of committing.[7]

A second congressional inquiry was taken up by the Joint Special Committee on the Condition of the Indian Tribes. Members of this committee traveled to the central plains to take testimony from witnesses at Forts Leavenworth, Riley, Larned, and Lyon, as well as in Santa Fe and Denver. While they were at Fort Lyon, Wynkoop led the committee members to Sand Creek where, he said, "the ground was still white with the bleaching bones of the slain."[8]

This committee issued a report entitled "The Chivington Massacre," which condemned the "wholesale massacre of Arapahos and Cheyennes by the Colorado troops under Chivington," and concluded that "these Indians were there encamped under the direction of our officers, and believed themselves to be under the protection of our flag."[9]

Still a third investigation took place. As the storm of Sand Creek broke across the nation, the army came under increasing pressure to account for Chivington's actions. Curtis, hoping to put the matter behind him, asked for and received the colonel's resignation on January 4, 1865. Nevertheless, Maj. Gen. Henry W. Halleck ordered Curtis to investigate Chivington's conduct.

The investigation was conducted by a military commission which took testimony in Denver and at Fort Lyon. Despite Chivington's efforts to have Samuel Tappan removed as the chairman because of past differences between them, the investigation proved thorough and fair: judicial procedure was followed and Chivington was given the right of counsel and the right to cross-

[7] "Cheyenne Massacre," p. v.
[8] Wynkoop manuscript, p. 37.
[9] "Chivington Massacre," p. 5–6.

examine witnesses. Because of its very fairness, this investigation proved the most damning to Chivington and the Colorado troops. Eyewitness after eyewitness testified about the duplicity and barbarity of the colonel and his men and remained steadfast in their accounts under cross-examination by Chivington himself. The report issued by the commission was entitled "Sand Creek Massacre."[10]

Despite the findings of these investigations, Evans and Chivington did not lack supporters. The faction that had always approved of the manner in which these two men had handled Indian matters closed ranks behind them. They dismissed the reports as having been based on the testimony of unscrupulous men like John Smith, whom even the Indians distrusted, they said, and who had reason to seek vengeance for the property he had lost at Sand Creek.

This faction also made much of the fact that the report entitled "Massacre of the Cheyenne Indians" had been issued over the signature of the committee chairman, Senator Ben Wade, who admitted he had neither heard any of the testimony nor seen any of the evidence. What Evans and Chivington's supporters overlooked, however, was that those committee members who had examined the evidence were the same men who issued the report, and that trustworthy men like Wynkoop, Cramer, and Soule had joined John Smith in condemning Sand Creek.

John Milton Chivington lived thirty years beyond Sand Creek, but the vitriolic congressional reports and public censure dogged his life. In 1867 his son drowned in the South Platte, and Chivington left Denver for San Diego soon afterwards. By 1872 he was back in Ohio managing a newspaper. At one point he ran for Congress only to have the shadow of Sand Creek cast upon his campaign, forcing him to withdraw. In 1883 he returned to Denver, where he became undersheriff and, later, coroner.

Until his death on October 4, 1894, Chivington justified his attack on Sand Creek in speeches to churches, or any other organization that would listen, as the necessary punishment of hostile Indians. He could never understand why the delivery of that punishment had not brought him the glory and promotion

---

[10] "Sand Creek Massacre"

similar attacks had brought other military leaders, including Brig. Gen. Patrick Connor.

Following Chivington's speech to the Eastern Star in Denver one day, a woman steered him over to a small, dark woman saying, "Mrs. Prowers, do you know Colonel Chivington?" Amache, the daughter of One-Eye, "drew herself up with that stately dignity, peculiar to her people, and ignoring the outstretched hand, remarked in perfect English, audible to all in the room, 'Know Colonel Chivington? I should. He was my father's murderer.' "[11]

If public opinion shifted against Chivington, it defended and finally ignored the role Evans had played in the Sand Creek affair. The governor justified Chivington's attack as necessary, but he claimed falsely that he had had no prior knowledge of it because he had been in Washington. In the eyes of his supporters that technicality absolved the governor from blame.

On July 18, 1865, President Johnson dispatched a letter to Evans asking for his resignation, and on August 1, the day the letter reached Denver, the governor complied.[12]

The question of statehood had surfaced once again. Residents of the territory, led by Evans's supporters in Denver—who were outraged by the president's request for his resignation—banded together to name him senator-elect from the proposed state of Colorado. Thus they served notice that Washington did not control affairs on the central plains. In late 1865, Evans left for Washington to take up new duties, but his friend President Lincoln had fallen before the assassin's bullet, and President Johnson was not disposed to admit Colorado into the Union. He vetoed the bill for statehood, rendering Evans a nonsenator from a nonstate.

Evans returned to Colorado Territory, free, at last, to devote his full time and energies to the financial opportunities which

[11] Mary Prowers Hudnall, "Early History of Bent County," *Colorado Magazine* 22 (1945):233–47; for a defense of Chivington's actions at Sand Creek, see Reginald S. Craig, *The Fighting Parson*, and the *Denver Republican*, October 5, 1894 (published with Chivington's obituary.)

[12] *Rocky Mountain News*, September 6, 1865.

had drawn him to the plains in the first place. In the next twenty years Evans built railroads across Colorado, railroads in which he maintained either controlling or part interest. Among the railroads he spearheaded were the Denver Pacific Railroad Company, which linked Denver with the Union Pacific that was routed through Cheyenne, Wyoming; the Kansas Pacific, which tied Denver to Kansas City; the Denver, South Park and Pacific; the Denver and New Orleans; and the Boulder Valley Railroad. Evans also built the Denver Electric and Cable Railway, later the Denver Tramway.[13]

Along the way Evans amassed a great amount of land, much of it through land grants bestowed on railroad companies. Under the Union Pacific Act, it should be recalled, railroad companies received ten sections of land on both sides of a railroad line for each mile of track they had laid. The Kansas Pacific, for example, received 832,822 acres on the plains of Kansas and Colorado, acres which increased in value as the railroad lines were completed. According to Evans's biographer, Edgar McMechen, he continually demonstrated his faith in Denver by investing in real estate; much of today's downtown Denver, including Civic Center, was part of Evans's portfolio.[14]

Before he died on July 2, 1897 at the age of eighty-three, John Evans, the empire builder of the plains, had fulfilled his life's dream of accumulating a great fortune. While fulfilling that dream, he had incidentally shepherded Colorado into an age of modern transportation, industrialization, and, in 1876, statehood. As Evans prospered, so did Colorado. In 1884 the historian Hubert Howe Bancroft interviewed Evans on his role in Colorado history and came away with the following impression, recorded in his private notes:

About Ex-Governor Evans and his son-in-law Judge Elberts [sic] there is much humbug. They are cold-blooded mercenary men,

[13] Thomas J. Noel, "All Hail the Denver Pacific," *Colorado Magazine* 59 (1973):91-116; Olga Curtis, "The Evans Dynasty: A Century of Power," *Denver Post*, February 23, 1969; Edgar McMechen, *The Life of Governor Evans.*
[14] McMechen, *Life of Evans*, pp. 105, 223.

ready to praise themselves and each other profusely, but who have
in reality but little patriotism.[15]

Silas S. Soule, the officer who refused to order his troops into
action at Sand Creek, was fatally shot in the streets of Denver on
April 23, 1865, by a member of the Colorado Second named
Squiers. Squiers was arrested later in New Mexico and brought to
Denver for military trial by Lieutenant Cannon of the New Mexico Volunteers. Before the trial could be held, however, Cannon
was himself found dead in his room at the Tremont House, mys-
teriously poisoned, and Squiers made good an escape to
California.[16]

Before he was killed, Soule had told his longtime friend, Capt.
George F. Price, that he feared he would be assassinated because
of his testimony against Chivington during the military investigation. He also thought that attempts would be made to
blacken his character after his death, destroying the effect of his
testimony. Immediately following Soule's death, Price testified
about this before the coroner's jury. Two weeks later on May 7,
1865, Chivington introduced a favorable witness before the
military commission, Lepman Meyer, a freighter, who testified
that Soule was a drunk, a thief, and a coward.[17]

Maj. Jacob Downing, Chivington's aide and defense attorney
during the military investigation, later ranched 2,000 acres east
of Denver. He is credited with introducing alfalfa and Hereford
cattle to Colorado and with developing vast sections of north and
east Denver, where a street is named in his honor. He also helped
in developing Denver's City Park. Sometimes cited as an example
of the progressive, civilized white men who had come to the
plains, Downing made no secret of his attitude toward the Indians, an attitude shared by many Denver townspeople. About
Sand Creek he said: "I tried to take none [no prisoners] myself,
but killed all I could. I think that was the general feeling in the

[15] Hubert Howe Bancroft, "Colorado Notes, 1884", Western History
Division, University of Colorado Library, Boulder, Colo.
[16] *Rocky Mountain News,* April 14, 24, 27, 1865; July 12, 15, 1865.
[17] "Sand Creek Massacre," pp. 186–87.

command. I think and earnestly believe the Indians to be an obstacle to civilization, and should be exterminated.''[18]

Maj. Gen. Samuel R. Curtis was relieved of command on January 30, 1865, and assigned to the Department of the Northwest. With the end of the Civil War he returned to civilian life and an appointment by President Johnson as inspector of newly laid Union Pacific Railroad tracks, a position that dovetailed with Curtis's long-standing interest in railroads. On December 26, 1866, he died while at his work.[19]

Maj. Scott Anthony was mustered out of the army and settled in Denver, where he became a surveyor and subcontractor for Evans's Denver Pacific Railroad Company. Later he became a prosperous Denver realtor and served as a director of the Denver Tramway Company, another of Evans's enterprises. He lived on toward the end of the century, a respected and influential member of Denver's community.[20]

Maj. Edward W. Wynkoop was appointed brevet lieutenant colonel in 1865 but resigned his commission to become agent to the Southern Arapahos and Cheyennes, whose welfare was his main concern for the next two years. In 1868 he returned to Philadelphia to enter business with his brother. Later, when the business failed, he again headed for the plains, this time to join in the search for gold in the Black Hills. He had some success in mining and thereafter worked at various jobs until 1890, when he was appointed warden of the New Mexico penitentiary. Following his death on September 11, 1891, at age fifty-five, newspapers across the plains eulogized him as "honest, brave and loyal to the core." His death went unnoticed in Denver, however, a city that Wynkoop had loved, his son said later, even while he was fighting against its "unworthy and unjust elements."[21]

[18] *Portrait and Biographical Record of Denver and Vicinity, Colorado,* pp. 1239-40; "Chivington Massacre," p. 70.
[19] Ruth A. Gallaher, "Samuel Ryan Curtis," *Iowa Journal of History and Politics* 25 (1927): 331-58.
[20] *Portrait and Biographical Record,* p. 340.
[21] Edward E. Wynkoop, "Edward Wanshier Wynkoop," *Kansas Historical Collections* 13 (1913-14):71-79.

In issuing the report titled "The Chivington Massacre," Sen. James R. Doolittle, chairman of the congressional investigating committee, addressed the causes of war on the plains: "The committee are of the opinion that in a large majority of cases Indian wars are to be traced to the aggressions of lawless white men, always to be found upon the frontier, or boundary line between savage and civilized life."[22]

On October 14, 1865, the surviving Southern Arapaho and Cheyenne chiefs met with government commissioners at Bluff Creek, forty miles south of the Little Arkansas River in southern Kansas. The mood of the council was heavy with sadness. Speaking for his people, Little Raven said:

> There is something very strong for us—that fool band of soldiers that cleared out our lodges, and killed our women and children. This is strong on us. There, at Sand Creek, is one chief, Left Hand; White Antelope and many other chiefs lie there, and our horses were taken from us there, and I do not feel disposed to go right off in a new country and leave them.[23]

Black Kettle also spoke of the hardships and sorrow of Sand Creek. What was the reason for it? he wanted to know. "We are different nations, but it seems as if we [are] but one people, whites and all." He also spoke sorrowfully of the people who had died at Sand Creek because they had trusted him. "My shame," he said, "is as big as the earth."[24]

Gen. John B. Sanborn, heading up the commission, told the chiefs, "We have all got to submit to the tide of emigration and civilization." In what amounted to a tacit acknowledgment by the government that the Fort Wise Treaty was not and had never been a valid treaty, Sanborn proposed that the two tribes relinquish their lands between the Platte and Arkansas rivers in exchange for land in southern Kansas and Indian Territory. When Little Raven asked how that could be, since land south of the

[22] "Chivington Massacre," p. 5.
[23] Charles J. Kappler, *Indian Affairs: Laws and Treaties*, 2:703, 2:887–89.
[24] Ibid., p. 709.

Arkansas belonged to the Kiowas and Comanches, Sanborn promised him that the problem would somehow be solved. In the meantime, the Southern Arapahos and Cheyennes, he said, could roam across their former lands so long as they did not camp within ten miles of the main roads, military posts, towns, or settlements.[25]

Despite the uncertainties in this proposal, the chiefs signed the Treaty of the Little Arkansas, agreeing to relinquish their lands in exchange for promises. Little Raven, Storm, Big Mouth, Spotted Wolf, Black Man, Chief in Everything, and Haversack signed for the Southern Arapahos; Black Kettle and Seven Bulls for the Cheyennes.

Article Six of the Treaty of the Little Arkansas, which took notice of the Sand Creek injustice, provided that the surviving chiefs were each to receive 320 acres of land. Another 160 acres were to be allotted to every widow and orphan of Sand Creek. There is no evidence that the chiefs ever received their allotments, but Amache, according to her daughter, received 160 acres in the Arkansas River valley.[26]

On October 16, 1867, the Southern Arapahos and Cheyennes assembled for another treaty council on Medicine Lodge Creek, sixty miles south of Fort Larned. At this council the two tribes were assigned a joint reservation between the Arkansas and Cimarron rivers in northwestern Indian Territory. But the reservation was smaller in area than what they were promised in the Treaty of the Little Arkansas because Kansas had refused to allow an Indian reservation within its boundaries.[27]

Within the year the Southern Arapahos under Little Raven left their traditional lands in Colorado and Kansas and moved southward toward the reservation; later Little Raven said that when they started out he was not even sure where the reservation was located. By April, 1869, other Southern Arapaho leaders,

[25] Ibid., p. 680.

[26] Hudnall, "Early History of Bent County," pp. 233–47; Kappler, *Indian Affairs*, 2:708–709, 889; *BIA Reports* (1868), House Exec. Doc. 1, 40th Cong., 3d sess., p. 35; see U.S., Congress "Amendments to Treaties," House Exec. Doc. 104, 40th Cong., 2d sess., 1868. The Left Hand who signed for the Apaches should not be confused with the Southern Arapaho Left Hand.

[27] Kappler, *Indian Affairs*, 2:760–64.

Yellow Bear, Storm, and Little Big Mouth, had also brought in their bands.

Neva was not among them. Following Sand Creek he had joined the hostiles, moving north and raiding white settlements. With him went No-Ta-Nee. On June 16, 1868, both men signed a second Fort Laramie Treaty, this one the counterpart of the Medicine Lodge Treaty, which called for the Northern Arapahos to accept part of the reservation in Indian Territory or move onto another reservation already given to the Sioux. In April, 1870, No-Ta-Nee was killed during an attack on white settlements near the Sweetwater in Wyoming. Neva simply disappeared.[28]

William Bent retired to his ranch at Big Timbers following the Little Arkansas Treaty Council. He lived quietly there until his death from pneumonia on May 19, 1869.

George Bent lived on the Oklahoma reservation, working as an interpreter and clerk in the agent's office at Darlington until his death, on May 19, 1918, in Colony, Oklahoma.

John Smith worked as an interpreter on the Oklahoma reservation until his death from pneumonia on June 29, 1871. He was sixty-one years old.

MaHom and her daughter Mary were taken to William Bent's ranch following Sand Creek. Eventually they made their way to Little Raven's band, since their own band had been destroyed. Mary later married a white man, Ben Keith.

Margaret Fitzpatrick Wilmarth, MaHom's eldest daughter and the widow of Thomas Fitzpatrick, served as an interpreter for the Southern Arapahos at the Medicine Lodge Treaty Council.

At the insistence of the Indians, the army finally returned two Cheyenne boys and one Southern Arapaho captured at Sand Creek.[29]

[28] *BIA Reports* (1868); Virginia Cole Trenholm, *The Arapahoes, Our People*, p. 233.
[29] Bent to Tappan, February 23, 1889, George Bent Letters, Colorado State Historical Society, Denver, Colo.

The half-blood children of John and Amache Prowers were educated in eastern universities, as were their grandchildren. In time, most of them returned to the plains, where they prospered in the county named for their family.

At dawn on November 27, 1868, as the band played "Garry Owen," Gen. George Armstrong Custer's Seventh Cavalry charged a Cheyenne camp on the banks of the Washita River in Indian Territory. When the attack ended, between eighteen and forty Cheyennes lay dead. Among them were Chief Black Kettle and his wife, Woman to be Hereafter.[30]

Kohiss, a Southern Arapaho woman, died in the 1940s at the age of 104, the last survivor of Sand Creek. She had tried to escape, she said, carrying her baby in one arm and dragging her other two children, who were too small to run, by the other. The children were killed.[31]

Little Raven continued to serve as principal chief of the Southern Arapahos until his death on the reservation in 1889, although he was described in newspaper accounts of the Medicine Lodge Treaty Council more than twenty years earlier as already in his dotage. During his waning years Little Raven came to rely upon the intelligence and energy of a rising young leader who succeeded him as principal chief and whose name happened to be Left Hand.

That a man named Left Hand became principal chief of the Southern Arapahos in 1889 has led some historians to conclude that somehow Chief Left Hand survived his wounds at Sand

---

[30] *BIA Reports* (1871), House Exec. Doc. 1, 42d Cong., 2d sess., p. 34; for additional unpublished details on the Battle of the Washita, see Bent to Hyde, September, 1905, George Bent Letters, Colorado State Historical Society; Bent to Hyde, August 28, 1913, Bent Letters, Coe Collection, Yale University, New Haven, Conn.; Bent to Tappan, February 23, 1889, George Bent Letters, Colorado State Historical Society; F. S. Barde manuscript, "Battle of the Washita," Indian Archives, Oklahoma State Historical Society, Oklahoma City, Okla.

[31] Trenholm, *Arapahoes*, p. 194.

Creek, recuperated for three years—until 1867, when the name Left Hand again appears in the tribal records—and eventually returned to his position of leadership.

Many similarities between the two men support that conclusion. Both were described by contemporaries as proud, dignified men, natural leaders and fine orators, who were always eager to mediate between their people and the white man. The description of Left Hand in 1872 as "handsome, lithe and athletic, and a man of strong personality and possessed of a large measure of magnetism when it came to enlisting the support and following of his tribesmen" is markedly similar to descriptions of the Chief Left Hand of the late 1850s and 1860s.[32]

But there were differences. The later Left Hand was a younger man, born in 1840, who was about twenty-four years old at the time of Sand Creek. Also, and most importantly, he could not speak English.[33]

The two Southern Arapaho chiefs with the same name were not related, according to George Bent. But there is reason to believe that they were connected and that the younger man adopted the name of the other. The Southern Arapaho Carl Sweezy wrote that the later chief, whom he had known as a youth, liked to tell of how he had been fired upon at Fort Larned when he had gone to offer assistance.[34] On that hot July day in 1864 when Chief Left Hand had approached Fort Larned, twenty-five of his "boys" rode with him. They were the young warriors who had followed him, believing in his policies, and who no doubt were influenced by his character. Some had probably died at Sand Creek, but others, who had decided to go with Little Raven that fateful November, had survived. One may have received Left Hand's name and later become a chief in his own right.

[32] John Murphy, "Reminiscences of the Washita Campaign and of the Darlington Indian Agency," *Chronicles of Oklahoma* 1 (1923):272.

[33] Ibid; *BIA Reports* from 1872 to 1900 contain numerous references to Left Hand's inability to speak English and of his need for an interpreter; "Left Hand's Autobiography," Indian Archives, Oklahoma State Historical Society. See also Hugh L. Scott, *Some Memories of a Soldier,* pp. 557-60 and U.S. Congress, "Cheyenne and Arapaho Indian Lands," House Exec. Doc. 43, 42d Cong., 3d sess., 1872, p. 65.

[34] Carl Sweezy, *The Arapahoe Way,* p. 22.

He would have received the name in a council held sometime after Sand Creek and before 1867, in those difficult years that were filled with great uncertainties for the Southern Arapaho people. The leading men would have called him to the center of the council, as was the Southern Arapaho custom. As he stood before them, encircled by the wise and respected elders of the tribe, with the other tribal members looking on from an outer circle, he would have been given the honored name.

The warrior was about twenty-seven years old and his reputation for courage and leadership was already sound. It was not for brave deeds he had received this honor, however, but for his generous spirit and a deepening wisdom that was believed to be much like that of the fallen chief.[35]

He would have accepted the new name as the sign he knew it to be, a sign that Left Hand's policies of peace and understanding remained the policies of his people and that his people wished them to endure.

[35] See Sister Inez M. Hilger, "Arapaho Child Life and its Cultural Background," Smithsonian Institution, Bureau of American Ethnology Bulletin no. 148 (1952), pp. 58–66, for explanation of name changes among the Southern Arapahos; See "Left Hand's Autobiography" (Indian Archives, Oklahoma State Historical Society) for facts on this man's early years and reputation. It was this Left Hand who led the Southern Arapaho warriors in the defense of the Cheyenne camp at the Battle of the Washita, 1868, surrounding and killing the troops under Maj. Joel H. Elliott, (F. S. Barde manuscript, Indian Archives, Oklahoma State Historical Society). The names of outstanding leaders in the past, including Left Hand's, are no longer found among the Southern Arapahos, perhaps, as one historian suggests, because of the difficulty of living up to their deeds and exemplary lives or because of the fear that other tribal members would consider the adoption of an esteemed name presumptuous (Dan W. Peery, "The Indian's Friend: John Seger," *Chronicles of Oklahoma* 10 [1932]: 348–63; 11 [1933]:709–732).

Bibliography

Manuscript Materials

Boulder, Colorado
   University of Colorado, Western History Division:
      Bancroft, Hubert Howe. "Interview with John Evans."
      _____. "Colorado Notes," including statements about
         John Evans, 1884.
      Bent-Hyde Papers, including original Bent map of Sand Creek.
      Bent, George. "Forty Years with the Cheyennes." Edited by
         George Hyde. Manuscript.
      William N. Byers Papers
      "John Evans, Pioneer on Two Planes." Pamphlet file.
      Hyde, George. "Last of Colonel Bent's Sons Dead."
      "Union Pacific: 100 Years in Colorado." Pamphlet file.
      Union Pacific Railroad Company *Annual Reports.*

Colorado Springs, Colorado
   Pioneers Museum:
      F. W. Cragin Collection. 28 notebooks.

Denver, Colorado
   Colorado State Archives:
      John Evans Collection: Indian Affairs
   Colorado State Historical Society:
      Scott J. Anthony Letters and Manuscript
      Alexander Barclay's Diary. Microfilm.
      George Bent Letters, including letters to George Hyde
         and Samuel Tappan.
      Byers, William N. "The Centennial State."
      Marshall Cook Manuscript
      Dawson Scrapbooks. 4 vols.
      John Evans Collection

Hafen, LeRoy R. "Historical Background and Development of the Arapahoe-Cheyenne Land Area."
_____. "The Indians of Colorado."
Shields, Lillian B. "The Arapahoe Indians: Their Association with the White Man." Master's thesis, University of Denver, 1929.
Samuel Tappan Diary and Manuscript.
Edward W. Wynkoop Manuscript.
Denver Public Library, Western History Division:
George Bent Letters to George Hyde.
W. Ferril Scrapbook, 1887.
Hyde, George. "Life of George Bent," including Bent-Hyde Letters. Typescript.
Federal Archives and Records Center, Office of Indian Affairs:
Upper Platte and Arkansas Agency Files, Letters Sent and Letters Received.

Norman, Oklahoma
University of Oklahoma Library, Manuscript Division:
Walter S. Campbell (Stanley Vestal) Collection
_____. "Resumé and Aftermath of Sand Creek."

Oklahoma City, Oklahoma
Oklahoma State Historical Society, Indian Archives:
Barde, F. S. "Battle of the Washita."
Census Records, Arapaho.
Cheyenne and Arapaho Agency Letterbooks.
Cheyenne and Arapaho Files on Agents, Battles, Captives, Celebrations, History, Legends.
Foreman Collection:
"Indian Pioneer History." Vols. 38, 52, 98, 104.
"Left Hand's Autobiography."

Topeka, Kansas
Kansas State Historical Society:
"Reminiscences of Robert M. Wright." Typescript.

Washington, D.C.
National Archives, Records of the Office of Indian Affairs:
Upper Arkansas Agency. Letters Sent and Letters Received.

Government Publications
and Records

Fort Wise Treaty. Record Group 75. Federal Archives and Records Center, Denver, Colorado.

Kappler, Charles J., comp. and ed. *Indian Affairs: Laws and Treaties.* 4 vols. 1904, 1913, 1927.

U.S. Congress. House. "Reports of Indians Taxed and Not Taxed in the United States." House Misc. Doc. 340. 52d Cong., 1st sess. 28 vols. 1892–1897.

_____. Senate. "Massacre of the Cheyenne Indians." *Report of the Joint Committee on the Conduct of the War.* Sen. Report 142. 38th Cong., 2d sess. 1865.

_____. Senate. "Sand Creek Massacre." *Report of the Secretary of War,* Communicating, in compliance with a resolution of the Senate of February 4, 1867, a copy of the evidence taken at Denver and Fort Lyon, Colorado Territory, by a military commision, ordered to inquire into the Sand Creek massacre, November, 1864. Sen. Exec. Doc. 26. 39th Cong., 2d sess. 1867.

_____. Senate. "The Chivington Massacre." *Reports of the Joint Special Committees on the Condition of the Indian Tribes.* Sen. Report 156. 39th Cong., 2d sess. 1867.

U.S. Department of the Interior. Bureau of Indian Affairs. *Reports of the Commissioner of Indian Affairs,* 1847–1906.

_____. *Biographical and Historical Index of American Indians.*

U.S. *Statutes at Large.* Vol. 12

U.S. War Department. *The War of the Rebellion: A Compilation of the Official Records of the Union and Confederate Armies.* Four series, 128 vols. 1880–1901.

Newspapers

Council Bluffs Bugle, Council Bluffs, Iowa. September, October, 1858.

Council Bluffs Non Pareil, Council Bluffs, Iowa. September, October, 1858.

Daily Camera, Boulder, Colorado. November 30, 1948; September 13, 1963.

Daily National Intelligencer, Washington, D.C. November 19, 1851 to March 28, 1863.

Denver Post, Denver, Colorado. February 23, 1969.

Denver Republican, Denver, Colorado. May 18, 1890; October 5, 1894.

Eufaula Indian Journal, Eufaula, Oklahoma. July 7, 1911.
Gazette Telegraph, Colorado Springs, Colorado. December 16, 1934.
Lawrence Republican, Lawrence, Kansas. May 22 to August 15, 1860.
Leavenworth Times, Leavenworth, Kansas. June 4, 1859.
Missouri Republican, St. Louis, Missouri. October 22, 1851; July 9, 1859.
New York Times, April 8, 1863.
Pueblo Star Journal and Sun Chieftain, Pueblo, Colorado. September 29, 1957.
Rocky Mountain News (weekly and daily), Denver, Colorado. April 25, 1859 to January 3, 1865.
Sunday Oklahoman, Oklahoma City, Oklahoma. March 4, 1968.

Books

Abert, James W. *Western America in 1846–1847: The Original Travel Diary of Lieutenant J. W. Abert.* Edited by John Galvin. San Francisco: John Howell Books, 1966.
Alter, J. Cecil. *Jim Bridger.* New and revised ed. Norman: University of Oklahoma Press, 1962.
Ames, Charles Edgar. *Pioneering the Union Pacific: A Reappraisal of the Builders of the Railroad.* New York: Meridith, 1969.
Andrist, Ralph K. *The Long Death: The Last Days of the Plains Indians.* New York: Collier Books, 1964.
Arps, Louisa Ward, and Elinor E. Kingery. *High Country Names.* Denver: Colorado Mountain Club, 1966.
Athearn, Robert G. *William Tecumseh Sherman and the Settlement of the West.* Norman: University of Oklahoma Press, 1956.
Baillie-Grohman, William A. *Camps in the Rockies.* New York: Charles Scribner's Sons, 1905.
Bancroft, Hubert Howe. *History of the Life of William Gilpin: A Character Study.* San Francisco: History Co., 1889.
Berthrong, Donald J. *The Southern Cheyennes.* Norman: University of Oklahoma Press, 1963.
Beckwourth, James P. *Life and Adventures of James P. Beckwourth.* Edited by T. D. Bonner. New York: Macmillan Co., 1892.
Bourke, John G. *On the Border with Crook.* New York: Charles Scribner's Sons, 1891.
Brown, Dee. *Bury My Heart at Wounded Knee.* New York: Holt, Rinehart and Winston, 1970.
Carriker, Robert C. *Fort Supply, Indian Territory.* Norman: University of Oklahoma Press, 1970.
Clark, William Philo. *The Indian Sign Language.* Philadelphia: L. R.

Hamersly, 1885.

Collins, Hubert Edwin. *Warpath and Cattle Trail*. New York: William Morrow, 1928.

Craig, Reginald S. *The Fighting Parson: The Biography of Colonel John M. Chivington*. Los Angeles: Westernlore Press, 1959.

Custer, George Armstrong. *My Life on the Plains*. St. Louis: Royal Publishing, 1891.

Dary, David A. *The Buffalo Book*. Chicago: Swallow Press, 1974.

De Smet, Pierre-Jean. *Life, Letters, and Travels of Father Pierre-Jean De Smet*. Edited by H. M. Chittenden and A. T. Richardson. 4 vols. New York: Francis P. Harper, 1905.

Downey, Fairfax. *Indian Wars of the U.S. Army, 1776–1865*. New York: Doubleday, 1963.

Dunn, Jacob P. *Massacres of the Mountains: A History of the Indian Wars of the Far West*. New York: Harper and Bros., 1886.

Dyer, Mrs. D. B. *Fort Reno or Picturesque Cheyenne and Arapahoe Army Life Before the Opening of Oklahoma*. New York: G. W. Dillingham, 1896.

Eggan, Fred, ed. *Social Anthropology of North American Tribes*. Chicago: University of Chicago Press, 1937.

Farnham, Thomas J. *Travels in the Great Western Prairies in Early Western Travels, 1748–1846*. vols. 28, 29. Edited by Reuben G. Thwaites. Cleveland: Arthur H. Clark Co. 1904–1905.

Frémont, John C. *Memoirs of My Life*. 2 vols. Chicago and New York: Belford, Clarke, 1887.

_____. *Narratives of Exploration and Adventure*. Edited by Allan Nevins. New York: Longmans, Green and Co., 1956.

_____. *Report of an Exploring Expedition to the Rocky Mountains*. Washington, D.C.: Blair and Rivers, 1845.

Fritz, Percy Stanley. *Colorado: The Centennial State*. New York: Prentice-Hall, 1941.

Gard, Wayne. *The Chisholm Trail*. Norman: University of Oklahoma Press, 1954.

Geffs, Mary L. *Under Ten Flags*. Greeley: McVey Printery, 1938.

Greeley, Horace. *An Overland Journey*. Ann Arbor: University Microfilms, 1966.

Grinnell, George Bird. *The Cheyenne Indians: Their History and Ways of Life*. 2 vols. New Haven, Conn.: Yale University Press, 1924.

_____. *The Fighting Cheyennes*. New York: Charles Scribner's Sons, 1915.

Hafen, LeRoy R. *Broken Hand: The Life of Thomas Fitzpatrick, Mountain Man, Guide, and Indian Agent*. Denver: Old West Publishing Co., 1931.

———, ed. *Colorado and Its People*. Vol. 1. New York: Lewis Historical Publishing, 1948.

———, ed. *Colorado Gold Rush Contemporary Letters and Reports, 1858–1859*. Glendale, Calif.: Arthur H. Clark Co., 1941.

———, ed. *The Mountain Men and the Fur Trade of the Far West*. Vol. 6, Glendale, Calif.: Arthur H. Clark Co., 1968.

———, ed. *Overland Routes to the Gold Fields, 1859: From Contemporary Diaries*. Glendale, Calif.: Arthur H. Clark Co., 1942.

——— and Ann W. Hafen, eds. *Relations with the Indians of the Plains, 1857–1861*. In *The Far West and the Rockies Historical Series*. vol. 9. Glendale, Calif.: Arthur H. Clark Co., 1959.

———, ed. *Reports from Colorado: The Wildman Letters, 1859–1865*. In *The Far West and the Rockies Historical Series*, vol. 13. Glendale, Calif.: Arthur H. Clark, Co., 1961.

Hall, Frank. *History of the State of Colorado*. 4 vols. Chicago: Blakely Printing Co., 1889.

History of Clear Creek and Boulder Valley, Colorado. Chicago: O. L. Baskin and Co., 1880.

Hoig, Stan. *The Sand Creek Massacre*. Norman: University of Oklahoma Press, 1961.

———. *The Western Odyssey of John Simpson Smith*. Glendale, Calif.: Arthur H. Clark, Co., 1974.

Howbert, Irving. *Memories of a Lifetime in the Pike's Peak Region*. New York: G. P. Putnam's Sons, 1925.

Hyde, George E. *Life of George Bent: Written from his Letters*. Edited by Savoie Lottinville. Norman: University of Oklahoma Press, 1967.

Jones, Douglas C. *The Treaty of Medicine Lodge*. Norman: University of Oklahoma Press, 1966.

Keim, DeB. Randolph. *Sheridan's Troopers on the Border: A Winter Campaign on the Plains*. Philadelphia, David McKay, 1891.

Kroeber, Alfred. *Cultural and Natural Areas of Native North America*. Berkeley: University of California Press, 1939.

Lass, William E. *From the Missouri to the Great Salt Lake: An Account of Overland Freighting*. Nebraska State Historical Society Publications, vol. 26. Lincoln: Nebraska State Historical Society, 1972.

Lavender, David. *Bent's Fort*. Garden City, N.Y.: Doubleday, 1954.

Leckie, William H. *The Military Conquest of the Southern Plains*. Norman: University of Oklahoma Press, 1963.

LeCompte, Janet. "John Poisal." In *The Mountain Men and the Fur Trade of the Far West*. vol. 6. Edited by LeRoy R. Hafen. Glendale, Calif.: Arthur H. Clark Co., 1968.

Levi-Strauss, Claude. *The Savage Mind*. Chicago: University of Chicago Press, 1966.

Marshall, S. L. A. *Crimsoned Prairie*. New York: Charles Scribner's Sons, 1972.

McMechen, Edgar Carlisle. *The Life of Governor Evans*. Denver: Wahlgreen, 1924.

Miles, Nelson A. *Personal Recollections of General Nelson A. Miles*. Chicago and New York: Werner Co., 1896.

Montaignes, François des. *The Plains*. Edited by Nancy Alpert Mower and Don Russell. Norman: University of Oklahoma Press, 1972.

Mumey, Nolie. *Early Settlements of Denver*. Glendale, Calif.: Arthur H. Clark Co., 1942.

National Cyclopedia of American Biography. New York: J. T. White and Co., 1937.

Nelson, Oliver. *The Cowman's Southwest: Reminiscences of Oliver Nelson*. Edited by Angie Debo. Glendale, Calif.: Arthur H. Clark Co., 1953.

Olson, James C. *History of Nebraska*. Lincoln: University of Nebraska Press, 1955.

Painter, Charles C. *Cheyenne and Arapahoe Revisited*. Philadelphia: Indian Rights Association, 1893.

Parsons, Eugene. *The Making of Colorado*. Chicago: A. Flanagan, 1908.

Pearce, Roy Harvey. *The Savages of America: A Study of the Indian and the Idea of Civilization*. Rev. ed. Baltimore: Johns Hopkins Press, 1965.

Portrait and Biographical Record of Denver and Vicinity Colorado. Denver: Chapman Publishing, 1898.

Richardson, Albert D. *Beyond the Mississippi*. Hartford, Conn.: American Publishing, 1869.

Sage, Rufus B. *Rocky Mountain Life*. In *The Far West and the Rockies Historical Series*, vol. 3. Edited by LeRoy R. Hafen and Ann W. Hafen. Glendale, Calif.: Arthur H. Clark Co., 1955.

Scott, Hugh L. *Some Memories of a Soldier*. New York: Century Co., 1928.

Seger, John H. *Early Days Among the Cheyenne and Arapaho Indians*. Edited by Stanley Vestal [Walter S. Campbell]. Norman: University of Oklahoma Press, 1956.

Seton, Ernest Thompson. *Life-Histories of Northern Animals*. Vol. 1. New York: Charles Scribner's Sons, 1909.

Shakespeare, Tom. *The Sky People*. New York: Vantage Press, 1971.

Smiley, Jerome C. *History of Denver*. Denver: Denver Times, 1901.

Sprague, Marshall. *Massacre: The Tragedy of White River*. Boston: Little, Brown and Co., 1957.

Stands-in-Timber, John, and Margot Liberty. *Cheyenne Memories*.

New Haven and London: Yale University Press, 1967.
Stone, Wilbur Fisk, ed. *History of Colorado*. Vol 1. Chicago: S. J. Clarke Publishing, 1918.
Sweezy, Carl. *The Arapahoe Way: A Memoir of an Indian Boyhood of Carl Sweezy as told by Althea Bass*. New York: Clarkson N. Potter, 1966.
Taylor, Colin. *The Warriors of the Plains*. New York: Arco Publishing, 1975.
Tebbel, John. *The Compact History of the Indian Wars*. New York: Hawthorn Books, 1966.
Trenholm, Virginia Cole. *The Arapahoes, Our People*. Norman: University of Oklahoma Press, 1970.
Turner, Katherine C. *Red Men Calling on the Great White Father*. Norman: University of Oklahoma Press, 1951.
Ubbelohde, Carl, ed. *A Colorado Reader*. Boulder: Pruett Press, 1962.
Villard, Henry. *The Past and Present of the Pike's Peak Gold Regions*. 1860. Reprint. Princeton: Princeton University Press, 1932.
Ware, Eugene F. *The Indian War of 1864*. Topeka, Kans.: Crane and Co., 1911.
Webb, Walter P. *The Great Plains*. 1931. Reprint. New York: Grosset and Dunlap, 1974.
Wharton, J. E. *History of the City of Denver from Its Earliest Settlement to the Present Time*. Denver: 1866.
Whitford, William Clark. *Colorado Volunteers in the Civil War*. Denver: State Historical and Natural History Society, 1906.
Wilson, Elinor. *Jim Beckwourth: Black Mountain Man and War Chief of the Crows*. Norman: University of Oklahoma Press, 1972.
Zamonski, Stanley W. and Teddy Keller. *The Fifty-Niners*. Denver: Sage Books, 1961.

Periodicals

Ashley, Susan R. "Reminiscences of Colorado in the Early Sixties." *Colorado Magazine* 13 (1936):219-30.
Athearn, Robert G. "Colorado and the Indian War of 1868." *Colorado Magazine* 33 (1956):41-51.
Bent, George. "Forty Years with the Cheyennes." Edited by George E. Hyde. *Frontier* 4 (October, 1905–March, 1906):3-7.
Bradley, Evelyn. "The Story of a Colorado Pioneer (Mrs. Charles A. Finding)." *Colorado Magazine* 2 (1925):50-55.
Block, Augusta Hauck. "Tower Boulder and St. Vrain Valley Home Guards and Fort Junction." *Colorado Magazine* 16 (1939):186-91.
Campbell, Walter S. (Stanley Vestal). "The Cheyenne Dog Soldiers."

Chronicles of Oklahoma 1 (1923):90-97.

Carey, Raymond G. "The Puzzle of Sand Creek." *Colorado Magazine* 41 (1964):279-98.

"A Century of Controversy." *Colorado Magazine* 41 (1964):278.

Curtis, Olga. "The Evans Dynasty: A Century of Power." *Empire Magazine, Denver Post*, February 23, 1969, pp. 8-12.

Dorsey, George A. *The Arapahoe Sun Dance: The Ceremony of the Offerings Lodge*. Field Columbian Museum Anthropological Series, vol. 5, no. 75 (1903).

_____ and Alfred L. Kroeber. *Traditions of the Arapaho*. Field Columbian Museum Anthropological Series, vol. 5, no. 81 (1903).

Ellis, Elmer. "Colorado's First Fight for Statehood: 1865-1868." *Colorado Magazine* 8 (1931):23-26.

Foreman, Carolyn T. "Colonel Jesse Henry Leavenworth." *Chronicles of Oklahoma* 13 (1935):14-29.

"Frontier Sketches." *Field and Farm*. July 25, 1908; July 8, 1911.

Gallaher, Ruth A. "Samuel Ryan Curtis." *Iowa Journal of History and Politics* 25 (1927):331-58.

Hadley, James Albert. "The Nineteenth Kansas Cavalry and the Conquest of the Plains Indians." *Kansas Historical Collections* 10 (1907-1908):428-56. Includes account of Maj. Joel H. Elliott's death, pp. 441-42.

Hafen, LeRoy R. "Charles Gardner: Big Phil." *Colorado Magazine* 13 (1936):53-58.

_____. "Fort St. Vrain." *Colorado Magazine* 39 (1952):241-55.

_____. "George A. Jackson's Diary, 1858-1859," *Colorado Magazine* 12 (1935):201-14.

_____. "Lewis Ledyard Weld and Old Camp Weld." *Colorado Magazine* 19 (1942):201-207.

_____. "Thomas Fitzpatrick and the First Indian Agency in Colorado." *Colorado Magazine* 6 (1929):53-62.

_____. "The Last Years of James P. Beckwourth." *Colorado Magazine* 5 (1928):134-39.

Hilger, Sister M. Inez. *Arapaho Child Life and Its Cultural Background*. Bureau of American Ethnology Bulletin 148 (1952).

Hill, Nathaniel P. "Nathaniel Hill Inspects Colorado: Letters Written in 1864." *Colorado Magazine* 33 (1956):241-76; 34 (1957):121-34.

Hudnall, Mary Prowers. "Early History of Bent County." *Colorado Magazine* 22 (1945):233-47.

Kingman, Samuel A. "Diary of Samuel A. Kingman in 1865." *Kansas Historical Quarterly* 1 (1932):442-50.

Kroeber, Alfred L. *The Arapaho*. American Museum of Natural History Bulletin 18 (1902-1907).

_____. "Symbolism of the Arapaho Indians." American Museum of Natural History Bulletin 13 (1900):69–86.

Lambert, Julia S. "Plain Tales of the Plains." *Trail* 7, 8, 9 (1916).

LeCompte, Janet. "Charlie Autobees." *Colorado Magazine* 35 (1958): 219–25.

_____. "The Hardscrabble Settlement: 1844–1848." *Colorado Magazine* 31 (1954):81–98.

_____. "Sand Creek." *Colorado Magazine* 41 (1964):317–35.

Mallery, Garrick. *Sign Language Among North American Indians.* Bureau of American Ethnology First Annual Report (1879–1880): 263–552.

Meserve, Charles Francis. "The First Allotment of Lands in Severalty." *Chronicles of Oklahoma* 11 (1933):1040–1043.

Michelson, Truman. "Narrative of an Arapaho Woman." *American Anthropologist* 35 (1933):595–610.

Mooney, James. "Arapaho." In *Handbook of American Indians North of Mexico,* edited by Frederick Webb Hodge. Bureau of American Ethnology Bulletin 30, 1 (1907):72–73.

_____. *The Ghost Dance Religion and the Sioux Outbreak of 1890.* Bureau of American Ethnology Fourteenth Annual Report, pt. 2 (1896):641–1110.

_____. "Little Raven." In *Handbook of American Indians North of Mexico,* edited by Frederick Webb Hodge. Bureau of American Ethnology Bulletin 30, 1 (1907):770–71.

_____. "Nawat." In *Handbook of American Indians North of Mexico,* edited by Frederick Webb Hodge. Bureau of American Ethnology Bulletin 30, 2 (1912):46.

Moore, Horace C. "The Washita Campaign." *Chronicles of Oklahoma* 2 (1924):350–65.

Murphy, John. "Reminiscences of the Washita Campaign and of the Darlington Indian Agency." *Chronicles of Oklahoma* 1 (1923): 259–78.

Newcomb, W. W. "A Re-Examination of the Causes of Plain Warfare." *American Anthropologist* n.s., 52 (1950).

Nicholson, William. "A Tour of Indian Agencies in Kansas and the Indian Territory in 1870." *Kansas Historical Quarterly* 3 (1934):348–49.

Noel, Thomas J. "All Hail the Denver Pacific." *Colorado Magazine* 50 (1973):91–116.

Palmer, H. E. "History of the Powder River Indian Expedition of 1865." Nebraska State Historical Society *Transactions and Reports* 2 (1887):103–52.

Parsons, Eugene. "Progress Among the Arapahoes." *Trail,* 7 (1916):

10-15.

Peery, Dan W. "The Indian's Friend: John Seger." *Chronicles of Oklahoma* 10 (1932):348-68; 11 (1933): 709-32.

Perrigo, Lynn I., ed. "Major Hal Sayre's Diary of the Sand Creek Campaign." *Colorado Magazine* 15 (1938):41-57.

Sanford, Albert D., ed. "Life at Camp Weld and Fort Lyon in 1861-1862: An Extract from the Diary of Mrs. Byron N. Sanford." *Colorado Magazine* 7 (1930):131-39.

Sayre, Hal. "Early Central City Theatricals." *Colorado Magazine* 6 (1929):47-53.

Scott, Hugh L. "The Early History and Names of the Arapaho." *American Anthropologist* n.s., 9 (1907):545-60.

Shields, Lillian B. "Relations with the Cheyenne and Arapaho in Colorado in 1861." *Colorado Magazine 4 (1927):145-54.*

Sievers, Michael A. "Sands of Sand Creek Historiography." *Colorado Magazine* 49 (1972):116-42.

Spring, Agnes Wright. "Rush to the Rockies, 1859." *Colorado Magazine* 36 (1959):82-129.

Swanson, Evadene Burris. "Friday: Roving Arapaho." *Annals of Wyoming* 47 (1975):59-68.

Sweezy, Carl. "A Long Way from the Buffalo Road." *American Heritage 17 (1966):22-25.*

Taylor, Alfred A. "The Medicine Lodge Peace Council." *Chronicles of Oklahoma* 2 (1924):98-118.

Thompson, George W. "Experiences in the West." *Colorado Magazine* 4 (1927):175-79.

Unrau, William. "A Prelude to War." *Colorado Magazine* 41 (1964): 299-313.

Voth, H. R. "Arapaho Tales." *Journal of American Folklore* 25 (1912):43-50.

Wissler, Clark. "The Influence of the Horse in the Development of Plain Culture." *American Anthropologist* n.s., 16 (1914):1-25.

Wright, Muriel H. "A Report of the General Council of the Indian Territory Meeting at Okmulgee, 1873." *Chronicles of Oklahoma* 34 (1956):7-16.

Wynkoop, Edward E. "Edward Wanshier Wynkoop." *Kansas Historical Collections* 13 (1913-14):71-79.

Index